Colombia's Military
and Brazil's Monarchy

Recent Titles in
Contributions in Latin American Studies

Modernization and Stagnation:
Latin American Agriculture into the 1990's
Michael J. Twomey and Ann Helwege, editors

State Formation in Central America: The Struggle
for Autonomy, Development, and Democracy
Howard H. Lentner

Cuba and the Future
Donald E. Schulz, editor

Ambivalent Anti-Colonialism: The United States
and the Genesis of West Indian Independence, 1940–1964
Cary Fraser

Mexico Faces the 21st Century
Donald E. Schulz and Edward J. Williams, editors

Authoritarianism in Latin America Since Independence
Will Fowler, editor

Colombia's Military and Brazil's Monarchy

Undermining the Republican Foundations of South American Independence

Thomas Millington

Contributions in Latin American Studies, Number 7

GREENWOOD PRESS
Westport, Connecticut • London

Library of Congress Cataloging-in-Publication Data

Millington, Thomas
    Colombia's military and Brazil's monarchy : undermining the
republican foundations of South American independence / Thomas
Millington.
        p.   cm. — (Contributions in Latin American studies, ISSN
    1054–6790 ; no. 7)
    Includes bibliographical references (p.   ) and index.
    ISBN 0–313–29806–8 (alk. paper)
    1. South America—Politics and government—1806–1830.   2. Brazil—
Politics and government—1822–1889.   3. Sucre, Antonio José de,
1795–1830—Political and social views.   4. Bolívar, Simón,
1783–1830—Political and social views.   5. Republicanism—South
America—History—19th century.   6. Monarchy—Brazil—History—19th
century.   7. South America—Relations—Brazil.   8. Brazil—
Relations—South America.   I. Title.   II. Series.
F2235.M63   1996
980.03'1—dc20   95–31341

British Library Cataloguing in Publication Data is available.

Library of Congress Catalog Card Number: 95–31341
ISBN: 0–313–29806–8
ISBN: 1054–6790

First published in 1996

Greenwood Press, 88 Post Road West, Westport, CT 06881
An imprint of Greenwood Publishing Group, Inc.

This book was designed and typeset by
Letra Libre, 1705 Fourteenth Street, Suite 391, Boulder, CO 80302

Printed in the United States of America

The paper used in this book complies with the
Permanent Paper Standard issued by the National
Information Standards Organization (Z39.48–1984).

10 9 8 7 6 5 4 3 2 1

For Rosario

The situation of the Brazilian Empire as the only monarchical government throughout the extent of the whole New World, exposes his Majesty [Pedro I] to peculiar difficulties and hazards ... jealousness will be more easily excited, and hostile combinations more easily formed, amongst the republics, his neighbors, against his Majesty's single power.

—George Canning, British Foreign Secretary, August 1826

[The Brazilian emperor's] true destiny is to be a friend of the neighboring republics.

—Simón Bolívar, President of Colombia and
Dictator of Peru, October 1825

The Colombian Second Division is ready for the campaign [against the Brazilian empire] and prepared to carry the standards of liberty or revenge to Rio de Janeiro itself.

—Antonio José de Sucre, Colombian General, May 1825

Contents

Photos follow page 96

Preface

THE PURPOSE OF THIS BOOK is to relate the decline of republican politics in South America to the existence of monarchic rule in Brazil. This monarchic rule, especially its continuation after Brazil achieved independence from Portugal, constituted a major setback to republican politics inside Brazil. It also undermined the commitment of the Spanish Americans to republicanism on the rest of the continent. It is striking, however, that no scholarly work has explored this aspect although the theme was explored in a polemical vein last century by the Chilean author J. V. Lastarria in his two volume work, *La América.*

The studies of South America's independence that have been done so far cover the following areas each of which obscures the view that the Brazilian monarchy had a disconcerting effect on Spanish-American republican development: (1) they treat the Brazilian monarchy as a separate case that had no bearing on the direction of the Spanish-American revolutions (e.g., the standard work by John Lynch, *The Spanish-American Revolutions, 1808–1826*); (2) they adopt a Brazilian historiographic perspective that presumes the moral and political aloofness of the monarchy from the Spanish-American republican governments (e.g., Ron Seckinger, *The Brazilian Monarchy and the South American Republics, 1822–1831*); and (3) they cite structural factors to explain the retardation of republican politics in Spanish-American societies after independence (e.g., the extensive works by Tulio Halperin-Donghi on Spanish-American postindependence societies).

The fact is, however, that if the European-influenced monarchy had been overthrown in Brazil at the time of independence (something that the South American republics, led by Colombian power, had within their means to accomplish), then the independence movements in Spanish South America would have been able to collaborate with emergent republican forces in Brazil to construct a continental, American system based on rejection of European influence. As it was, European influences and the aristocratic concept became enshrined in the Brazilian monarchy. By failing to challenge the monarchy in Brazil, the South American republics lost an important opportunity to disavow European principles of elitism in the New World. This contributed to a loss of republican momentum among the Spanish Americans and explained part of their willingness to rely on the United States to take the responsibility for repudiating European influences in the New World.

This book should be read as a critical interpretation. It is not an archival study, although some archival material is used. The book essentially seeks to uncover the corollary of the continued, postindependence existence of the monarchy in Brazil. This is the disuniting of the Spanish Americans by the South American international system as it was forged in the late 1820s. In this system, it did not matter to the South American republics that Brazil was the only monarchy in South America and that it stood for things diametrically opposed to what they, as independent republics, stood for and fought for. What "mattered" in this system was the balance of power among states, not the quality of domestic structures. However, this book rejects the prevailing view that the Spanish Americans were too distracted by questions of maintaining order in their own new societies to be concerned about the implications of the continued existence of the monarchy in Brazil. Rather, this was *made* to not matter to them with the result that it became possible to create an international system based on balance of power principles rather than political principles. In the course of the nineteenth century the Spanish Americans become predators on each other's territory in the name of balance of power principles. It is not accidental that Chile, who pioneered this system in South America, relied on close support from the Brazilian monarchy. Further, the continued existence of the Brazilian monarchy caused the Spanish Americans to approach the internal problem of order in their own societies in more particularized and authoritarian terms than would have been the case if the international system they were operating in was unified by republican principles. How these untoward outcomes for the Spanish Americans in South America originated in a identifiable decision-making process hinging on the conflict between Sucre and Bolívar is the subject of this book.

The circumstances in which the idea for using a conflict between Sucre and Bolívar as a framework for exploring this subject developed in the following manner.

In 1976–1977, I had the opportunity to be an adviser to the Bolivian Ministry of Finance on debt and budgetary policies. In the course of my duties in the ministry, I undertook a statistical analysis of the budgetary structures in the central and decentralized sectors of the Bolivian government. While working at the ministry on current debt strategy, I became quite interested in the historical origins of state debt policy. I arranged to spend substantial periods of 1977 in the state archives at Sucre, Bolivia. I determined that there was adequate archival material to do an analysis of Bolivia's debt policymaking in the years 1825–1828. I eventually published a book on this subject in 1992.

During the course of my archival research in Bolivia, I became interested in the international political position of Bolivia's head of state at the time, Antonio José de Sucre. Sucre was a Venezuelan general who, under Simón Bolívar's orders, commanded the invasion of Bolivia (Upper Peru) in early 1825 and liberated the area from Spanish control. Sucre's subsequent efforts to develop a foreign policy for Bolivia were prompted, in my view, by a divergence of opinion that had developed between him and Bolívar, who was at the time acting as the dictator of Peru. I began to see that Sucre was attempting to position Bolivia to be free of Peruvian control and, therefore, free of Bolívar's Peruvian dictatorship. In order to accomplish this, he tried to ally Bolivia to Argentina in the latter's war against the newly independent empire of Brazil, which was organized around a European-supported, constitutional monarchy based on Portuguese royalty. To be sure, the conflict between Sucre and Bolívar developed independently of the monarchy question; it was rooted in differences of attitude toward the purposes of the overthrow of Spanish power that Colombian military power was achieving on the continent. Those differences became apparent with the liberation of Ecuador. They grew during the liberation of Peru and Bolivia. These differences were therefore defined before the question of the Brazilian monarchy appeared on the horizon of Colombian power. Yet, I began to see that the existence of the Brazilian monarchy was a crucial factor in the conflict between Sucre and Bolívar during the months when that conflict became centered on Bolivia. At play in the struggle between Sucre and Bolívar to decide Bolivia's political future were these wider questions: Should the Spanish-speaking states accept the Brazilian monarchy as a legitimate domestic political structure in the South American system? Should they seek to exclude it on the grounds of its anomalousness within the essentially, antimonarchic, antiEuropean, antichurch, antinobility, antislavery structure of the independence struggle waged on behalf of Spanish-speaking populations on the continent? Should they ignore it and let the ideological difference between Brazil and the Spanish-speaking states go by default?

The question for me was how important this perspective was given Ron Seckinger's major archival study, *The Brazilian Monarchy and the South American Republics, 1822–1831*. Seckinger's book is obviously based on a greater familiarity with the Brazilian monarchy than with the politics of the Spanish-speaking republics. Although he addresses the internal politics of the Spanish-American republics, he does so in a manner that is much less detailed and convincing than the manner in which he treats the monarchic politics of Brazil. In his characterization of Sucre's governmental activities in Bolivia, he relies largely on William Lofstrom's well-known work, *The Promise and Problem of Reform: Attempted Social and Economic Change in the First Years of Bolivian Independence,* and makes virtually no mention of Sucre's extraordinary conflict with Bolívar as a factor in Sucre's domestic and foreign policies. His book betrays no awareness that Sucre was attempting to implicate Bolívar in Argentina's war against Brazil in a determined effort to extricate Bolívar from his Peruvian dictatorship. This effort, in my view, is the key to understanding Sucre's activities in Bolivia.

While Seckinger's book is a serious and useful work, I could not help but wonder how the relations between the Brazilian monarchy and the Spanish-speaking republics would appear if they were interpreted from the political perspective of the Spanish-speaking republics rather than from a biased Brazilian historiographic perspective; from a perspective that, moreover, took account of the internal political situation in Bolivia and the nature of Sucre's ongoing conflict with Bolívar concerning the proper direction of the independence process and whether Colombian power would or should be used against the monarchy.

Having determined to write on this subject, I decided to structure it around the elements involved in the relationship between Colombia's growing military predominance on the continent (with the capability that this gave to challenge the Brazilian monarchy) and the internal dynamics of the monarchy (whose survivability depended on keeping the Spanish-speaking republics from allying against it). The question at the core of the conflict between Sucre and Bolívar is this: Should Colombia's military power be used to challenge the Brazilian monarchy and thereby strengthen the cause of republican government on the continent (including inside Brazil)? Or, should such a challenge to the monarchy be deliberately avoided in order to pave the way for Bolívar to introduce some of the authoritarian features of the Brazilian system (order and progress) into the governments of the Spanish-American states. Within this thematic framework, I concentrate on the internal political situation of Sucre in Bolivia, where he commanded Colombian military forces and disagreed with Bolívar over making these forces hostile toward the Brazilian monarchy. I suggest that the failure of Sucre to "win" this core conflict with Bolívar resulted in more fear of Bolívar's authoritarianism than the monarchy in Brazil, and this is what ultimately discouraged the formation of a republican alliance against the monarchy under Colombian auspices in the late 1820s. These events in turn laid the foundation for the nineteenth-century South American balance of power system, with its chief feature being the fighting among the Spanish-speaking populations (in both their domestic and international affairs), while the Brazilian elites remained smugly at peace under their imperial monarchy, all the while scolding the Spanish Americans for their lack of political "maturity."

——————

Chapter 1 describes the consequences of the relocation of the Portuguese court from Lisbon to Rio de Janeiro, Brazil, during the years 1808–1822. This chapter describes the inherent conflict between American and European affiliations that accumulated around the court at Rio and then took shape during the reign of Brazil's first independent monarch, Pedro I (1822–1831).

In Chapter 2, Colombia is introduced into the analysis by examining the contradiction between its republican structure and the strategic goals of its military expansion. Emphasis is on the ways in which Sucre and Bolívar sought at this early stage to manage this conflict. The conflict which arose between them is outlined. This conflict influences the later concern of what was to be done about the Brazilian monarchy, given the growth of Colombian liberating power on the continent. The final section of this chapter examines the Colombian intervention in Peru in terms of Bolívar's authoritarian, pro-British disposition of Colombian power there. Bolívar's moves in Peru necessarily made him more tolerant of the authoritarian features of the Brazilian monarchy and less patient with republican politics. This emerges explicitly in his correspondence at the time and further distances his thinking from that of Sucre.

With Colombia's military machine at its borders, urgency was given to deciding whether the monarchy's continued existence, unchallenged by the Spanish Americans collectively, was acceptable to them. In this context, the introduction of a new politics in Buenos Aires, the progress made by British Foreign Secretary, George Canning, in legitimating the Brazilian monarchy, and Pedro's move toward a war with Argentina exerted powerful, contradictory influences. This is the subject of Chapter 3.

Chapter 4 examines the Colombian invasion of Upper Peru in terms of Sucre's strategy for preventing the spread of Bolívar's Peruvian dictatorship. He used the Colombian invasion of Upper Peru to separate it from Peru and to constitute it as the independent republic of Bolivia. Sucre sought the support of neighboring Argentina in this endeavor.

Chapter 5 explores Sucre's effort to challenge the Brazilian monarchy through the formation of an offensive alliance between Bolivia and Argentina in the wake of an obscure incursion of Brazilian military forces into western Bolivia. Sucre made a bid to shore up Bolivia's independence by joining it with Argentina in a war against the monarchy. This was done in the face of Bolívar's determination to structure the independence of Upper Peru in a way that would facilitate its integration into his Peruvian power base and thereby avoid confrontation with the monarchy. The result of these cross purposes, which is the subject of Chapter 6, was that relations of the Spanish-American republics toward the monarchy were allowed to drift out of the alliance scenario; the monarchy was accepted by default. This was the effective result of the negotiations held between Bolívar and the Argentines at Potosí in late 1825.

Chapter 7 describes South America's system of international relations from the perspective Sucre's new plan to accommodate the monarchy within an overall American equilibrium. Sucre's subsequent overthrow in Bolivia opened the door to a series of armed struggles (the first one consisting of Peru against Colombia) that over the course of the nineteenth century pitted the Spanish Americans against each other more than they were ever pitted against Brazil. This system of rivalry and military conflict over territory was a gross caricature of what Sucre had hoped for from an American equilibrium. South America was, however, made politically safe for the Brazilian monarchy. But the Spanish-American unity that had been forged at the cost of so much blood and treasure in the struggle for independence was destroyed. This nineteenth-century South American system of what Robert Burr calls "power politics" was, in effect, a Brazilian system. It secured the monarchy by the mechanism of Spanish-American fragmentation.

Acknowledgments_____

THIS BOOK WANDERED IN THE WILDERNESS for many years until two scouts stumbled across it and pointed it toward academic civilization. These are James Wilkie and Robert Burr, outstanding historians of Latin America and colleagues at the University of California at Los Angeles. Professor Burr observed that "not all scholars will agree with all of Millington's interpretations." That is undoubtedly true since the argument offered here is a new one. Not only that, but the current writing on the nineteenth century in Latin America emphasizes economic and social structures. Studies of politics and ideology, such as my book, go against the grain. I would like to think, however, that my approach in this book is justified not only because I am a political scientist but because historians themselves are beginning to recognize—Charles Hale is a notable example—that a return to the study of politics is long overdue in the historiography of the nineteenth century in Latin America. To Professor Hale, my thanks for his encouragement of my project.

My debts to Bolivians, in whose country I have done most of my field research including much of the research for this book, are too numerous to mention. I would, however, like to acknowledge the late Gunnar Mendoza, head of the state archive at Sucre, Bolivia. He was a hard man to get a reaction out of but I remember one day very clearly when I did succeed in goading him. I was working in the archive on financial policy in Bolivia during the administration of Antonio José de Sucre. It was late in the afternoon and most of the staff had left. I strolled over to *Don* Gunnar, barely able to see him behind the huge piles of old documents on his desk. I made a comment about Sucre being widely seen as a political novice who relied on his mentor and boss, Simón Bolívar, to tell him what to do. This did get a rise out of *Don* Gunnar. "Go and read what Sucre told the Brazilian commander who had crossed the border with his troops into Bolivia and go look into the whole Brazilian matter. Then we will see if you have the temerity to come back and tell me that Sucre was doing what Bolívar wanted him to do." Suffice it say that I did take a look and that look eventually became this book. The quotation by Sucre in the front matter of the book is from the language *Don* Gunnar referred me to.

I can't mention my work in Bolivia without mentioning my brothers-in-law who have in myriad ways opened doors for me: The Vivado brothers, Raúl, Manuel, Juan Carlos, Alfredo, and Fernando. I did a lot of my research and writing for this book on various occasions in Manuel's office in La Paz. I would also like to recall a talk I delivered on this book in La Paz in August of 1995. This was arranged by Cecilia Córdoba of the U.S. Information Service. Many of Bolivia's outstanding historians and public figures were present, including Jacobo Libermann, Valentín Abecia, Juan Lechín Suarez, Jorge Siles, Freddy Velasco, Marcelo Araúz, and Raúl Mariaca. They made lively and knowledgeable comments that caused me to go back and check some things.

This book was so long in the writing and research that it taxed unduly the resources and patience of the reference staff at Hobart and William Smith Colleges where I teach. The librarian William Crumlish has been a boon to my scholarly activities. Michael Hunter, Joseph Chmura, and Dan Mulvey have provided indispensable help with sources.

At Hobart and William Smith the teaching enterprize is pervaded by a self-conscious interdisciplinarity that I have found very stimulating. My own scholarly approach has been colored by this atmosphere. I would like to mention particular colleagues at HWS with whom I have carried on extended conversations over the years about matters political, historical, theoretical, and philosophical. These are Joseph DiGangi and Maynard Smith (political science), Francis O'Laughlin and Marvin Bram (history), and Steven Lee (philosophy).

My student Benjamin Ramsey proofed my proofing and found many errors that I had missed and some that I did not know were errors! Doris Kenny, the social sciences secretary, handled very efficiently all of the correspondence I carried on in connection with the book.

At the Greenwood Publishing Group I have received efficient and professional collaboration from James Dunton (acquisitions), Marcia Goldstein (permissions), Desirée Bermani (production), and Carol Blumentritt (copyediting). I have been most fortunate to have the professional services of Andrew Davis and Jon G. Brooks. Their company, *Letra Libre*, in Boulder, Colorado, did an outstanding job of composition. My friend and director of Orbis Books, Robert J. Gormley, had his oar in the project at various stages.

The current Argentine ambassador to the United States, Raúl Granillo Ocampo, took a lively interest in my book and facilitated permissions to print material from the Argentine archives as well as the photograph of a painting of Rivadavia. Horacio Mendez, the cultural affairs officer of the Argentine embassy, was very helpful with Argentine permissions. The current Ecuadorean ambassador Edgar Terán secured permission from his government to print a photo of a painting of Sucre that currently hangs in the foreign chancellery in Quito.

The map of South America in 1825 in the book was drafted by my son Kenneth, an accomplished illustrator, and it was put into computer graphics by my student Alexei Deshevoi.

When I first began working on this book in 1976 in La Paz, Bolivia my two sons Ken and Tom were just youngsters and the third, Greg, was barely in the thought process. Now they are young men embarked on their own lives and careers. They have been very patient with my labors although I have tried to not let my work intrude on the family project. This book probably could have been finished ten years earlier but I am glad it wasn't. It is a better family and a better book because of the "delay." My wife, Rosario, has been an unremitting source of inspiration and commentary concerning Latin American matters generally and those Bolivian in particular. This one is for her.

South America in 1825

Map by Kenneth Millington

Introduction_____

FROM THE END OF THE SIXTEENTH CENTURY until the second
decade of the nineteenth century, the South American continent was
dominated by a dual structure of colonial rule consisting of the Portuguese in Brazil and the Spanish in virtually all other areas of the continent. The continent was partitioned initially between the Spanish and
Portuguese by a treaty negotiated at Tordesillas, Spain, on June 7, 1494,
and was approved subsequently by the Pope. The Tordesillas line of
demarcation became the starting point from which the Portuguese
empire expanded through relentless, outward movements of the Brazilian population and government officials. Through a treaty made in 1750,
Spain ceded to the Portuguese an amount of South American territory
that nearly doubled the size of Brazil under the old Tordesillas boundary.
On the eve of independence, the great sprawl of Brazil was bordered to
the northwest by the Spanish Viceroyalty of New Granada with its capital
at Bogotá, to the west by the Viceroyalty of Peru with its capital at Lima,
and to the southwest by the Viceroyalty of Plata with its capital at Buenos
Aires.

The onset of the independence movements in the two South American empires in the last decades of the eighteenth century had some
common causes. Politically, the example of the successful colonial revolt
in North America and the egalitarian, democratic ideology of the French
Revolution prompted some segments of the Portuguese and Spanish-
American populations to question their own continued colonial subju-
gation. Economically, the restricted, monopolistic trade practices
imposed within the Spanish and Portuguese empires were being out-
grown by the South American colonial economies; the wider markets,
cheaper manufactured imports, and the more rapid growth predicted by
free trade doctrines exerted a seductive appeal among many colonial
producers, consumers, and merchants. In addition, during the second
half of the eighteenth century, both Spain and Portugal attempted to
centralize their South American empires by imitating current Bourbon
administration in France. These reforms, although increasing the levels
of efficiency and accountability in the administration of the empires,
tended to erode the affective ties of colonial populations to their kings

that had grown up in the earlier periods of royal paternalism and decentralization.

Despite these background similarities, the actual process of achieving independence differed markedly between Brazil and the Spanish Americans. The institution of monarchy provided the framework for the Brazilian independence movement. Ultimately, the Brazilians were able to nationalize a powerful branch of the ruling Braganza dynasty of Portugal and make it the basis for their independence from Portugal. This strengthened the monarchy as a focus for the loyalties and aspirations of the Brazilians at both the elite and popular levels. By contrast, the subject of monarchy in the Spanish-American colonies became the source of tremendous division. The ruling Bourbon monarch of Spain, Ferdinand VII, had fanatically sought to repress the Spanish-American independence movements when he returned to the throne, following his deposition by Napoleon. Certain sectors of the Spanish-American colonial population believed that the purpose of independence was to form republican societies and to repudiate the legacy of monarchy so deeply entrenched after 300 years of living under rule by the Spanish Hapsburgs and the Bourbons. Ferdinand's obduracy only heightened their feelings. However, other sectors, if they did not believe in continued loyalty to the Spanish Crown, did believe that constitutional monarchies were needed in the emerging states in order to prevent rampant social disintegration.

Nominally, the republican ideology prevailed, and the collapse of Spanish viceroyalties resulted in the creation of the self-proclaimed republics of Argentina, Chile, Paraguay, Bolivia, Peru, and Colombia. Yet, the republican victory in these states was uncertain from the beginning. Republican principles were inevitably tenuous in vastly backward and racially heterogenous societies, which were totally unaccustomed to them. Further, the enormous dislocation of economic structures and the general militarization of society that occurred during the long struggle for independence made it difficult to believe that fledgling, representative governments would possess enough authority to impose stability and order.

The steady progress of monarchic government in Brazil posed another unsettling question: Hadn't monarchy in Brazil, which was admittedly ruling a slave-oriented and much less populist society than the Spanish-American societies, nevertheless held Brazil together as it gained independence from Portugal—an independence that had avoided armed conflict among Brazilians and between Portugal and Brazil? By contrast, hadn't the Spanish-American efforts to maintain a republican, antimonarchic rationale for their own independence struggles contributed to an escalating war with Spain, to a denial of their governments' internal legitimacy, isolation from Europe, and a strain on their relations with Brazil? Worse yet, it appeared that the Brazilians under their monarchic rule were intent on fashioning a society that was in some respects more liberal than what was apparently achievable by the other republic-minded South Americans.

In view of all of this, how much confidence could the Spanish Americans have in the applicability of republican principles to their revolutions? Didn't those principles presuppose exactly what their revolutions were missing—a bedrock of civil society and consensus? Weren't republican principles suffering from irrelevancy to Spanish-American realities?

1

Monarchic Factors in the South American Independence Movements

Migration of the Portuguese Monarchy to Brazil: Spillover Effects on the Argentine Revolution

Great Britain was responsible for the installation of the Portuguese monarchy in Brazil in 1810. It was this structure that provided the framework of the Brazilian independence movement.

The maintenance of Portuguese independence in the face of the expansionist tendencies of the Bourbons ruling in neighboring Spain was a cardinal tenet of Britain's policy of the European balance of power in the seventeenth and eighteenth centuries. Britain had signed various treaties of alliance with the Portuguese ruling family, the Braganzas, during this period. As a result of Napoleon's invasion of the Iberian peninsula in 1807–1808, the British removed the royal apparatus from Portugal across the Atlantic to Brazil, Portugal's colony in South America. The queen, the Prince Regent Don John, his wife Carlota, and their two sons Miguel and Pedro, along with thousands of the extended royal family, state bureaucrats, and military personnel were escorted by British men-of-war across the Atlantic. The British intended to return John to Portugal after Napoleon was defeated and the European balance was restored. The Spanish Bourbons fared worse than the Portuguese Braganzas during Napoleon's invasion. Napoleon placed his brother, Joseph, on the Spanish throne, forcing the Spanish king Carlos IV and the heir apparent, his son Ferdinand VII, to abdicate. They were held prisoners in the suburbs of Paris until Napoleon was defeated.

In the meantime, the Portuguese court was officially established in Rio de Janeiro, where it functioned as the government of Brazil, introducing myriad reforms, upgrading the colonial administration, and opening all of the Brazilian ports to free trade. The new free trade regime created access to much wider markets for landowning and commercial

Brazilian elites. It heavily undercut those monpolistic concerns in Portugal and Brazil, which were privileged by the restricted colonial trading system. On December 16, 1815, John elevated Brazil to the status of a kingdom united to Portugal. He officially became king of both Portugal and Brazil in 1816. Ministries of state were also established in Brazil at this time; they represented an important *de facto* step in the direction of framing an independent state structure in Brazil.[1]

In regard to Brazil's relations with the Spanish-American viceroyalties on the South American continent, an inevitable split had developed in the court at Rio. On the one hand, there were the Portuguese Europeanists who, having accompanied John to Brazil, were biding their time until it was safe for the court to return to Portugal. On the other hand, there were the Americanists, consisting of some Portuguese but increasingly of Brazilians. The Americanists wanted to link the court at Rio to the internal politics of the Spanish-American viceroyalties in order to promote an American role for Brazil and thereby to separate it from the European system. The "political state of this part of South America" was changed irrevocably by the planting of the Portuguese court in Brazil, John was told by his Americanist advisors; he should capitalize on this change by using the prestige of the throne to build political relations, separate from Europe, with the Spanish-American colonial populations.[2] By contrast, the influence of the Portuguese Europeanists depended on convincing John that his primary political obligations were in Europe, not America, and that Napoleon could not last forever. Both sides recognized the reality of the situation: The more Brazil became involved in Spanish-American politics, particularly as those politics veered toward independence, the more it would tend to separate itself from Portugal and from Europe.[3]

John's wife, Carlota, was behind the court's first major political overture to the Spanish viceroyalties. Unable to rule as a regent or as a queen in Spain or Portugal, Carlota was inspired to rule as regent over the Spanish-American viceroyalties, thereby offering to the Spanish-American populations a legitimate alternative to French colonial rule during the captivity of Ferdinand. With John's consent, a large volume of letters and a large number of agents were sent out by Carlota from Rio to the South American viceroyalties and even to the distant Viceroyalty of New Spain (Mexico).

Carlota's initiative was intended to appeal to independence-minded Spanish Americans. It did so especially in Buenos Aires, where a movement toward independence was already well under way. In a effort to seize the port of Buenos Aires and deny it to the French enemy, the British invaded it only to be repulsed by a popular army under the charismatic leadership of a French officer in the Spanish service, Santiago Liniers. He overthrew the Spanish viceroy, proclaiming himself the new viceroy. A revolutionary leadership had sprung up in Buenos Aires in the wake of these events, which included Manuel Belgrano, Juan José Castelli, Juan Martín de Pueyrredón, Mariano Moreno, and Bernardino Rivadavia. They were distrustful of Liniers because of his Frenchness and his upstart authority. To them, it was preferable to obey Carlota as an heir to the legitimate ruling dynasty of the Spanish Bourbons rather than an adventurer like Liniers, who was suspected, moreover, of harboring French loyalties. Firm in their belief that the time for independence had arrived, they preferred to make a state based on a popular bonding of the people to a royal sovereign such as Carlota, thereby achieving independence without the risk of breaking the viceroyalty apart under the surge of a revolutionary, democratic politics.

John felt that he was losing control over Carlota's far-flung schemes. He withdrew the court's support and prevented her from going to Buenos Aires to be invested as she wanted. According to Brazil's foremost historian of period, Manuel de Oliviera Lima, if Carlota had gone to Buenos Aires, "she would have been deliriously acclaimed by the people, at least by the nationalistic portion of the population ... as the legitimate successor of the imprisoned monarch (Ferdinand), and as the incarnation of incipient separatist aspirations." The Argentines would have been spared the chaos and internecine fighting that their efforts to achieve independence through a republican politics, self-consciously opposed to the Brazilian monarchy, left them vulnerable to. "Loyalty to a legitimate dynasty was an element on which all the Spanish Americans could have relied with security ... those which aspired to independence but which came to it through the creation of unstable republics, would have been much better served by emancipating themselves and constituting a constitutional monarchy which would not have felt the need to challenge the great stable power of the Kingdom of Brazil, one hundred times superior to the (absolutist) Kingdom of Portugal."[4]

After Carlota's initiatives terminated, and Ferdinand was placed on the Spanish throne by the Allies, following their defeat of Napoleon, John offered to use his personal tutelage and military resources to shield the populations of the Plata viceroyalty against any attempt by Ferdinand to wreak revenge on them for their continued revolutionary activity. He made various offers to independence leaders in Buenos Aires and also in Santiago, Chile, to provide them with Braganza princes so that they might found monarchies and join in the formation of an "Empire of South America," independent of European politics. He confided to an agent of Buenos Aires in Rio that he was coming to "understand the necessities of the New World" and that he "acted like an American

Monarch." But, increasingly, Brazilian foreign policy under John was becoming centered on the Eastern Bank question.

The Eastern Bank was a province belonging to the Plata viceroyalty that lay south of Brazil on the eastern banks of the Uruguay and the Plata rivers. The Portuguese and Brazilians owned considerable property in the Eastern Bank. The Eastern Bank was of vital strategic importance because it lay astride the Plata river system, which drained large portions of the Brazilian interior. For these reasons, repeated diplomatic, political and military efforts were launched from Brazil during the colonial period, with the approval of Lisbon, to separate the Eastern Bank from the Plata viceroyalty and annex it to Brazil. These efforts were vigorously resisted by the viceroyalty in the larger seesaw struggle over the old Tordesillas boundary. The fact that the Eastern Bank became a major military battlefield between Argentina and Brazil in the postindependence period was a continuation of this earlier pattern of rivalry between the viceroyalty and Brazil. But the conflict over the Eastern Bank assumed major ideological significance in the postindependence period because it was there that the alternative ways in which the Spanish-American republics might relate to the Brazilian monarchy were defined and tested.

An independence movement had broken out in the Eastern Bank in the form of an insurgency led by José Artigas. He directed the uprising against Spain and also against the Portuguese. Artigas's forces frequently attacked across the border into Brazil. On the Eastern Bank, he regularly confiscated Brazilian property. The independence leaders in Buenos Aires viewed Artigas as leading a separatist movement—a traitor to the cause of creating the united nation of Argentina out of the Plata viceroyalty. John's Americanist advisers urged him to use the pretext of attacking Artigas on the Eastern Bank as a means of currying favor with the revolutionary leadership in Buenos Aires. At the same time, he wanted to create a buffer between Brazil and the revolutionary politics of Buenos Aires and to maintain Brazil's access to the Plata River system. Originally, John had preferred to try to keep Spanish viceregal rule intact in the Plata basin in order to block the extension of Buenos Aires's revolutionary rule there or, alternatively, to seek to control the littoral Spanish provinces— Entre Ríos, Corrientes, Paraguay, the Eastern Bank—as client states of Brazil. It was not only the fear of democratic contagion, but also the possibility that Napoleon might use the Spanish territories against the Braganzas, that pushed John toward intervention in the Plata area.[5]

In July 1811, a Portuguese army invaded the Eastern Bank and occupied Montevideo in order to rescue the Spanish viceroy from capture by revolutionary troops from Buenos Aires and, at the same time, to prevent him from joining forces with the patriots to recapture the border area of Misiones, which the Portuguese had seized from the Plata Viceroyalty in 1803. In order to keep his options open with the revolutionaries, John let them know that he was willing to see the power of the Spanish viceroy diluted. Paraguay could stay under its Spanish governor, and the viceroy would stay in control of the Eastern Bank and Entre Ríos, but the rest of the viceroyalty could come under the rule of Buenos Aires.[6]

In April 1812, Britain mediated the Eastern Bank dispute in order to secure the evacuation of John's forces and stop the collaboration between Buenos Aires and the court at Rio against their common enemy, Artigas. British Foreign Secretary, Robert Stewart Castlereagh, was becoming extremely concerned that John was encouraging revolutionary elements in Buenos Aires in his efforts to overthrow Spanish rule. John did succumb to the importunings of Lord Strangford, the British mediator, to withdraw his army. The evacuation of Portuguese forces from the Eastern Bank allowed Artigas eventually to establish his supremacy, to the chagrin of Buenos Aires, which had hoped to bring the area under its control after the Portuguese evacuation. Artigas's rule was short-lived, however. Taking advantage of the growing political opposition to Artigas in the Eastern Bank and also renewed contacts with Buenos Aires, John sent in another Portuguese army of occupation, this time under General Carlos Frederico Lecór. This occupation by Portuguese troops led to the annexation of the Eastern Bank to Brazil in 1821, thereby bringing a Spanish-American population forcibly under Portuguese sovereignty.

This peremptory action had ideological and chauvinistic overtones in that occupation rights were asserted in the Eastern Bank on the basis of the alleged inferiority of republican principles to those of monarchy. Lecór clearly manifested these sentiments when he invaded the Eastern Bank in 1817 and made particularly disdainful and provocative remarks about how inept the Spanish Americans had become, especially the Argentines, as a result of their efforts to set up popular governments and how better off they would be if they submitted to monarchic Portuguese rule like the Eastern Bank population. Lecór's comments caused even the monarchic-minded Pueyrredón, Argentina's Supreme Director, to characterize them as those of "a foreigner who commits hostilities on the soil of the nation, who subjugates our brothers and who prefers threats which impoverish the name American."[7] This monarchic chauvinism was to become prominent in Pedro's bellicosity toward the Eastern Bank for several years following 1825, when his newly raised imperial army replaced the Portuguese army of occupation there.

Another basic current in Brazilian policy that placed power structure issues ahead of the ideological issues was directed toward dividing the Argentine provinces against each other. In this way, Brazil could create a regional power structure that was favorable to the extension of its economic and military control over the Plata River system. Widespread distrust of Buenos Aires among the Argentine provinces provided Brazil— under John and under Pedro—with fertile ground for this divide and rule policy. Brazilian control over the Eastern Bank could be made to appear to the Argentine provinces as a means of preventing Buenos Aires from gaining control over the Eastern Bank and using it to augment its already disproportionate power over them in the projected Argentine state. Long-standing hostility between the independence governments in Buenos Aires and Paraguay provided Brazil with the opportunity to reinforce its claims to the Eastern Bank and to break down the diplomatic isolation of Paraguay, which dated from 1813. Achieving an alliance with Paraguay and possibly with other littoral Argentine provinces against Buenos Aires was a cornerstone of Brazil's Eastern Bank policy under both John and Pedro; it can be dated from 1808. After his imperial forces replaced the Portuguese in the Eastern Bank in 1825, Pedro accelerated attempts to lure Paraguay into an alliance to cover Brazil in the event of war with Buenos Aires over the Eastern Bank.[8]

British policy nudged Rio's policy away from ideological concerns toward the maintenance of a balance of power in the Eastern Bank. First were the efforts of Castlereagh to defuse the conflict in the Eastern Bank in order to prevent a rift in the British-Spanish-Portuguese alliance system. John's continued presence in America was perceived by the brooding, reactionary British statesman to be detrimental to the legitimist basis of the European peace. In the first place, the political relations that John was developing with he neighboring Spanish-American populations, particularly with the revolutionary leadership at Buenos Aires, interfered with the Allies' attempt to shore up Ferdinand's legitimacy as the Spanish king. What Castlereagh called pejoratively the "American politics at the Court at Rio" was making it difficult to get the Spanish-American populations to "unite with their (Spanish) brethren in Europe in acknowledging their allegiance to their lawful sovereign Ferdinand VII and in contributing ... to the efforts now making in Europe to uphold the integrity of the Spanish Monarchy." In Castlereagh's view, integrating the Spanish monarchy into the European peace required the maintenance of the Spanish empire in South America; it was impossible to build up Ferdinand in legitimist Europe and then to permit him to lose control of his colonies in South America at the same time. Castlereagh feared that John's American policy would insulate South America from the political forces of the post-Napoleon European peace in which Britain was implicated. The British envoy in Buenos Aires touched a raw nerve in Castelreagh's diplomacy when he wrote that "the objective of John's policy was to destroy all European influence on (his) neighbors."[9] Castlereagh pressed John in 1820 to give up his American politics and return to Portugal. Britain would help John to re-establish Braganza rule, which had been inevitably weakened due to his prolonged absence in America.[10] He increased his opposition to John's continued presence in Brazil in the aftermath of the Napoleon's defeat.

Subsequently, Castlereaugh's successor as Bristish Foreign Secretary, George Canning, attempted to prevent any escalation of the conflict between Brazil and the Argentine provinces into a war of principles—monarchy versus republics, Europe versus America. The underlying objective of British diplomacy was to negotiate an equilibrium of power and expectations in the Eastern Bank, first between Spain and Portugal and then between Argentina and Brazil. The British objective eventually became the creation of a buffer state in the Eastern Bank to ensure a free trade regime for the Plata River system; neither the Brazilians or Argentines would have to see themselves as "losing" the Eastern Bank to the other side. As such, the British hoped that the Eastern Bank could become the precursor of other balance-of-power arrangements to be wrestled into shape along Brazil's endless borders with the Spanish Americans. By this means, the relations between the Spanish Americans and the Brazilians could be molded by pragmatic, geopolitical logic and not by the principles of ideological difference. In this perspective, the task was not necessarily different from creating balance-of-power relations between the Spanish-American states, among whom, disparities of size and military power were prevalent and needed equilibration. Conceivably, Brazil might have to join with some Spanish-American states against others in shifting, balanced, regional power structures that would maintain stability and avoid interruption of free trade flow—balancing power and boosting trade with the outside world were part of this same continuum of British policy. "Unnecessary" wars needed to be avoided. In the perspective of British policy in South America, Brazil would move from suspect monarchy for the Spanish Americans to player in the process of rotating the international power structures on the South American continent in the interest of maintaining equilibria—always under the attentive eyes of British diplomats and entrepreneurs. If the Spanish Americans could develop more conservative social and political systems so much the better—prudential, balance-of-power foreign policies were best pursued by political aristocracies, not popular majorities.

This British approach had scored a major coup in the Eastern Bank when the British minister to Brazil, Lord Percy Clinton Strangford, negotiated the withdrawal of a Portuguese army of occupation in 1812. But it suffered a setback in 1817 when Lecór's army reinvaded, driving Artigas into exile in Paraguay and forcibly denying the centralists in Buenos Aires any access to the area. This created a provocative imbalance of power that moreover incited Argentine ideological hostility toward the monarchy. Between the evacuation of the Eastern Bank by Lecór's army and the introduction of imperial forces in the area, British diplomacy under Canning became committed to creating a buffer state in the Eastern Bank as a means of equilibrating the international power structure and thereby allowing the ideological issue to be defused.

In addition to British pressure on him to return to Portugal, John was under pressure to return from the leadership of a liberal constitutionalist movement, which had broken out in Lisbon in 1820. This movement revealed the considerable estrangement that had occurred between the Portuguese population and their expatriate king. Although politically liberal, the leaders of this movement sought to recreate the old colonial ties between Portugal and Brazil. They insisted that John's continued presence in Brazil was fueling the Brazilian aspiration for independence. The immediate return of John to Portugal would have the threefold advantage of (1) deflating the Brazilian independence movement; (2) giving John the opportunity to regain his political relevance in Portugal on the basis of a constitutional monarchy; and (3) setting the stage for the reincorporation of Brazil into the Portuguese empire, with new rights of legislative representation, but with abrogation of the free trade regime adopted since 1808 in Brazil.

On April 26, 1821, John ended his thirteen year American sojourn and departed Rio for Lisbon, declaring his son Pedro regent of Brazil, a decision that set the stage for Brazil's independence from Portugal. Pedro, having grown up in Brazil and counting Brazilians among some of his closest friends and advisers, promised to be even more of an "American Monarch" than his father.[11]

Spanish-American Liberators and Monarchism

The strong antimonarchic, secular mood of the Spanish-American independence movements was fueled by a contempt for Ferdinand, the obtuse and reactionary Spanish monarch, and for zealous loyalists who were urged on, in many instances, by fanatical Catholic priests. The early hallmark of the Spanish-American independence movements had been their liberal, republican, democratic rhetoric modeled after both the North American and the French revolutions. Nevertheless, confidence in this rhetoric began to erode as the large-scale popular mobilizations incident to the fighting led to a militarization of life. In this spiral of fighting, patriot *caudillos* (chiefs) with grass roots followings rose up to challenge the authority of fledgling republican orders. This intense, internecine squabbling between the *caudillos* and the elected leaders (Páez versus Santander in Colombia and Bustos versus Rivadavia in Argentina were the classic cases) produced apprehension among the leaders of the professional armies fighting for the patriot cause. Impatient with liberal reforms and fearful that republican government was not stable enough to cope with the social problems unleashed by the struggle against Spain, military leaders advocated the imposition of authoritarian, monarchic orders as the basis for organizing the political independence of the colonies.

Agustín de Iturbide evinced this thinking in Mexico, although in a reactionary way. Mexico had begun to feel the effects of the liberal revolution that broke out in Spain on January 1, 1820, and led to the re-establishment of the parliamentary *Cortes* and the Constitution of 1812. The constitution was declared in effect for Mexico, and Mexican delegates were elected to attend the *Cortes*. The colonial class structure of the Mexican colony was attacked by numerous new edicts promulgated by the *Cortes*—the enfranchisement of popular sectors; elimination of privileges and *fueros* (statutory exemptions) of the church and the militia; and the undermining of the socioeconomic authority of the landowning oligarchy by outlawing primogeniture, entailments, and the use of forced Indian labor.

Iturbide's answer to the liberal revolution that broke out in Spain in 1820 was to devise a conservative "revolution" in Mexico. His famous *Plan de Iguala* committed Mexico to political independence on the basis of adoption of a national monarchy to be invested by a Spanish prince. It promised equality for all races and equal access to the offices of the monarchy between Spaniards and Mexicans. At the same time, it stipulated the protection of the social structure and the property rights and the church's privileges that existed under the colonial regime. The motto of the plan, and of Iturbide's army, was union, independence, and religion. On August 24, 1821, Juan O'Donojú, the new Mexican viceroy appointed by the Spanish liberals, signed a treaty with Iturbide at Córdoba incorporating the *Plan de Iguala* and calling on Spain to send a prince to Mexico.[12] On September 28, 1821, Iturbide's forces, which had absorbed large portions of both the guerrilla armies fighting for independence and the royalist armies, occupied Mexico City. Iturbide declared Mexico an independent empire. He placed himself at the head of a regency and insisted that he be addressed as "your highness." Perfunctorily, he called for congressional elections. The new congress which went into session in February 1822 was composed of Bourbonists, *Iturbidistas*, and republicans. When it became apparent that the Spanish government would not ratify the Treaty of Córdoba, Iturbide decided to make himself emperor of Mexico.[13] In May 1822, he was crowned as Agustín I in the presence of his own military regiment, the thoroughly intimidated members of congress, and dutiful members of the church.

Iturbide proceeded to close the congress and to rule in a dictatorial manner, further alienating political opinion in the Bourbonist and republican camps and, more significantly, in the lower echelons of the military, where resentment festered among Mexicans over the continuation of Spaniards in the officer ranks. Mexican military ringleaders began to systematically challenge orders from the royalist officers in ways that bordered on mutiny. Disavowed by Iturbide, they joined widespread Bourbon and republican conspiracies against Iturbide's despotism. In the end, republicans, Bourbonists, and opportunists all joined together against Agustín I, forcing his abdication on March 19, 1823. Iturbide's abdication, however, sharpened the possibility of a military intervention by Ferdinand's concerned friends in the reactionary Holy Alliance—Russia, France, Prussia, Austria-Hungary—to restore the monarchic principle in Spain's colonies before it was too late.

In the meantime, the South American Liberators—Bolívar and San Martín—were giving up democratic principles in favor of monarchy, not only to internally stabilize the revolutions unfolding around them but also, externally, to entice European support for independence. San Martín's and Bolívar's drifts toward monarchic principles also reflected the fact that, for the Spanish Americans on the South American continent, the monarchy in Brazil was an existential reality.

———✦———

José de San Martín dabbled briefly in revolutionary politics after his return to his native Argentina in 1812 from his service with the Spanish against Napoleon. The revolution hatched in Buenos Aires against Spain was four years old. Its internal politics were rent by vituperative splits in the revolutionary ranks and by opposition from the interior provinces, where the revolutionary authority of Buenos Aires was totally overshadowed by the growing power of the local *caudillos*. The government in power at the time of San Martín's return was zealously committed to a utilitarian ideology, ruthless domination of the provinces from Buenos Aires, and strict adherence to the principle of civilian supremacy over the military.

Bernardino Rivadavia's intellect and will drove this government. It was, however, vigorously opposed by royalist plotters and the *caudillos* in the provinces. San Martín organized a military faction that overthrew

Rivadavia. The new executive installed by San Martín, however, fared poorly because of opposition organized in the rejuvenated legislature by the followers of Artigas. Worse, the armies of Buenos Aires suffered serious setbacks in the war against the Spanish in Upper Peru and the Eastern Bank began to slip from its control because of the arrival of Spanish reinforcements in Montevideo, the lengthening shadow of Brazilian occupation and annexation, and the ongoing insurgency of Artigas. In an effort to recoup its fortunes, the government gave San Martín command of its army fighting in Upper Peru.

In the four years since his return to Argentina, the stern, introverted San Martín had become disillusioned with the republican prospects of the Argentine revolution. Between the "loud mouthed politicians" in Buenos Aires and the regional jealousies that gave the *caudillos* their appeal, San Martín held out small hope for a national unification. He had come to believe that the pursuit of a republic, particularly if it took a federal form, would simply produce anarchy of which the "royalists would be the masters" by default.[14] San Martín did not particularly like the Braganza rule in Brazil, but his biographer, Ricardo Rojas, who was anxious to deny the attribution of monarchic aspirations to San Martín, overstates his antipathy.[15] San Martín was above all a realist when it came to discerning the relevance of monarchic rule in Brazil to the form of government that Argentina should adopt. He put it this way in a statement that is particularly important because it illustrates the thesis of this book, namely, that the existence of the Brazilian monarchy heightened the Spanish American's sense of how unsafe and unworthy they would be alongside Brazil if they tried to be republics.

> The inhabitants of the United Provinces have had no other object in their revolution than to emancipate themselves from Spanish rule and to establish a nation. Are we able to establish a republic without provoking the opposition of Brazil? (An Argentine) republic without arts, sciences, agriculture, inhabitants, and with a large extent of territory which may be properly called a desert, is not a good neighbor for a monarchy.[16]

In other words, *as a republic* Argentina could not hope to be the political and cultural equal of the Brazilians under their monarchy.

San Martín decided that the Spanish were unbeatable in the Upper Peruvian theater. He was dubious that the Argentine revolution in Buenos Aires could ever unify the provinces. He decided to abandon his command of the northern army, leave the service of Buenos Aires and start building his own army in his native province of Mendoza. Turning his back on Argentina, he planned to cross the Andes and undertake the liberation of Chile, and then Peru, from Spanish control. His army became galvanized by the spectacular crossing of the Andes, which San Martín engineered. It was an externalized Army of the Andes that liberated Chile. As such, that army was not going to play an internal role in the Argentine revolution.

The Supreme Director in Buenos Aires, Pueyrredón, refused to accept this fact. For him, the military machine that San Martín had created needed to be brought back to Argentina and thrown into the looming fray in the Eastern Bank in order to recoup the fortunes of the government at Buenos Aires—against the imperial army of Brazil if necessary; against the "traitor" Artigas if possible. Neither of these prospects interested San Martín since he had concluded that Argentina's experience with a "wasteful revolution and ruinous war has cooled the passions incident to all political changes, and men's minds, by this time more settled, aspire solely to an emancipation from Spain, and the establishment of some solid form of government whatever that may be." San Martín determined to supply the answer to the "whatever that may be" in Peru after he liberated it. His attempt to create a monarchy in Peru as the basis for its independence was an expression of his disillusionment over the fratricidal strife that had broken out among the Argentines as a result of their efforts to make some kind of a democracy out of their independence movement.[17] On the eve of his invasion of Peru, after liberating Chile, San Martín broke off relations with Pueyrredón.

In the case of Peru, San Martín believed that Spain would cede its independence under a Spanish prince. He wanted to avoid major fighting in the country. This was partly because of the numbers—his 5,000 men against 12,000 men in the royalist ranks. But he also believed that he could persuade the Spanish viceroy and his commanders to establish a ruling *junta* pending the arrival of a Spanish prince. He believed that Peru, under a monarchy, would be able to maintain social order in the postindependence period and avoid demagogic, populist politics that would be particularly dangerous, given the large masses of Indians and blacks at the bottom of the social pyramid. Achieving independence by conducting large scale fighting against the Spanish army would cause dislocations and only make it harder to maintain the social order in the aftermath of victory.[18]

Negotiations with Peruvian viceroy Joaquín de la Pezuela were held at Miraflores on September 25, 1820, while San Martín was at his headquarters in the Peruvian coastal city of Pisco. The negotiations were unsuccessful; the stumbling block was San Martín's insistence on the independence of Peru, Spanish prince or no Spanish prince. San Martín then decided to lay siege to Lima. He moved his army to Ancon on

November 1 and then above Lima to Huacho in order to cut the capital off from the agricultural produce of northern Peru. In the meantime, Thomas Cochrane, a mercenary British admiral in San Martín's service, set up a sea blockade of Lima, and a division was sent into the interior to harass royalist outposts.

Even though most northern Peruvian *creoles* (Spaniards born in America) did not support independence outright and preferred to work for Peruvian autonomy in a Spanish framework, they were reassured by San Martín's social conservatism, his predilection for monarchy, and the expectation that his military forces would be able to guarantee social order during the transitional period. Led by Torre Tagle, a Peruvian aristocrat and governor of Trujillo, pronouncements from local *cabildos* (town councils) covering the whole of northern Peru were made in favor of independence under the protection of San Martín's Army of the Andes.

Facing a crisis of confidence in his leadership, Pezuela ceded the viceroyship to one of his military commanders, José de La Serna, with whom San Martín promptly opened negotiations at Punchauca on May 4, 1821. The two leaders met there on June 2. San Martín proposed his idea of establishing a *junta*—he called it a regency—to rule Peru pending the dispatch of a prince from Spain and official acceptance by Madrid of Peru's independence. The new viceroy was not interested; the talks ended in failure.

On July 6, 1821, La Serna left Lima with his army for the mountains. On July 10 San Martín entered Lima. On July 14, the Lima *cabildo* declared independence. It gave power to San Martín on July 28. On August 3, he took the title of Protector, with absolute civil and military powers. He made an official declaration of independence.

Undaunted by the failure of his negotiations with the viceroy, San Martín set about laying the foundations for the creation of a throne in Peru, the most conspicuous aspect of which was his creation of the noble Order of the Sun on October 1821. In November 1821, he dispatched a secret mission to Europe, via Brazil,[19] to find a prince for the Peruvian throne and to push recognition of Peru's independence in the European Courts. He did not have a constitutional monarchy in mind for Peru, but, rather, a kingdom, the first of a number of kingdoms hopefully to be established in the former Spanish colonies with the aid of British mediation and coordinated, necessarily, with the Portuguese dynasty that ruled in Brazil. It is significant that the emissary chosen by San Martín for this mission was a former agent of Carlota who had well established contacts in the court at Rio.[20]

In reality, San Martín's military position in Peru was weakening. The Spanish army had retreated from Lima but it remained intact in the mountains and was being strengthened by heavy recruitment of the indigenous population. Spanish military power continued to grow, while San Martín's army around Lima fell apart due to idleness.[21] Given the apparent ability of the Spanish army to deny San Martín's army the capacity to extend its control beyond the coastal areas of the country, the Protector's declaration of Peruvian independence in 1821 had a hollow ring. With his overtures to the Spanish viceroy stalled, his mission to Europe uncertain, and his loss of the military initiative, he was forced to consider relying on military forces from Colombia to break the stalemate. This raised the question of whether common political ground could be found between Bolívar and San Martín, given the latter's overt monarchist orientation. There was some precedent: Bolívar already had to explore common political ground between him and Iturbide in Mexico.

In 1820, San Martín was forty-two years old. He was very tall by the South American standards of the day, of white complexion, thin lipped, with blue eyes and a large, impassive face. He was reserved and hard to read. He despised histrionics. His favorite targets were "loud-mouthed politicians." He preferred working secretly, conspiratorially, on his plans. He was a Mason and he had a severe narcotics addiction. Recurrently, he lived in a world all his own. San Martín presented a stark contrast, both physically and temperamentally, to his formidable counterpart from the north, Simón Bolívar.

In 1820, Bolívar was thirty seven years old. He had long sideburns and a mustache, enormous black eyes, an even set of white teeth and a churlish mouth. Like most members of the "white" Venezuelan aristocracy of Spanish descent, he had a considerable endowment of Indian and black genes. He was was small—almost diminutive—but he cut a dashing figure. He was very athletic, an excellent horseman, and a graceful and indefatigable dancer. He drank wine only rarely, did not smoke, and allowed no cigars in his presence. He had no spontaneous sense of humor, although he had a flair for satire. He was not amiable, which he conceded. He had a terrible temper and he was utterly ruthless, but also magnanimous and generous, as long as it was he who was doing the giving. His will was his sovereign. Desk work was abominable to him; he seemed to be always going someplace. He needed very little sleep, a trait that he exploited to the fullest. His manner was always very agitated and he spoke in rapid cadences, with the disconcerting habit of not looking at the person he was talking to. His French was fluent, and he always used it when dealing with Europeans. He understood some English but insisted that the North Americans he encountered speak Spanish, or

French, if they preferred, with him. His relationships with North American envoys throughout his career were invariably much less forthcoming than those with European diplomats.[22]

Bolívar was the scion of a wealthy, landowning Venezuelan family. He was born on July 24, 1783. He lost his mother to illness at the age of nine. His father had died, also from illness, when Bolívar was just two years of age. He was raised on the family plantation, surrounded by servants and tutors, with his younger sister and his brother. Two maternal uncles continued to act *in loco parentis* as they had essentially done since the death of Bolívar's father. At age eleven, they sent him to Madrid to live with a well connected uncle and continue his studies. Bolívar managed to make a quick trip to Paris in early 1802. He also married the daughter of a wealthy Caracas couple living in Madrid.[23]

Bolívar and his wife returned to Caracas where she fell ill and died abruptly on January 22, 1803, just eight months after she and Bolívar were married. He returned to Europe and lived there for the next three-and-a-half years. He spent time in Paris, where he lost himself in the life of the *bon vivant* and is said to have observed the coronation of Napoleon as emperor in the cathedral of Notre Dame on December 2, 1804. He traveled to Europe and to England in the company of one of his former tutors, the eccentric romantic, Simón Rodríguez. Under Rodríguez's guidance, Bolívar began to read widely in classical literature and the French Enlightenment. He also developed a particular admiration for the British parliamentary monarchy, which he observed while in London with Rodríguez.[24]

Upon his return to Caracas, politics became Bolívar's life. He was a major figure in the independence movement, which broke out in Caracas in 1808. He subsequently led a diplomatic mission to Britain, where he sought to secure backing for Venezuela's bid for independence. His meeting with Foreign Secretary Richard Wellesley was not successful. Bolívar struck Wellesley as too impetuous and the subject of revolution in Spain's American colonies was embarrassing, in any case, to the British policy. At that particular time, Britain was taking steps to join the Spanish against Napoleon. Despite the diplomatic rebuff, Bolívar continued to study British political life. He felt that the British had the best of both worlds—the stability of monarchy and the robustness of democracy.[25]

Bolívar returned to Venezuela from Europe in late 1810 after a brief and inconsequential stop in Charleston, South Carolina. He was in Caracas in time to criticize the long-winded and dialectical debates over the writing of a constitution that preceded the formal decision to declare independence from Spain and establish the first republic of Venezuela. He joined the army and played an active role in the effort to save the republic from a loyalist uprising, which had spread from the coastal city of Coro in 1812 and eventually engulfed Caracas. Bolívar escaped to Cartagena, in New Granada, and published a postmortem on the fall of the ephemeral Venezuelan republic.

In his Cartagena Manifesto, Bolívar excoriated the republic for its failure to form a strong central government, its infatuation with the federalist model, and its liberal permissiveness that allowed the counter-revolution to build in Coro with impunity. He sounded one of the imperatives of his later political thought: the need for Spanish-American unity. All of the independence movements, especially that in New Granada, had to learn from the Venezuelan failure and to opt for stronger governments in order to avoid falling prey to loyalist reactions. "Coro is to Caracas, as Caracas is to all (Spanish) America."[26]

The Cartagena Manifesto is significant for our purposes because of Bolívar's prediction of disastrous effects that would result from a Spanish emigration to Venezuela to escape the the establishment of French rule on the peninsula.

> It is probable that following the downfall of the peninsula there will be a tremendous emigration of men of all classes, particularly of cardinals, archbishops, bishops, canons, revolutionary clerics ... all capable of subverting our incipient, faltering states. ... (T)he religious influence, the rule of civil and military domination and all of the prestige they can bring to bear will be the ... instruments which they will use in subjugating these countries ... Nothing will stand in the way of this Spanish emigration. It is conceivable that England will cover the escape of a group whose departure would partially weaken the forces of Bonaparte in Spain and tend to increase and add new life to their own party in America. The (first wave of émigrés) will raise fifteen or twenty thousand men, whom their leaders, officers, sergeants, corporals and veteran soldiers will rapidly drill and discipline. This creation of this army will be followed by another arrival, yet more terrible, of ministers, ambassadors, councilors, magistrates, all of the ecclesiastical hierarchy and the grandees of Spain whose trade is deceit and intrigue, and all bearing imposing titles designed to dazzle the multitude. And descending like a torrent, they will overrun the land tearing [Venezuela's] tree of liberty down to its very roots. The troops will fight on the field, but this army will battle us from their desks, using seduction and fanaticism for arms.

This scenario is similar to the flight of the Portuguese, under British protection, to set up their affairs in Brazil. But the contrast is more telling. The Portuguese royal line was transferred intact to Rio, in the shape of the reigning queen, the heir apparent, John, and his two sons. They were transferred to Brazil by the British with the explicit intent of returning them to Portugal after Napoleon was defeated. In the Spanish case that Bolívar contemplated, Ferdinand and his father, the reigning king, had been captured by Napoleon. Therefore the emigration would not preserve the royal line but would consist of the flotsam of the wrecked monarchy, hangers-on, and "men of all classes." In Venezuela, Bolívar predicted that this renegade group would raise an army to crush the patriotic armies in order to pave the way for the arrival of the Spanish Bourbon apparatus which would add a dimension of decipt and intrigue to the task of repressing the patriotic movement in Venzuela. In Brazil, by contrast, the arrival of the Braganzas was a patriotic event. There was no independence movement underway. Rather, there was a colony that was energized politically by the Braganza rulers. The movement toward the creation of Brazil as a viable, separate state began from the moment Braganza feet touched Brazilian soil; the Braganza rule in Brazil provided the foundation for the eventual creation of a liberal monarchy with patriotic support among the people that would lead them successfully to independence. The sterile and repressive effects of the hypothetical Spanish-Bourbon emigration to Venezuela that Bolívar predicted represented almost the opposite of the Braganza impact on Brazil. Because it provided such a sharp contrast to what Bolívar expected from Spanish-Bourbon royalty coming to Venezuela, he perhaps viewed the Braganza project in Brazil with fascination at first and then respect. If this portion in the Cartagena Manifesto is read as the "antithesis" to the Braganza "thesis" in Rio, we can interpret it as a dialectical relationship in what Nestor de Santos Lima refers to as "the evolution" of Bolívar's "image of Brazil."[27]

Bolívar recruited an army in New Granada, invaded Venezuela, crushed the loyalist forces, and established a dictatorship. Another loyalist uprising—this one in the interior and more sanguinary—broke out in 1813 and drove Bolívar out, with instances of extreme horror and cruelty perpetrated by both sides. Bolívar showed himself capable of trading atrocity for atrocity.

Bolívar fled again to Cartagena, where he tried to recruit forces to reinvade Venezuela. He was unsuccessful this time, largely because of the imminent arrival of the expeditionary army that Ferdinand had dispatched from Spain. Bolívar departed Cartagena just before a group of Venezuelan refugee officers arrived to oversee preparations for the city's defense against the assault by Ferdinand's forces. These Venezuelans, including Sucre, escaped just before the city fell to the Spanish. They followed Bolívar to the West Indies, where some plotted another campaign with him while others, including Sucre, returned to Venezuela on their own to engage in guerrilla activities.

In September 1815, Bolívar was in Kingston, Jamaica, where he composed a historic letter to an English merchant who had asked him to analyze the prospects of the Spanish American independence movement at that time.[28]

In his Jamaica Letter, written in August 1815, Bolívar exclusively addresses the Spanish-American independence movements. But, by implication, he was not excluding the Brazil of the Braganzas from a league of American states. "I do not favor American monarchies," Bolívar stated categorically. Nevertheless, he observed, there are in America large areas to be governed, and monarchies were best suited in these cases. As a result, some monarchies would be "inevitably" established. In the other areas, republics—some with central governments and some with federal—would emerge. This legitimate variety of political form did not have to mean the political fragmentation of America. On the contrary, Bolívar passionately desired its unity in the form of a league of states like the Amphyctionic League of the ancient Greek states. "Would to God," he wrote, "that some day we may have the good fortune to convene . . . an august assembly of representatives of republics, kingdoms, and empires to deliberate on the high interests of peace and war, with the nations of the other three quarters of the globe."[29]

Bolívar was not contemplating a closed hemispheric entity; the thought was cosmopolitan, global. Yet Bolívar's perfunctory references to the North Americans in the Jamaica Letter suggest that his vision of unity excluded them. Bolívar admired the sturdy republican citizenry of the United States, but it only served as a glaring reminder to him of how deficient in republican virtue his own countrymen were. Three hundred years of bureaucratized, secretive rule by Spain had denied them even the rudiments of an understanding of governmental affairs. As a result, he wrote, "Institutions which are wholly representative are not suited to our character, customs and present knowledge. ... As long as our countrymen do not acquire the abilities and political virtues that distinguish our brothers of the north, wholly popular systems, far from working to our advantage, will ... bring about our downfall."

Bolívar looked to Europe for political models; democratic traditions were less entrenched there, and the elite art of legitimizing government was highly developed. The Jamaica Letter exudes a yearning for European recognition of America's independence as a means of offsetting Ferdinand's fanatical zeal to crush the revolts in his colonies. Spain, in Bolívar's view, although once the mightiest of nations, was now too weak to rule its American empire or even hold its own in Europe. Ferdinand's project of reconquering his empire was motivated by blind revenge. Europe was more enlightened. How could it not block Ferdinand's lunacy? "(S)hall Europe, the civilized, the merchant, the lover of liberty, allow an aged serpent, bent only on satisfying its venomous rage, to devour the fairest part of our globe (America)? What! Is Europe deaf to the clamor of its own interests? Has she no eyes to see justice?"

Although the rise of the Holy Alliance and its strengthening effect on Ferdinand's stubbornness discouraged Bolívar over the course of the next decade, he held to his faith that Europe would outgrow a narrow-minded legitimacy and would eventually support the Spanish-American independence project: "Europe is not Spain." To permit the United States to define the Spanish-American independence project in terms of a New World republican solidarity against Europe would be tantamount to imposing a servitude to the United States on the Spanish Americans. Without the benefit of European influence, particularly that of Great Britain, to counterbalance the growing power of the United States, Bolívar feared that the Spanish-American states would become fragmented, politically unstable, and subject to manipulation and eventually to domination by the United States in its guise of leading the hemisphere toward democracy.

Bolívar looked toward Europe because he did not have confidence in republican government as something that the Spanish Americans should aspire to until the attributes of citizenship were much more widely diffused among the populace. But he vehemently opposed legitimist principles as having any right to a place in the New World. What he sought were monarchies, or quasi-monarchies, that were rooted in the patriotic support of the people and that would be capable of receiving support from liberal Europe, not the reactionary Europe of the legitimists.

Bolívar had returned to Venezuela from exile in the Caribbean in 1816 to begin the process of consolidating his authority over the whole revolutionary movement—something that had eluded him before, particularly in the Venezuelan east. He made the town of Angostura, located on the Orinoco River in the eastern part of Venezuela, his military headquarters. The Angostura location was a safe distance from the coastal areas held by the Spanish, and it gave Bolívar access to the vast *llanos* (plains) where he was determined to recruit heavily for his armies. He also installed a congress at Angostura made up of delegates from Venezuela and exiled New Granadians and charged it with the responsibility of drafting codes for the republic-in-exile.

Bolívar was ready to implement his plan to unite New Granada and Venezuela. In his address to the Angostura Congress (February 15, 1819), he called for unification, and he outlined a constitution for the vast new state. Bolívar hoped that his Angostura Address would provide the guidelines for drafting a constitution for the new state of Colombia. In the address, he argued that Colombia's new charter should correct the flaws of federalism and legislative dominance in the original constitution of Venezuela. He advocated a centralized national government with a strong executive branch based on a president and a cabinet. He outlined a hereditary senate in imitation of the British House of Lords, and a lower elective house modeled after the House of Commons. He added a novel fourth branch, consisting of censors to set examples of probity and watch over public morals. Bolívar did not endorse either monarchy or aristocracy, as such. "On the other hand," he asked rhetorically, "have not aristocracy and monarchy held great and powerful empires together century after century? Is there any government older than China? What republic lasted any longer than Sparta and Athens? Did not the Roman Empire conquer the earth? Did not France have fourteen centuries of monarchy? Is there any nation greater than England? Yet these nations have been or still are aristocracies and monarchies?" These truths he asked the legislators to bear in mind as they evaluated his recommendation for writing a constitution. He was to be bitterly disappointed. The elitist, authoritarian thrusts of the Angostura Address ran against the grain of liberal political opinion that predominated among both Venezuelan and New Granadian delegates.[30]

Bolívar's reactions to Iturbide's experiment in Mexico illuminate his monarchist tendencies during this period. Bolívar was favorably disposed toward Iturbide when he learned of his sudden eruption in Mexico. He was at Cúcuta, New Granada, when he wrote Iturbide on October 10, 1821, that through him the "people of Mexico has essentially demonstrated that it wants to belong to itself and not to somebody else. Its future is marked by its good fortune and its glory and you have made it come to pass."[31]

But Bolívar soon became disillusioned with Iturbide when he learned that the *Plan de Iguala* was meant to pave the way for the Treaty of Córdoba and for placing a Spanish prince on the Mexican throne. (It is not certain that when Bolívar congratulated Iturbide he already knew of the text of the *Plan de Iguala*.) He perceived a new and insidious danger to the cause of Spanish-American independence if it were to be achieved by means of accepting Bourbon princes on American thrones. Even the Constitution of Colombia, which was being drafted at Cúcuta along liberal, republican lines that ignored his Angostura Address, seemed to Bolívar to be preferable to this eventuality. "A Bourbon monarchy in Mexico will have close relations with Spain's rulers and the European powers will support the Mexican throne out of their particular and general interest. ... This Mexican monarchy will challenge Colombia across its border, use espionage and eventually invasion, after having already divided it, fomenting class struggles and even destroying our republican system." (This is one of the few times Bolívar unequivocally defended a republican system for Spanish Americans.) To prevent this from happening, Venezuelans must stay united and loyal to the national government at Bogotá in order to defeat monarchic intrigue among them emanating from Mexico.[32]

Similarly, Bolívar wrote to San Martín in Peru. He predicted that

> if the Spanish Government ratified the Treaty of Córdoba, similar pretensions will be entertained regarding the other free governments in America and (Spain will) desire to terminate its differences with them along the same lines as Mexico ... These Bourbon princes, supported by the monarchs of the Old World, could cause very regrettable alterations of the interests and the political systems adopted by the Spanish-American states ... it is necessary to finish the expulsion of the Spanish from the whole continent, to close ranks and to guarantee ourselves mutually, in order to defeat the new enemies and the new methods that they may seek to employ."[33]

Yet, when he learned that the Spanish liberal government was unlikely to ratify the Treaty of Córdoba, Bolívar said in a letter to Francisco de Paula Santander, the New Granadian general elected vice president of Colombia, that "it would be the best thing in the world if Iturbide declares himself Emperor."[34] Bolívar felt that a popularly based Mexican empire would put an end to Bourbon schemes and also to republican agitation backed by the neighboring United States. Instead of founding a throne based on the weak foundations of borrowed European royalty, Bolívar hoped that Iturbide could now found his own throne on the basis of the sovereignty of the people. (This ultimately became Bolívar's expectation for the Braganza project in Brazil.) As such, the empire would shield Mexico against the Holy Alliance and against the United States. Although the letter is somewhat cryptic and evidently hastily written, this construction is a plausible one. Bolívar refers to the U.S. desires for Mexico by using a pejorative colloquial expression. His fears about North American democracy being a trap for Latin Americans were well known even by this time. His apprehensions about Bourbon plotting in Mexico are clearly expressed in his letters to Santander, San Martín and Carlos Soublette, a Venezuelan confidant of Bolívar.

Bolívar soon recognized, however, that Iturbide was nothing more than a dictator in a monarchic disguise. From his vantage point in New Granada, Bolívar predicted that Iturbide, with no popular support, would fight the people instead of royalists—and inevitably fall from power. He predicted the same fate for San Martín in Peru, whom he also accused of "thinking more about laying the basis for a throne than in defeating the royalists on the field of battle. And so we will have two monarchies on our flanks which will come to a bad end, because they started bad, unless Colombia took a hand in their affairs." This seems to mean that the monarchies in Peru and Mexico could come to a better end if Colombia got involved.[35]

Europe's Monarchic Orientation

While Europe was at war with Napoleon, and in the immediate aftermath of his defeat, British policy under Castlereagh sought to protect Spain's empire in South America. He feared that the increasing strides toward independence in the Spanish colonies would place them at odds with the popular movement that had arisen in Spain against the French occupation in 1807–1808. Britain was seeking to use this revolt as a base for waging war against the French on the Spanish peninsula. In the aftermath of Napoleon's defeat, and the introduction of a post-Napoleonic system in Europe, Castlereagh became even more solicitous of the need for Spain, with its newly restored Bourbon monarch, Ferdinand VII, not to be challenged by rebellions in its American colonies. This new European system was militantly conservative. It was dedicated to erasing the French Revolution from the European psyche. The restoration of the world based on hierarchy as it existed in the monarchic societies of Europe before the deluge of *liberté, égalité, fraternité* was perceived to be the philosophical as well as political challenge of the day. Legitimist principles permeated the discussions at the Congress of Vienna and provided the moral framework for the political and territorial arrangements made there and signed into treaty on January 22, 1815. The doctrine of legitimacy—the belief that the right to rule was hereditary and not elective—was the spearhead of the restoration. Re-establishing the French and Spanish Bourbons on their respective thrones received top priority in the legitimist program.[36]

The discussions in Vienna were cut short by Napoleon's dramatic return from his captivity on the island of Elba and the onset of the "Hundred Days." The finale at Waterloo sealed Napoleon's fate and created the occasion for the allies to reassemble, this time at Paris in the fall of 1815, in order to finish their deliberations and to address, in particular, the question of whether the wartime alliance should be transformed into a permanent political concert. The Holy Alliance treaty was signed at Paris by Russia, Austria-Hungary and Prussia (France joined subsequently) at Tsar Alexander's instigation. It envisaged the signatories acting as one to protect the embodiment of Christianity in European monarchic rule. The doctrine of legitimacy was to receive its most militant and reactionary expression in the Holy Alliance.

Political opinion in Great Britain was uneasy about joining the island state with a strong parliamentary tradition to a permanent concert in Europe based on the principles of legitimacy. It feared being implicated in the schemes of the continental dynasties for repressing popular movements, wherever they broke out in Europe, in the name of protecting the peace. Traditionally, British security had been linked to the maintenance of a balance of power in Europe. Castlereagh's new understanding with Prince Metternich, the Austrian chancellor, shifted Britain's policy toward participation in a permanent political concert on the continent as opposed to playing the role of "balancer." Although Castlereagh rejected British membership in the Holy Alliance, he did sign a treaty that renewed the wartime alliance of Britain, Austria, Russia, and Prussia. This Quadruple Alliance treaty proposed periodic meetings of the allied ministers to review the peace arrangements made at Vienna. This implicated Britain in the monarchic principle as the basis of the European peace.

Since the meeting of the Quadruple Alliance in 1818 at Aix-la-Chapelle, Ferdinand had been pressing the allies to aid him in quashing the Spanish-American revolutions. Increasingly, his entreaties were directed toward the Holy Alliance as opposed to the Quadruple Alliance.

Tsar Alexander became concerned about Ferdinand's plight after he was virtually taken prisoner by the liberals in 1820. French diplomats were keenly aware of the tsar's concerns. For their own part, they perceived the Spanish army, backed by liberal propaganda, to be aimed against the ruling monarchies of Europe, beginning with the restored Bourbons in France, instead of against the Spanish-American revolutionaries. A distinct chill settled over French-Spanish relations in the wake of the liberals' overthrow of Ferdinand. By championing the cause of Ferdinand, France sought to increase its political leverage within the Holy Alliance as a basis for recovering its traditional European diplomatic leadership. More particularly, it sought to increase France's own standing with Alexander, while embarrassing his relations with Britain.[37]

This reactionary shift in French policy occurred in the immediate aftermath of Clemens Talleyrand's departure from the French cabinet. Ironically, as Louis XVIII's minister, Talleyrand had given the concept of legitimacy a more moderate basis than the Christian mysticism of Tsar Alexander; he had hoped to align France more with Britain than with Russia. But Talleyrand was despised by the powerful ultraconservatives in the French House of Peers. After he left office, French policy underwent a pronounced shift toward the Holy Alliance and against Britain. Talleyrand's successor, Armand de Richilieu, was much more pro-Russian and responsive to the *ultras* in his handling of foreign policy. He was conservative on the whole question of whether France should recognize the independence of Spain's colonies. The *ultras* exerted pressure to make French foreign policy less sensitive to British balance-of-power concerns and more in accord with the agenda of the Holy Alliance.

Joseph de Villèle rose from a provincial Chamber deputy to a minister in the Cabinet in 1820. He was then called on by the king to form a new cabinet in 1821. An outsider to *ultra* circles, Villèle was against allowing the Holy Alliance to define French policy. He was not convinced that France should intervene in Spain. In regard to the question of Spain's colonies, he felt that French policy might better be coordinated with the British in support of constitutional monarchies for the colonies, rather than tied to the reactionary purposes of the Holy Alliance. Such coordination, he felt, would help curb the republican appeal of the United States in the New World to the mutual advantage of the British and French.[38]

By contrast, Duc de Montmorency was a reactionary monarchist and pro-Russian. Villèle, however, had named him foreign minister in his new Cabinet. Montmorency had allies on the far right in both houses and was very friendly with Count Pozzo di Borgo, the Russian ambassador at Paris. He firmly believed that by rescuing Ferdinand in Spain with the tsar's backing, French policy could redeem itself in Europe's eyes for the sins of its own revolution.

At the Congress of Troppau in October 1820, Austria, Prussia and Russia, agreed to admit France formally to the Holy Alliance. They also were determined to begin military intervention in any European state facing revolution against hereditary monarchic rule, starting with the kingdom of Naples, where King Ferdinand IV had been shoved off his throne by a constitutionalist movement. At the Congress of Laibach, held in January 1821, Austria, Prussia and Russia ordered the armed intervention in Naples. It was also agreed that the four powers would convene the next year at Verona to consider the interventionist agenda. In the meantime, an Austrian army of 60,000 men invaded the kingdom of Naples and restored the king to power. No one applauded louder than Ferdinand. In anticipation of the Congress of Verona, the Spanish king requested the Holy Alliance powers to authorize a French intervention to overthrow his liberal oppressors in the manner of the Naples intervention. If the Holy Alliance restored Ferdinand to absolute power as the result of armed intervention in Spain, would that be a precedent for restoring his rule in the rebellious colonies? Or, could France use its new influence over Ferdinand to persuade him to grant independence to the colonies under Bourbon monarchies? The latter course would pacify the colonies before the revolutions proceeded to the point where it was impossible to make political arrangements with them that were favorable to the legitimist principles of the alliance.

At Verona the British envoy, the Duke of Wellington, suggested to Montmorency joint action in favor of recognizing of the independence of the Spanish colonies. Montmorency feared that recognition of the extant governments in Colombia, Peru, Chile, and Argentina, following the U.S. decision to recognize these governments in March 1822, would interfere with establishment of Bourbon monarchies in those places. He also feared that acceptance of Wellington's offer would create an insurmountable obstacle to the imminent French intervention in Spain. Austria, Prussia, and Russia agreed with Montmorency at Verona to militarily support France in its invasion of Spain if Great Britain sought to aid the Spanish liberals in retaliation. Vicompte Francois-René Chateaubriand, the former French ambassador to Britain, replaced Montmorency at Verona and extended his initiatives by making a personal pledge to the tsar that France would intervene in Spain to rescue Ferdinand.[39]

Villèle felt that by committing France to an invasion of Spain at Verona Montmorency had exceeded his instructions. Montmorency resigned, but in late December 1812, Villèle was pressured by the *ultras* to name Chateaubriand as foreign minister. Less reactionary, more imaginative and opportunistic, Chateaubriand felt that France could play a leading role in finding a monarchic solution for Spanish-American colonies if it could pull off a successful intervention in Spain, get rid of the liberals there, and gain control over Ferdinand. Under pressure from the *ultras* and the king, Villèle eventually acquiesced in the invasion plan. French naval vessels in Latin American waters were ordered to attack Spanish ships but not the ships of insurgent colonies, in case of a French-Spanish war in Europe. The French began operations to invade Spain in early 1823, and in April 1823, the French army crossed the Bidassoa River and took up offensive positions along the border. At this time, Chateaubriand delineated French policy toward Spain's colonies in anticipation of the restoration of Ferdinand. He sought to take account of the situations created by Iturbide in Mexico and San Martín in Peru, although he was unaware of the latter's monarchic plans for Peru.

> There are some colonies, like Cuba and Puerto Rico, which ask only to be protected by the mother country in preserving the advantages that time and circumstance have given them. Peru could easily be brought back and retained under the domination of the King, for only the towns along the coast have declared themselves independent. The interior of that country has remained loyal. As yet, Mexico is only imperfectly separated from Spain. By the exercise of care, reason, and skill, it would perhaps be possible to establish in America great monarchies governed by princes of the House of Bourbon. In this manner we could combat the waxing system of republics, while Spain would retain the sovereign power as well as immense advantages in those fine colonies which are about to escape from her control.[40]

The French army swept over liberal forces and occupied Spain. By autumn French soldiers had put Ferdinand back on the throne and crushed the liberal movement. These events caused Villèle to take another look at France's role in organizing Spain's former colonies into monarchies. He wrote the commander of the French forces in Spain that three Spanish Bourbon princes should be placed in Mexico, Peru-Chile, and Argentina-Paraguay, and they should be recognized as independent states, although in reality they would be European dependencies. France would be ensured of unrestricted trade relations with the new sovereignties. It also would supply ships and some soldiers and funds to pull off this operation which, Villéle wrote, "should be favored by the different Cabinets of Europe in order to defend peace and order in the New World, to honor by a useful conclusion our intervention in Spain and to make (the invasion costs) more tolerable to France by this consideration and by the new markets furnished to our products." Cuba, Puerto Rico and the Philippines would be allowed to stay in Spain's colonial system.[41]

On November 1, 1823 Villéle told the French ambassador in London, Prince de Polignac, that recognition of the independence of the Spanish-American colonies should be the result of mediation by the Holy Alliance between Spain and the colonies; that their emancipation should take place on the condition of the establishment overseas of Spanish princes whose position should resemble that of Pedro in Brazil.[42]

This prospect of French intervention in Spanish America to establish Bourbon monarchies alarmed George Canning, Castlereagh's successor as foreign secretary. He saw in this eventuality an intolerable obstacle to the expansion of British influence in the New World, both as a counterweight to the United States and as a means of allowing Britain to gain the upper hand over the Holy Alliance in Europe by denying it the ability to incorporate the Spanish-American colonies into its political system. He hoped to bring New World states into existence not as dependencies of the European courts, but as sovereign constitutional monarchies, thereby countering U.S. influence in New World politics and redressing the balance in the Old World, which had become dangerously skewed toward the reactionary legitimism of the Holy Alliance. The Braganza situation in Brazil would become the main focus of Canning's Latin American policy.

Brazil's Monarchic Independence: A Model for the Rest of South America?

Pedro's regency was supported by a powerful anti-Portuguese group of Brazilian landowners and merchants based on the import-export economy. Pedro's Brazilian supporters wanted independence from

Portugal in order to preserve the advantages that had accrued to them from the free trade regime. They were fearful that with John back in Lisbon, the Portuguese liberals would try to reimpose on Brazil the old colonial institutions that restricted the landowners and merchants to inadequate Portuguese markets. But they wanted to maintain the traditional structure of agrarian production based on African slave labor and the *latifundio* (large landed estates); they had steadfastly resisted British pressure to abolish the slave trade. They wanted, therefore, to achieve independence under Pedro's monarchic rule so that mass mobilizations, inevitably involving the large slave population, could be avoided.

This elite group controlled and monarchized the Brazilian independence process, retarding the development of republican politics and placing Brazil squarely out of step with the Spanish-American independence process. Republican ideas had not advanced very far in Brazil, due largely to the stability of Braganza rule in the period from 1808 to 1822 and to the perception that Pedro's regency could be used as a vehicle for the achievement of independence from Portugal. Various anti-Portuguese independence movements had broken out—the so-called *Inconfidencias* of Minas Gerais in 1789, Rio in 1792, Bahia in 1798, and Pernambuco in 1817. French ideas of social equality and radical political democracy were bruited about in these rebellions and even disseminated among the illiterate classes, including the slaves. But none of these rebellions amounted to much more than urban plots and intrigues, with the exception of the one at Pernambuco which actually created a republic in the northeast based on a fairly large popular mobilization, involving slaves as well as men of property, before it was crushed by Portuguese troops and its leaders punished.[43]

Pedro was a very romantic, self-indulgent, haphazardly educated, boorish man—the product of enormous pampering in his royal upbringing both in Portugal and Brazil. He had a large body and a swarthy face. He was totally uncouth. Yet there was a robust streak in the young monarch. He had come to terms with his congenital epilepsy. Proud of having made his way through Virgil's *Aneid,* he liked to draw a parallel between his father's decision to create a new kingdom in Brazil and Aneus's arrival among the Etruscans: Both were efforts to create civilized rule in a wild, politically virgin environment. He took on his new regency in Brazil very energetically. He pictured himself flamboyantly as the incarnation of Brazilian nationalism. He also thought of himself as a liberal reformer. Indeed, he despised slavery, a trait that did not endear him to conservative Brazilians. But Pedro's basic problem was that he was a foreigner attempting to structure Brazil's nationalism; his Portugueseness ultimately was his fatal flaw as Brazil's ruling monarch.[44]

In the beginning, Pedro encouraged the growth of Americanist advice around him. He intended to behave as an American monarch, rather than as an extension of a European dynasty in America; he wanted his rule in Brazil to be seen not as a dynastic right but as the choice of the Brazilian people. The chief advice that Pedro received in 1820 came from the Brazilian-born, European-schooled José Bonifácio de Andrada e Silva. Disturbed by the popular radicalism of the French Revolution but imbued with the rationalist teachings of the Enlightenment, Bonifácio convinced Pedro to declare the independence of Brazil on the foundation of a constitutional monarchy. Bonifácio was conservative politically but progressive in his social and economic policies.

Pedro duly proceeded to "Brazilianize" his royal authority by three acts of policy. First, he made a declaration of independence from Portugal, declared Brazil an empire, and denied to his father any rights of sovereignty over it. Second, he created a Brazilian electoral college to name him "Emperor of Brazil, by acclamation of the Brazilian people" and had himself crowned. Third, he convoked a convention, under Bonifácio's management, to devise a constitutional monarchy for the new empire and pledged himself to exercise the imperial rule within the framework of that document.

Pedro's abrupt actions were denounced promptly in Lisbon by the liberal imperialists. Although they advocated an inclusion of Brazil's delegates in the new legislature in Lisbon, as allowed under the new Portuguese constitution, the liberals vehemently resisted anything smacking of independence for Brazil and attacked Pedro as a revolutionary. Nevertheless, Pedro was determined to expand his political base in Brazil by appearing to his new countrymen as the architect and defender of Brazilian independence against the liberals in Portugal. Initially, it was of no great importance to him whether Britain supported him in this endeavor or not—Britain was committed in Europe and Pedro apparently preferred to be on autonomous American ground. Thus his foreign minister, speaking in French to the British envoy in Rio, informed him that British recognition of Brazil was immaterial since the "emperor was resolved not to mix in the *politique torteuse* of Europe, and would not allow Europe to interfere in those of Brazil or of South America."[45]

Pedro made preparations for war against liberal Portugal if it refused to grant independence peacefully. But he clearly preferred to achieve Portugal's consent to Brazilian independence through negotiations and to stake patriotic support for his monarchy on that achievement, not on fighting against Portugal. The fact that he was a Braganza, facilitated political communication between Rio and Lisbon. Brazil, through Pedro's monarchy, preserved a blood tie to the Portuguese crown, notwithstanding the feuding between father and son and notwithstanding the political subordination of the crown in Lisbon. This buffered the independence movement in Brazil; it made it less revolutionary and provided the conservative interests in this sprawling, slave-infested society with a rallying point.

Even though independent, Pedro's monarchy was the only one in South America. The second fact was even more important than the first in the Holy Alliance's calculation of that continent's future relationship to Europe. The argument that Pedro was not "really" rejecting European political standards, gained considerable currency as the result of his marriage to the daughter of the Austrian emperor. Metternich, the emperor's Chancellor, was personally set at ease about Pedro's purposes as a result of his bridal choice.[46]

If Europe would approve the independence of Brazil as achieved by dynastic arrangement with Portugal and thereby preserving the monarchic principle on the South American continent, Pedro was prepared to follow a Europe-first policy. At bottom he preferred to define the politics of his monarchy by relations with Europe and separation from the Spanish Americans. He contemptuously turned his back on the American politics indulged in by his father—to the chagrin of Canning. The last thing Canning wanted was for Pedro to goad the Spanish Americans into making a common cause against his monarchy. Such a development could not but split the New World off from the Old, the great *bête-noire* of the cagey British statesman.

Canning succeeded Castlereagh at the same time that Pedro succeeded his father in Brazil. The whole dynamics of the relationship between Brazil and Europe shifted as a result of these two simultaneous changes. One era had been distinguished by Castlereagh's opposition to John's robust American politics. The new era was marked by Canning's efforts to push Pedro into cultivating his relations with the Spanish Americans. Increasing the acceptability of Pedro's behavior in the eyes of the Spanish Americans was Canning's major objective. If Pedro were placed on the defensive in the New World, he would be of less use to the Old World in Canning's scheme. "The situation of his Empire," Canning told his envoy in Rio, "as the only monarchical government throughout the extent of the whole New World, exposes his Majesty to peculiar difficulties and hazards; ... jealousness will be more easily excited and hostile combinations more easily formed amongst the republics, his neighbors, against his Majesty's single power." Great Britain, Canning continued, "feels a deep interest not only in the welfare and stability of the House of

Braganza, but in the stability of a Government which forms the strongest connecting link between the Old World and the New."[47]

Canning's objective was to have the Spanish Americans, by virtue of their acceptance of Pedro, move toward the adoption of constitutional monarchies—or at least toward the adoption of conservative political systems—that would be compatible with the monarchic orientation of Europe and beyond the reach of republican seduction by the United States. If Pedro's monarchy in Brazil could become the vehicle for achieving Brazil's independence in spite of the Holy Alliance, its standing should surely increase among the Spanish Americans, and Canning's scenario might acquire plausibility.

George Canning is mainly known for his tenure (1822–1827) as the British Foreign Secretary—a position he seemed to erupt into from the relative obscurity of a decade of service as a member of Parliament representing his native Liverpool. Actually, Canning had already been foreign secretary from 1807–1809. He was the main architect of the British plan to move the Braganza Court from Lisbon to Rio to escape Napoleon. That Canning should have been the prime mover in this plan that subsequently caused Castlereagh so much embarrassment, was simply one fold in the relationship between the two men that was fraught with mutual contempt and rivalry. Although Canning had an aristocratic education, his origins were distinctly middle class. A certain amount of class tension therefore lurked in his relationship with Castlereagh, the Marquis of Londonberry. Their antagonism was evident already during Canning's first tenure as foreign secretary when Castlereagh was the minister of war. This antipathy toward each other culminated in a famous duel in 1810 after both had left the government. When Castlereagh became foreign secretary in 1812, Canning emerged as his main detractor in the Parliament and his only rival in mastery of foreign policy questions. Canning was his distinct superior both as a debater and orator. Upon Castlereagh's death, Canning was the logical choice to be his successor, although the king and his Tory advisers in the Cabinet were adamantly opposed to his appointment. But appointed he was.[48]

A large part of Canning's foreign policy was designed to dismantle Castlereagh's entailment of British policy in the reactionary politics of Europe. His tool for this was the New World. He most famous utterance was made in a speech in Commons on December 12, 1826. Canning was at the apex of his fame. He was also terminally ill; his death was only six months away. His speech was in the form of a testament. "I called the New World into existence," he told a mesmerized audience, "to redress the balance in the Old." He was referring to his engineering of Britain's recognition of the Spanish-American states in 1824. He was also referring to his Brazilian policy.[49]

Canning's New World policy was motivated not only by his disdain for the forces of legitimacy but also by his disdain for the boisterous democracy of the United States—"Yankeeland" as he called it in his private letters. Canning was more liberal than Castlereagh, to be sure, but he was still a monarchist. He was fearful that the rising profile of the northern republic would challenge Britain's world position. Not only was the United States a noncolonial maritime power, but its republicanism, if it spread to the rest of the hemisphere, threatened to divide the Old and New worlds. Britain would not likely be able to side politically with either; the U.S. was too democratic and anticolonial and Europe to too legitimist and reactionary. The key, hence, to Canning's policy was to try to develop a political accommodation between the Old and New worlds and to have Britain regulate their relations.

It was essential to Canning's policy to achieve a European acceptance of Brazil's independence under Pedro's monarchic auspices. Canning faced Holy Alliance efforts to encourage John to resist Pedro's move toward independence and thereby to buttress Brazil as a legitimist bastion against the Spanish-American republics. Yet, Canning reasoned, if British mediation could lead to the achievement of Brazilian independence on the basis of Pedro's monarchy being recognized and consented to by John, how could even the Holy Alliance then withhold its own consent? If the monarchic independence of Brazil could be achieved, the Spanish Americans could be enticed to accept the monarchy's place on the continent and, perhaps, to trim their republican sails accordingly. Canning, thus, saw in the Brazilian monarchy a means of drawing the Old and New worlds together. Rather than finding itself at the periphery of events in a situation where the Old and New worlds split ideologically—the one republican and led by the United States and the other legitimist and led by the Holy Alliance—Britain would rather be at the center of events in a new world order. The Brazilian monarchy also represented to Canning a political counterbalance to the United States in the New World. But it could only challenge the United States so long as the monarchy was able to reconcile itself with the Spanish Americans, which depended, in turn, on Europe's willingness to recognize Brazil's independence and thereby establish its credibility among the Spanish Americans. Canning felt that the price of failing in his effort to mediate Brazil's independence would be the opposition of the New World against the old under the leadership of "Yankeeland." His great nightmare, he wrote to a friend, was the "division of the world into Europe and American, republic and monarchy, a league of worn out governments, on the one hand, and of youthful stirring nations, with the United States at their head on the other."[50]

Lisbon, however, stubbornly insisted on continued sovereignty over Brazil. Pedro, equally stubborn, was commited to the principle of Brazilian independence. For a time, Canning tried to disguise independence by designing a temporary commonwealth relationship between Lisbon and Rio. His formula for achieving this was to press Pedro to accept the overlordship of his father, so that the crowns of Brazil and Portugal would be seen as reunited on the head of John until his death, when Pedro would succeed to the Portuguese crown and possibly send an heir to rule Portugal as his viceroy. In the meantime, Pedro needed to accept John's assumption of title of emperor of Brazil; Pedro would be the king of Brazil. The semantics here got complex.

Canning eventually succeeded in arranging mediation of the dispute in London. But Pedro complained that Canning was being too solicitous of the Portuguese. Britain had not stood up for Ferdinand's rights in his colonies nearly so arduously as it was pressing John's rights in Brazil. Pedro wanted British recognition of Brazil regardless of Portuguese recognition. Canning exhorted Pedro not to allow himself to become an outcast of Europe, presiding over a renegade monarchy in America. If Pedro turned his back on Portugal, he would be excluded from his succession rights to the Portuguese crown and seen in Lisbon as having "bartered his inherited for his acquired right." He might choose not to exercise his succession rights, but his honor required that this "should be done by voluntary renunciation rather than that he should appear to be deprived of it by a sentence pronounced upon him, in the face of the (European) world, as a punishment for rebellion against his father."[51]

Canning wanted to make sure that the Holy Alliance had no choice but to accept the use of British mediation, based on Portuguese consent to Brazilian independence. He found that Pedro's father-in-law, the Austrian emperor, would support Brazil's independence if Pedro did not openly revolt against his father. Canning was aware that John was being subjected in Lisbon to French and Russian pressure to deny Portuguese recognition of Brazilian independence. Yet he was optimistic that, once the talks were underway, "even those Powers that are most desirous of thwarting any compromise by which (as they apprehend) the principle of legitimacy would be soiled," would yield the field to British mediation.[52]

The British envoy in Rio was instructed to join his efforts with those of the Austrian envoy in order to encourage Pedro's negotiators to be cooperative in the London talks. Pedro, however, became impatient with British toleration of any formula that would leave Portugal with sovereign rights in Brazil, however temporary. He found British policy toward Brazil certainly more enlightened than that of either France or Russia, but it also manifested "a greater friendship for Portugal than for Brazil." The 1810 commercial treaty, which John had signed with the British had, in effect, secured British protection of Portugal in Europe by granting monopolistic privileges in Brazilian trade. Pedro had hinted that he would renegotiate that treaty and repeal the British privileges if it did not recognize Brazilian independence. As for the supposed political advantages of gaining rights of successorship to the Portuguese crown, Pedro pretended to see this as a liability. In one interview with the British envoy, he theatrically played the American card from his father's deck. Pedro rose to his feet and, extending one leg behind the other, supported himself precariously on the toe of his extended leg and announced that this was a posture he wanted to avoid. "He intended," according to the British envoy, "to fix himself firmly in Brazil and . . . not weaken his footing by keeping an insecure position in Portugal, where, without any advantage, he should be exposed to all the evil inseparable from any connection with that kingdom of Europe, and all of its wars and tortuous politics and the concomitant evil springing therefrom."[53]

Aside from the hope of Europe's acceptance of Pedro, Canning's policy was on even more unstable ground in its second essential objective: producing a détente between the Brazilian monarchy and the Spanish-American republics. He had to recognize that the subject of monarchy had become a divisive matter for the Spanish Americans, given the fierce struggle between monarchists and republicans that had turned their independence movements into civil wars. Even though a monarchic consensus was no longer possible as a result of these civil wars, nominally won by the republicans, neither was a republican consensus clearly within grasp. In fact, the creation of the American monarchy in Brazil made the republican consolidation of the Spanish-American states that much more problematic, particularly if, as was to be expected, the monarchy's stability and legitimacy evoked admiration in the unstable republics and, worse, if the monarchy actively plotted to undermine the republics. Carlota's initiative was widely perceived among Spanish Americans as a Trojan Horse that disguised a Braganza plot to take political control of the viceroyalties. The Chilean Senate on November 11, 1819, referring to John's kingship in Brazil, noted that "for Chile, which ... has become independent of Spain after a costly war, the establishment of a king in America was a matter of concern even to the most naïve of souls." The senate advocated sending an agent to Brazil to observe the monarchy and to "manifest our rights and block all suspicions and intrigues" that it might be sponsoring against the Chilean republic.[54] The Spanish Americans harbored ambivalent, even paranoid, attitudes toward the monarchy in Brazil.

Preventing this ambivalence from turning into open hostility depended, in Canning's view, on moderating Pedro's behavior toward the Spanish Americans, especially toward the Argentines with whom Brazil was in the closest contact. Any challenging, chauvinistic behavior by Pedro would assuredly, in Cannings's view, "furnish an inducement for the new states of Spanish America to unite themselves sooner or later in a common cause against Brazil."[55] If Pedro were placed on the defensive in the New World, and if hostile combinations were formed against him, the stability of his monarchy would be undermined, and it would not be able to serve efficiently as the "connecting link between the Old World and the New."

There was little room for Canning to influence the Spanish-American revolutions by mediating their conflict with Ferdinand. Not only was the gap between Ferdinand and the Spanish-American revolutionaries unbridgeable, but also Britain lacked the kind of leverage over Ferdinand that it had over John; Ferdinand was "owned" by the Holy Alliance. This forced Canning to preserve Castlereagh's conservative policy to some extent; he was not prepared to identify British policy with the principle of revolution *de facto* in the New World by recognizing the new states in spite of Spain and Europe. The best he could do for several years, until well into 1824, was to hold out the promise of recognition until opinion in Europe changed. Canning's hope was that Colombia's expanding military power might exercise a conservative, organizing influence on the Spanish-American revolutions that it came into contact with and thereby make them perhaps more acceptable to Europe. In fact, Canning's whole policy rested on two increasingly apparent pillars: (1) Pedro's monarchic authority in Brazil; and (2) Bolívar's military power in the rest of South America. Canning's fear was the entry of Colombian armed forces into the Eastern Bank conflict on the side of the Argentines.

Notes

1. Memorandum, Jose Rabello, Brazilian envoy to Washington, April 20, 1824, in William Manning, *Diplomatic Correspondence of the United States Concerning the Independence of the Latin American Nations.* New York: Oxford University Press, 1925, II: 779–80. This document contains a useful chronology of events surrounding John's arrival in Brazil, with emphasis on the groundwork laid for the independence of Brazil from Portugal. The exodus of John's court, as well as the overall story of the Braganza advent in South America, is depicted in Neil Macaulay, *Dom Pedro: The Struggle for Liberty in Brazil and Portugal, 1798–1835.* Durham, N.C.: Duke University Press, 1986. For more diplomatic analysis of the exodus see Alan K. Manchester, *British Preeminence in Brazil: Its Rise and Decline.* Chapel Hill: University of North Carolina Press, 1933.

2. Henry Chamberlain to Castlereagh, November 2, 1822, in Charles Webster, *Britain and the Independence of Latin America.* London, 1938, I: 215–16.

3. Thomas Sumpter to Robert Smith, July 23, 1810, Manning, II: 670.

4. Olviera Lima, *Manuel de Dom João VI no Brasil.* Rio de Janeiro, 1945, I: 272.

5. John Hann, "Burr's Model Applied: The Balance of Power in the Rio de la Plata." *Proceedings of the Pacific Coast Council on Latin American Studies.* 3:1974, 31–34.

6. Ibid., 33

7. Bartolomé Mitre, *Historia del Belgrano y de la Independencia Argentina.* Buenos Aires, 1927. III: 39.

8. Hann, "Burr's Model," 31–34. See also Ron L. Seckinger, *The Brazilian Monarchy and the Spanish American Republics.* Baton Rouge: Louisiana State University Press, 1984, 103–05.

9. Castlereagh to Chamberlain, December 19, 1816, in Charles Webster, *Britain and the Independence of Latin America.* London, 1938, II: 179–80; Chamberlain to Castlereagh, October 8, 1816, in ibid., I: 178–79; July 20, 1816, in ibid., I: 175–180; December 19, 1816, in ibid., I: 179–80.

10. Castlereagh to Chamberlain, December 19, 1816, in Webster, II: 179–80; Castlereagh to Edward Thornton, May 5, 1820 in ibid., I: 196–7 and May 15, 1820, in ibid., I: 203–04.

11. Calogeras Pandiá, *A Política Exterior do Império.* Rio de Janeiro, 1962, II: 25 ff., 380 ff.

12. James Smith Wilcocks to John Quincy Adams, October 25, 1821, in Manning, III: 1599–1614. Biased, but gives excellent detail on Iturbide-O'Donojú relations and the Plan de Iguala framework.

13. William Spencer Robertson, *France and Latin American Independence.* New York: Octagon Books, 1967, 202–013.

14. Robertson, 187.

15. Ricardo Rojas, *San Martín: Knight of the Andes.* Trans., Herschel Brickell and Carlos Videla. New York: Doubleday, 1945, 261–65.

16. Robertson, 186–88. Quotation from a letter to a close friend, Tomás Godoy Cruz, May 24, 1816, in Robertson, 186–88.

17. San Martín to James Duff, December 6, 1817. in Webster, I: 557. Ricardo Piccirilli, *San Martín y la Política de los Pueblos.* Buenos Aires, 1960, 239–300.

18. Mariano Felipe Paz Soldan, *Historia del Peru Independente, 1822–1827.* Madrid, 1919, I: 1–73. R. Vargas Ugarte, *Historia General del Peru.* Lima, 1962, VI: 186–92.

19. Seckinger, 31–32.

20. San Martín's envoys to Europe were Juan García del Rio and James Paroissien, the latter an old Brazilian hand and one-time agent of the Braganzas. Paroissien's career and role as envoy: R. A. Humphreys, *Liberation in South America, 1806–1827: The Career of James Paroissien.* London, 1952.

21. R. Vargas Ugarte, *Historia del Peru.* Buenos Aires, *1958,* VI: 186–194.

22. Bolívar's physical appearance and address: Captain Andrew, *Journey from Buenos Aires to Potosí.* London, 1827, 95–96. See also Angel Grisanti, *Retratos de Bolívar y Sucre.* Caracas, 1969. Bolívar's comparison of his personality to Sucre's, emphasizing Sucre's more likeable qualities: letter to Sucre, April 26, 1825, *Cartas de Bolívar,* edited by R. Blanco-Fombona, Madrid, 1921, 94–95. Bolívar's negative relations with North American ambassadors were epitomized in his dealings with William Tudor, envoy to Peru in the 1820s, and the future American president and ambassador to Colombia in the late 1820, William Harrison.

Both men became arch-enemies of Bolívar and shaped many attitudes toward him held in Washington. Bolívar had Harrison declared *persona non grata* in 1829.

23. Standard English biography of Bolívar: Gerhard Masur, *Simón Bolívar,* rev. ed. Albuquerque: University of New Mexico, 1969. Bolívar's early life details and family lineage: Vicente Lecuna, *Crónica Razonada de las Guerras de Bolívar.* New York: Colonial Press, 1950, I: x–xii; Gil Fortoul, *Obras Completas.* Caracas, 1953, I: 309–20.

24. Simón Rodríguez's influence on Bolívar: Lecuna, *Crónica,* I: xiv–xvii; European travels with Rodríguez and personal taste for British political system: Fortoul, 321–22.

25. Wellesly-Bolívar meeting: Lecuna, *Crónica,* I: xiv–xvii.

26. *Selected Writings of Bolívar,* edited and translated by Vicente Lecuna and Harold Bierck, New York: Colonial Press, 1951, 1:24–26.

27. Nestor dos Santos Lima, *La Imágen de Brazil en las Cartas de Bolívar.* Caracas, 1978.

28. Text of Jamaica Letter: Lecuna and Bierck, I: 103–22

29. Ibid., 115.

30. Text of Angostura Address: Lecuna and Bierck, I: 173–l97.

31. Bolívar to Iturbide, October 19, 1821. *Obras Completas.* Ed. by Vicente Lecuna and Elizabeth Barret de Nazaris, Havana, Cuba, 1947, I: 598.

32. Bolívar to Carlos Soublette, November 22, 1821, in ibid., 608–09.

33. Bolívar to San Martín, November 16, 1821, in ibid., 607.

34. Bolívar to Santander, February 9, 1822, in ibid., 628.

35. Bolívar to Santander, September 13, 1822, in ibid., 680.

36. Henry A. Kissinger, *A World Restored.* New York: Grosset and Dunlap, 1964.

37. Robertson, 129–78.

38. Ernest R. May, *The Making of the Monroe Doctrine.* Cambridge, Mass.: Harvard University Press, 1975, 106.

39. Robertson, 208–09; May, 93–94, 97, 102–03.

40. Robertson, 261.

41. Ibid., 262.

42. Ibid., 281.

43. Emilia Viotti da Costa, *The Brazilian Empire: Myths and Histories.* Chicago: University of Chicago Press, 1974, xix, 7, 8, 10.

44. Influence of epilepsy on Pedro: Macaulay, 36, 65. Aspects of personality and influence of the Aneid: Ibid., 22, 45. Another sketch of Pedro's personality emphasizing his boldness and feistiness: Stuart to Canning, September 5, 1824, Webster, II: 286–88.

45. Chamberlain to Canning, November 2, 1822, Webster, I: 214–16.

46. Metternich's favorable albeit mixed view of Pedro's monarchy: William Spence Robertson, "Metternich's Attitude toward Revolutions in Latin America," *Hispanic American Historical Review,* 1941, 22: 533–34; 550–56. Pedro's marriage to the daughter of Emperor Franz Joseph: Macaulay, 57–59.

47. "Hostile combinations": Canning to Richard Gordon, August 1, 1826, Webster, I: 311–312.

48. Canning's role in the Braganza exodus to Brazil and his antagonism with Castlereagh: Leslie Bethell, *George Canning and the Independence of Latin America*. London, 1970, 3–4.

49. William W. Kaufman, *British Policy and the Independence of Latin America*. New York: Anchor Books, 1967, argues that Canning used his Latin American policy to destroy the Holy Alliance and bring into existence a new world balance. For another interpretation of Canning's policy in America: Harold Temperley, *The Foreign Policy of Canning, 1822–7; England, the Neo-Holy Alliance and the New World*. 2nd ed. London, 1925.

50. Canning to John Frere, January 8, 1825, in Bethell, 9.

51. Canning to Chamberlain, January 12, 1825, in Webster, I: 248–55.

52. Ibid., 254.

53. Joint British-Austrian pressure on Pedro: Canning to Chamberlain, August 5, 1823, in Webster I: 226–27 and December 10, 1823, 225–30; "Not to weaken his footing": Chamberlain to Canning, February 12, 1825, in Webster, I: 157–261.

54. Juan José Fernandez, *La República de Chile y el Imperio del Brasil*. Santiago, 1959, 19–20; Alfredo Valladão, *Brasil e Chile Na Época do Império: Amizade Sem Exemplo*. Rio de Janeiro, 1959, 77.

55. "Common cause": Canning to Ponsonby, British mediator between Brazil and Argentina, March 18, 1826, in Webster, II: 141.

2

Colombia's Military
Against Republican Politics:
Sucre and Bolívar

THE VAST STATE OF COLOMBIA was created by the unification of the two adjacent colonial districts of Venezuela and New Granada. Even though the republican ideology was prominent in both the New Granadian and Venezuelan revolutions, the wars for independence shaped different political experiences in the two areas, bringing to the surface underlying differences in racial structures and colonial tradition. These differences severely strained the republican constitution on which the Colombian union was based. Also, the size of Colombia's military establishment in the 1820s under Bolívar began to menace the republican government of Colombia. In fact, a tacit alliance against the Colombian republican constitution began to take shape between Bolívar and his ally against the Spanish, José Antonio Páez, the leader of the Venezuelan *llaneros* (plains fighters). Páez led the cause of Venezuelan secession from the Colombian union in the 1820s. There was an inherent contradiction between Bolívar's ability to support republican principles elsewhere in South America and his encouragement of Páez's efforts to overthrow the republican constitution of Colombia. It was a contradiction that Sucre, Bolívar's ablest general, was well aware of. He attempted to resolve it against Páez. Sucre favored the creation of republican states in South America free of monarchic influence, in general, and European influences, in particular. Significantly, Páez and his supporters sought to tempt Bolívar to become the monarch of Colombia. In this way, the Páez faction could jettison the republican structure, which in their view was controlled by the New Granadians at Venezuela's expense.

Colombia's Republican Gamble

New Granada's racial structure consisted largely of white and Indian populations with only a relatively small black population concentrated along the coasts. The plantation system employing black slave labor never spread to the interior of the country, where the feudal *encomienda* system, Indian communal lands, and free-holdings prevailed. Racial mixture among blacks and whites had produced a mulatto population in the coastal towns while a mixture of Indians and whites produced a substantial mestizo population in the interior highlands. New Granadian creoles from in the central highlands, an area known as Cundinamarca where the viceroyalty was centered, were much less racially mixed than Venezuelan *creoles*. Furthermore, they held the mixed-blood segments of the population firmly in check through an elaborate network of religious, social, economic, legal, and political devices. Although the mixed-bloods in New Granada were widely recruited into the patriot armies, dominant political power remained in the hands of the Cundinamarcan creole class after the overthrow of Spanish rule. The major challenges to the Cundinamarcan control of New Granada came from separatist movements started by largely white commercial elites in coastal areas, especially in Cartagena.[1]

In Venezuela, however, it was different. The *pardos* (mixtures of black, Indian, and white) constituted by far the majority of the population. They emerged as a major political force in the wake of the independence wars. Venezuela lacked the tradition of lawfulness which was characteristic of New Granada, especially in Cundinamara; Bogotá was the seat of the viceroyalty, the *audiencia* (royal territorial court) and a major university. Venezuela was more haphazardly ruled by Spain. It shifted in and out of various Caribbean jurisdictions before becoming attached to the viceroyalty of New Granada. It was only given semi-autonomous status late in the colonial period, when it was elevated to a captaincy-general. Furthermore, Venezuela's whole economy was based on the plantation system using black African slave labor.[2]

The war for independence in Venezuela was marked by enormous bloodshed, social destruction, and racial revenge. A precarious equilibrium between the few whites and the many *pardos* had been maintained by Spanish policy during the colonial period. The colonial officials secured some social rights for the *pardos* in order to gain their allegiance to the crown and to play them off against local whites. With the outbreak of the independence movement, that equilibrium broke down. The Venezuelan white property owners either were exterminated or they fled into exile. Attacks were mounted against them by the *pardos*, who were incited to a genocidal frenzy by renegade loyalists. Enormous property holdings were "liberated" during rampage. To a great extent, the war in Venezuela functioned as a social and racial revolution, creating a specter that haunted Bolívar's political thought throughout his career. It was the mobilization of the *pardos* living around the coast that fueled a rebellion in Coro, which in turn led to the overthrow of the first Venezuelan republic. A much larger uprising of the *pardos* living in the interior plains ensued.[3]

New Granadian elites next door feared the ascendancy of the *pardos* in Venezuela. They viewed with particular horror the prospect of mobilized outcast portions of the population becoming the basis of a new political and social order—"*pardocracia*." They were especially fearful of the *llaneros*.[4] The Cundinamarcans held the belief that their own independence movement was a legal rebellion, with its roots in an earlier, community-based tax revolt against royal despotism; as such, it was not a social revolution. The intellectual and political leader of the independence movement in New Granada was Camilio Torres, a Cundinamarcan lawyer and scholar who achieved considerable notoriety during the colonial period as a critic of royal taxation policies. Torres's group eventually triumphed over other factions and inaugurated a federal government in 1812. Its period of rule, however, was ineffectual and brief. A Spanish expeditionary army occupied New Granada in 1815 and liquidated the leadership of the federal government. Camilio Torres was among those executed. However, a legalistic ethos survived among the Cundinamarcan creoles that accentuated their sense that Bolívar's countrymen were crude and morally inferior. The particular barbarism of the Venezuelan wars served to prove this thinking.[5]

Despite the enormous social and political differences that existed between New Granada and Venezuela, they were mutually bound to Bolívar. The military campaigns that he conducted against the Spanish in both lands over a period of twelve years led cumulatively to the final, almost simultaneous collapse of Spanish power in Venezuela and in New Granada. Bolívar's victories gave him prestige and authority in both countries, and this paved the way for his plan to unify them politically.[6]

Bolívar launched a campaign from Angostura that culminated in a major victory over the Spanish expeditionary forces in the battle of Boyacá (August 7, 1819) in New Granada. This spectacular event turned the military tide against the Spanish. Vast cavalry forces made up of Venezuelan *llaneros* under the leadership of their own *caudillo*, Páez, had swung definitively over to Bolívar's side. The incorporation of this sector of the population widened the military base of the Venezuelan independence movement but also made its political and social dynamics more unpredictable.

The delegates at Angostura proclaimed the union of New Granada and Venezuela, along with Ecuador. Ecuador was an area to the south of New Granada. Although it had been ruled judicially by the *audiencia* seated at Quito, it was administered as part of the Viceroyalty of New Granada in the colonial period. The Angostura Congress also named

Bolívar as president of the new Colombian state and Francisco Antonio Zea, a New Granadian who was prominent in the Angostura Congress, as his vice-president. It also named Santander as provisional vice-president of New Granada. Vice-presidencies were also created for Venezuela and Ecuador, the latter to be filled when the area was liberated from the Spanish. The congress also called a constitutional convention to meet at Cúcuta, a small town in New Granada near the Venezuelan border, on January 1, 1821.

The delegates at Cúcuta from Cundinamarca dominated intellectually the convention. They exhibited considerable apprehension about uniting New Granada to Venezuela. One key Cundinamarcan delegate, Vicente Azuero, voiced his concerns. He felt that despite its ill-fated experience with federalist government under Torres, the federal form was safer for New Granada if it had to be joined to its neighbor. It would provide a buffer against Venezuelan revolutionary influences that intruded themselves into the body politic of New Granada. A centralized state would be more dangerous because "with Venezuelans exercising direct influence over our domestic administration, they would end up disorganizing almost all of the social bonds (of the New Granadians) as has occurred in Venezuela, where the right of property is scarcely even known and there is not a moment of security."[7]

Azuero and his fellow New Granadians at Cúcuta eventually accepted a centralized state under pressure from Bolívar and his adherents. But they gambled on the hope that through a republican constitution based on the rule of law, New Granada might be able to exercise a tutelary influence over Venezuela and channel its revolutionary energies into the structures of representative government.

The Cundinamarcans' problem in this endeavor was not only Páez; it was also Bolívar's authoritarian tendencies. His enormous, personalistic authority based in the professional military had obvious dictatorial and praetorian overtones. Bolívar had clearly indicated that the moral censors in the fourth branch of government that he advocated in the Angostura Address should be composed originally of the Venezuelan liberators. By firmly rejecting the idea of any hereditary caste in government, and by enshrining the principle of civilian supremacy over the military, the Cundinamarcans hoped to create a constitution that would domesticate Bolívar's power. The decision made at Cúcuta to locate the capital of Colombia at Bogotá in the heart of Cundinamarca fueled this hope. The Cúcuta Constitution was a high-stakes gamble by the Cundinamarcans that their constitution could make a republican citizen out of Bolívar—and out of Páez.[8]

In the constitution that was finally drafted, the federal form of government was rejected in favor of the centralized state that Bolívar favored. But the authoritarian overtones of Bolívar's Angostura Address were deliberately rejected. The constitution made Colombia into a purely representative republic. All of the offices in the government were for limited tenure and subject to periodic election by the people. The powers of the executive branch (a presidency, a vice-presidency, and ministries) were distinctly subordinated to the legislature, which was clearly the dominant branch of the government. There was a strong preference for legislation, as opposed to an executive decree or administrative ruling, as the means of regulating society and the government's role therein. The body assembled at Cúcuta, in fact, acted much more like a legislature than a constitutional convention. It drafted and promulgated an enormous array of laws and codes that touched every aspect of social life, as well as regulated the military, the Church, the educational system, and economic practices. The zeal for perfecting society through liberal reforms in the Benthamite sense, rather than a concern for making the law relevant to a society's ethos in Montesquieu's sense, dominated the outlook at Cúcuta. This put the drafters completely out of tune with the model of government that Bolívar had adumbrated in his Angostura address.[9]

Ultimately, the political challenge facing the New Granadians was to legitimate the Cúcuta Constitution in Venezuela by isolating Páez. The standard-bearer of this strategy (which was a defensive strategy as much as an offensive one) was Santander, himself a native of Cúcuta. The Cundinamarcan delegates at Cúcuta had already begun to group themselves around Santander as their leader, in whom they vested their best hopes for holding the raw power of Páez at bay. Santander and Páez knew perfectly what was at stake; they had had this confrontation—law versus power—before.[10] The test this time was the Cúcuta Constitution: Would Páez break it or be broken by it? There was also the related question of Bolívar's military power. Could it be subordinated to the constitution? Could it even be prevented from converging with Páez's power to overthrow it?

Bolívar's Strategy of Power

Bolívar began to deliberately construct an extra-constitutional structure of power—for which the expansion of Colombia's military power in South America would be the vehicle—from the first moment that he became aware of the results of the deliberations of the Cúcuta Assembly. He was furious that the lines that he had laid down in his Angostura Address—the hereditary senate, the powerful president, the fourth branch of censors—were rejected. Bolívar saw the Cúcuta Constitution as a make-believe structure that mocked the real needs of Colombia for a strong, paternalistic government to give it a sense of cohesion and firm rule after the enormous upheavals produced by the fighting against Spain. The learned, legalistic community of elite Cundinamarcans (Bolívar referred to them as a "debating society") was a tiny fragment in the wild, militarized state of Colombian society. "If it is not the *llaneros* who exterminate us," he wrote Santander, "it will be the suave philosophers of a perfectible Colombia."[11]

Largely to placate Bolívar, the Cúcuta Congress elected him president of Colombia. Bolívar said privately that he could not be a citizen in a state whose laws he disagreed with; that the condition for his citizenship in Colombia was the adoption of his Angostura program as the basis for the constitution. Yet publicly he agreed to lend his name to the Cúcuta project by accepting the presidency. But he insisted that he remain at the head of the army and that a clause be written into the constitution giving him extra-constitutional dictatorial powers with which to govern in those areas where his armies were still fighting or which were just recently liberated by them. He also made known his support for Santander to whom he intended to delegate his presidential responsibilities. Bolívar intended to occupy himself with the remaining military campaigns against the Spanish. He wished the vice-president well (the two men had a very close relationship at this time), but Bolívar privately doubted that Santander would be able to handle the Venezuelans.[12]

Bolívar returned to Venezuela in mid-1821 to join forces with Páez's army for the final assault on the Spanish, who were largely entrenched around Caracas at that time. This campaign produced the victory at Carabobo (June 24, 1821), which effectively terminated the war in Venezuela. Páez and his patrons in Venezuela almost immediately started a campaign to discredit the Cúcuta Constitution in the name of a *llanero*-based movement. A connection developed between the erstwhile loyalist whites, who returned from self-exile after the war, and the native elements of *caudillo* rule, which developed during the war and had coalesced around Páez. The politics of this connection took the form of the cooptation of Páez by the returning exiled whites and the manufacturing of all manner of charges against the national government of Bogotá. For a while, Venezuela remained loyal to the national government. In fact, the party behind Páez was the only thing that held Venezuela together politically. Eventually the claims that emanated from his backers, calling variously for a monarchy or an empire to replace the Cúcuta republican order, became steadily more insistent. It was clear that in their efforts to create a *llanero* militia to serve as a political base, Páez and his patrons intended to undermine the authority of the professional army that Bolívar had built up. By writing letters to Bolívar over Páez's signature, Páez's backers hoped to turn Bolívar against Santander and thereby lay the groundwork for a political takeover of Venezuela in the name of "loyalty" to Bolívar. When Bolívar was headlong into his invasion of South America, Páez "wrote" him that the people of Venezuela were not suited to pseudo-republican government, Cundinamarcan style. "Something else" was needed. This was like Napoleon being asked back from Egypt to save France from the Directory. In this case, Bolívar was being asked back to save Colombia from the "conspiracy of paper-pushers" at Bogotá.[13]

Santander soon felt trapped in a vice. On the one side, there was the problem of Páez. His growing power threatened to become the basis for a separatist movement. Santander embraced the hope that "liberal" sentiments would gain some ascendancy in Caracas and cause the separatist-monarchist movement to disappear. Páez and his supporters "know they cannot reach high positions in the present political structure of Colombia," he wrote to Bolívar. "They therefore have to consider appealing to another system to see if one day they can replace us."[14]

On the other side, there was the problem of Bolívar's disposition to make freelance use of his extra-constitutional powers. He expected Santander to continue to raise troops for his armies without legislative approval, even after the combat theaters moved outside of Colombian borders. Santander soon felt the strain of trying to serve two masters. "Your theater of operation" he wrote Bolívar in his sanctimonious style, "is defined by your own free will and the goals you set. Mine, by the constitution and the will of the legislators." It began to appear to Santander that Bolívar's command of Colombia's army on the basis of the extra-constitutional powers, and Páez's command of his *llaneros* in Venezuela were cut from the same cloth. Allowing Bolívar to stay outside of the constitution made it that much harder to bring Páez into it.[15]

Bolívar's alienation from the Cúcuta Constitution as the basis for the Colombian state took the form of his determination to construct an external political power structure. He planned to diplomatically form the American league of states. At the same time, he planned to use the Colombian army to build up a military empire outside of Colombia in the course of chasing down and defeating the remaining Spanish armies on the South American continent.

In his Jamaica Letter of 1814, Bolívar had sounded the call for convening an assembly of Spanish-American states in Panama to construct an American league. Eight years later, after Venezuela and New Granada had been liberated and united, he sent emissaries to Peru, Chile, Argentina, and Mexico to negotiate bilateral alliance treaties between those states and Colombia and also to secure their pledges to send representatives to Panama in order to form the league. The league idea was vigorously pursued by Pedro Gual, as the foreign minister of Colombia.

Gual was particularly concerned that the United States be in Panama to preside over the meeting as its titular leader and the New World's republican model.[16] Bolívar, for his part, felt that it was a mistake to invite the United States. His concept of the American league of states, as we saw in his Jamaica Letter, certainly did not praise republican ideology nor did it contemplate any political combination of Spanish America with the United States based on the exclusion of Europe; quite to the contrary on both points.[17] The lengthy instructions to his agents, sent to Spanish-American capitals in 1821 to negotiate bilateral treaties of alliance with Colombia and also to invite their participation in the assembly of states in Panama, studiously avoided any normative reference to republican or even liberal principles of government. Instead, the instructions envisaged the American states as *de facto*, territorially controlled entities. There was no implication that the American states were or should be united by a commitment to representative institutions or liberal government. They had become "separated in the exercise of their sovereignty" by virtue of the "course of human events" generated by the armed struggle for liberation from Spanish rule. Where they were united was on the question of "sustain(ing) themselves against the aggressions of foreign powers." Sovereignty, thus, rested essentially on territorial control achieved by military effort, not on the consent of the governed. This explains the emphasis placed on the principle of the last effective colonial occupier (*uti possidetis juris*) in the instructions. The future member states were required to commit themselves to the defense of this *de facto* principle as the basis of organizing their borders and arbitrating disputes. Bolívar, therefore, did not intend to base the league on the principles of representative government. Even in the Chilean instructions where Bolívar had recommended the creation of an "American nation of Republics," he cautioned O'Higgins against drafting a constitution along liberal lines. Stronger governments were needed in America, he reminded him.[18]

Bolívar might theoretically have decided to challenge the Colombian Constitution from Venezuela. He doubted, however, that he could establish effective political control over a land that was in the throes of a social and racial revolution. Furthermore, if he established a power base in Venezuela, he would be pushed into making a premature choice between the Cúcuta Constitution and the *llaneros*. On the one hand, to oppose the Cúcuta Constitution in Venezuela would mean basing himself in the unpredictable currents of the Venezuelan revolution. On the other hand, to have to pledge his support for the constitution in Venezuela would mean a confrontation with the large movement that was being mobilized around Páez. It seemed preferable to let Páez dislocate the new constitutional order unchallenged, thereby allowing Bolívar to pose as the savior of Colombia on his terms, returning from distant theaters of military triumph. His extra-constitutional military dictatorships in Ecuador and points south, where he took his armies in search of the Spanish foe, would anchor Colombia and serve as its bulwark against being torn asunder by Venezuela. The price, ultimately, that he would ask for "saving" Colombia would be the substitution of the Cúcuta Constitution.

This drift in Bolívar's thinking is revealed by a military metaphor for the Colombian state that he used at this time. Venezuela was the "vanguard," Cundinamarca was the "center" and Ecuador was the "reserve." Bolívar said Venezuela was where the real challenges to the Colombian "ship of state" existed, but it was also the place of greatest volatility. He concluded that his own capacity to stabilize the Colombian state therefore required him to operate in the south, where he could liberate Quito, the ruling city of Ecuador, and annex the Pacific port of Guayaquil as a staging area for the invasion of Peru. In Venezuela, he "could not do more than ride on the sea in the storm in which I could capsize with my ship, while navigating the Pacific I can anchor when I want to and secure the ship in the best port with the best assurances. ... The south can serve as (Colombia's) basis for salvation."[19]

While he was undertaking the final campaign against the Spanish in Venezuela, Bolívar wanted the groundwork laid for a campaign against Quito. He particularly wanted a campaign opened through the port of Guayaquil in order to pave the way for the annexation of that province to Colombia, along with the rest of Ecuador. Bolívar envisaged the campaign against Quito as a pincer movement: One line of attack was to be mounted from Guayaquil and the other, to be directed by him, from the south of New Granada after he finished the war in Venezuela. Bolívar had lost confidence in a Venezuelan general whom he had put provisionally in charge of the Quito campaign. He decided to let him languish until he could arrive from Venezuela with reinforcements. In the meantime, he gave Sucre the responsibility for opening up the campaign to liberate Quito via Guayaquil. Sucre's meteoric rise to fame began in the swamps around this sultry, Peru-oriented Pacific port.

Sucre's American Republicanism

Antonio José de Sucre was the fifth of nine children, born on February 3, 1795, to Vicente Sucre and Manuela Alcalá. They lived in the small Caribbean port of Cumaná, located on the eastern coast of Venezuela. The name in its original spelling, Succre, can be traced back to various towns in the Spanish Netherlands; the House of Succre had a seat in the Flanders parliament. The line can be followed further back to Juan de

Succre who served the House of Borgona in Spain in the fifteenth century. His son, Andrés, was a tutor to Spain's second Hapsburg king, Phillip II. Further back, the line can be traced to Jewish ancestors who evidently converted to Christianity under the pressure of the Spanish Inquisition. This seems to be a problem for some of Sucre's race-conscious biographers, who point defensively to the family's Flanders seat as a sign that it had passed the test of *limpieza de sangre,* that is, blood lines that were not subject to Arab or Jewish "contamination." During Sucre's life, his foes made allegations against his bloodlines, including the charge of illegitimacy. Bolívar seems to have squelched these "rumors."[20]

The Alcalá family name was rooted in Málaga, Spain. Antonio was in the sixth generation of both the Sucre and Alcalá lines in Venezuela. The death of his mother occurred when he was just seven—and caused his childhood to be, as Sucre looked back on it, "a little sad." His father remarried and moved Antonio and his brothers and sisters into another house with their new mother. Six new children were born of this marriage. In this situation, Sucre gravitated toward his uncle, José Manuel, who took over the responsibility for his education and taught him to think of Venezuela as his *patria* (fatherland). In his childhood, Sucre was already detached; he stood apart from the normal games and general "messing around" of his peers. He was too reflective and stiff—"*muy comedido y parco*" in the words of his uncle—to join in their activities. "He was very taciturn and seemed to be in a dialogue with himself," the uncle added about his young charge.[21]

Sucre's life was seared by war. The war against Spain was particularly vicious in Venezuela as it mingled with racial hatreds, social revolution, and sickening atrocities. In the bloodletting, Sucre lost three brothers—two executed by the Spanish on the field of battle and one murdered by rampaging *llaneros.* His ailing sister was raped and killed in her hospital bed by the *llaneros.* His stepmother committed suicide to avoid falling into their hands. Two more sisters died in flight. Before coming into Bolívar's wake in 1816, Sucre had fought for eight years with the insurgents in his home province of Cumaná. He entered the ranks at age thirteen, after returning to the east in 1808 from Caracas where he had been sent to study engineering. He barely escaped with his life on more than one occasion in countless skirmishes with loyalist forces.[22]

Sucre rose in the eastern ranks more by virtue of his planning abilities than his exploits on the field of battle. He commanded an artillery unit in one of his first assignments in Cumaná and a demolition squad in another. In order to advance his military expertise, he was sent to Caracas to serve under the republican general Francisco Miranda. Back in Cumaná, he served as a "scientific officer" on the staff of the voluble eastern *caudillo* and future foe of Bolívar, Santiago Mariño. Sucre instructed him on matters of military discipline. He subsequently became the one-person brain trust of the wild and wooly Venezuelan guerilla leader, Francisco Bermúdez. Sucre planned Bermúdez's campaigns, managed his politics, and wrote his correspondence.

Bolívar's initial contact with Sucre appears to have occurred during an inspection trip he made to the Venezuelan east in 1814. A unit trained by Sucre impressed Bolívar with the precision of its maneuvers, and he asked who had trained it. Sucre's profile was raised in the course of mediating, at Bolívar's request, a dispute between Mariño and Bermúdez to the advantage of the latter. Bolívar was pleased. He employed Sucre to cultivate support for Bermúdez at the expense of Mariño, since the latter was more resistant to accepting Bolívar's leadership in the east.[23]

By 1816, Sucre had concluded that only Bolívar had the stature to unite the disparate patriot forces in the east under a single command. Sucre decided, even while it was not certain that Bolívar would be able to establish his authority over the eastern *caudillos,* to join his forces; it was more an act of faith than a tactical move. Sucre never veered from his loyalty to Bolívar. He became famous for one of his phrases: "*Contra Bolívar—nada.*" But Sucre was very self-determining. He had a prickly sense of his honor and his probity. He was ruled by his own conscience and he relied on his own thinking.

Sucre was, however, acutely concerned about advancing his military career. On one occasion, his zeal got him ahead of Bolívar's timetable for his ascent up the military ladder: He engineered his own promotion to general, while Bolívar was at the front in New Granada. Still stationed in eastern Venezuela after the main theater of the war had shifted to the west, Sucre had been elected a deputy to the congress in Angostura. Although he never formally accepted the post because he was too young, he managed to play a role in the politics at Angostura. A rebellion against Bolívar's authority had broken out among the delegates. Sucre sided decisively with the pro-Bolívar faction. For his intervention, Vice-President Zea awarded him the rank of brigadier general without clearing it first with Bolívar. While Bolívar was returning to Angostura after his victory over the Spanish at Boyacá, he encountered Sucre on the Orinoco River. He had received word of Sucre's "political" promotion, and Sucre was en route to inform Bolívar of the events at Angostura. A tense confrontation occurred between the two of them, by no means the last one. Bolívar had been informed that he was being hailed by "General" Sucre. Bolívar bellowed that there was no "General" Sucre in the army. Once on board Bolívar's craft, Sucre advised Bolívar that he had accepted the promotion contingent on Bolívar's approval. He argued that not to have accepted it would have demoralized Bolívar's adherents at Angostura. Bolívar fulminated. Sucre talked. By the time they returned to Angostura, Sucre still had his new general's epaulets on his shoulders.[24]

Despite their altercation on the Orinoco, an affectionate friendship had developed between Sucre and Bolívar. It had ripened at Angostura before Bolívar left for the western front in 1818. Bolívar's letters to Sucre, starting with the one written on October 17, 1817, exude a paternalistic affection; Sucre's to Bolívar show a filial desire to please.[25]

After his return to Angostura, Bolívar assigned Sucre the critical task of purchasing munitions and rifles in the West Indies for his armies. Upon delivering this consignment to the front in New Granada, Bolívar placed Sucre on his general staff, made him interim minister of war during the illness of the incumbent, and gave him responsibility for negotiating a truce with the Spanish commander, and also a treaty that put an end to the barbaric practices that had developed in the armies on both sides. His star was rising, as Bolívar wanted it to. Daniel O'Leary, Bolívar's Irish right-hand man, remembered one particular afternoon in 1821 when he was out with Bolívar reconnoitering Spanish lines in New Granada. O'Leary saw a lone rider approaching them and asked Bolívar who he was. "He is one of the best officers in the army," Bolívar responded. "Strange as it may seem, he is not well known, nor does anyone suspect his capabilities. I am determined to bring him out of obscurity, for I am convinced that some day he will rival me."[26]

In early 1821 when he received his instructions from Bolívar for the Ecuadorean campaign, Sucre was twenty-six years old. He was five feet, six inches tall and of slight build. His complexion was ruddy and pockmarked. His hairline had receded sharply above his temples, giving his prominent forehead a winged aspect. His eyes were almond shaped; the drooped lids gave him a benign, placid countenance, which, combined with his deferential manner, helped to put people immediately at ease with him. Like Bolívar, Sucre was very abstemious; he never smoked and seldom drank. He laughed infrequently, although, unlike Bolívar, he did have a sense of humor and was often jocular in correspondence with his friends in the military. He was introspective, occasionally diffident, and very sensitive to personal slights. He often sulked. He was a facile and incessant writer. The archive of his letters and military orders consists of ten large volumes. His letters to Bolívar alone number almost one thousand. Many are long and most are in Sucre's own hand. His prose was not decorated with striking allusions and metaphors like Bolívar's; it was oriented by common sense. The language was generally succinct and vigorous, but often idiomatic and occasionally petty. The grammar was marginally deficient. Like Bolívar, he worked voraciously, often right through the night, drawing minutely detailed maps, writing correspondence, military orders, decrees, and dispensations. During these marathon sessions, he had the absentminded habit of placing his quill pen behind his ear and staring into space, totally lost in his thoughts. His secretary found this a particularly amusing sight.[27]

Although he had a temper and on occasion would break into barracks language, normally Sucre had an open and unassuming way about him. Although certainly not handsome, women found him considerate and his liaisons became frequent. He was very fastidious about his responsibilities to his natural children, as indeed he was about everything. Compared to his virility-conscious comrades in the military service, Sucre lacked the qualities of *machismo:* he was too polite, too laid back, too much the "nice guy." These qualities are summed up in the Spanish word *dulzura* which Bolívar applied to Sucre. It means literally "sweetness." Bolívar liked to parody this quality of Sucre, noting that his last name was the same as the word for sugar in French. Yet Bolívar had a high regard not only for Sucre's remarkable gifts as a military strategist but also for his analytical capabilities and incisive intelligence. He once wrote him that "if it is not you, I do not know who can help me with his intellectual resources." Although he intended to groom Sucre as his successor, Bolívar was worried that he might not fit into the mold because of "the independence of his ideas." Alluding to Sucre's seeming political naiveté, Bolívar observed somewhat ruefully that Sucre "wants to be seen as being simple ... but in reality he is not."[28]

A deep skepticism concerning everything European pervaded Sucre's outlook. This put him at odds with Bolívar in evaluating the significance of European developments for Spanish-American independence. For example, on January 1, 1820, a revolt occurred among the troops in a large expeditionary army that Ferdinand was preparing to send to America. One of the leaders of the revolt, Antonio Quiroga, formed a new government, reinstated the Constitution of 1812 and the parliament (the *Cortes*) that had been devised during Ferdinand's captivity. He also advocated peace with the new Spanish-American states and less reliance on the Holy Alliance powers. Bolívar held out high hopes for these events. They signaled to him that the Spanish army and the people had enough of the war in America. "The liberals," he reasoned, "being interested in the propagation of liberal principles will encounter such opposition (to a continuation of the war) in Spain and throughout Europe that the *Cortes* will have to decide in our favor." Spain was now part of a wider liberal consensus in Europe that acknowledged the inevitability of American independence. This was one reason why he had Sucre negotiate an armistice with the Spanish.[29]

Sucre's reaction to these events (which so excited Bolívar's political imagination) was skeptical. He noted that not much difference in Spanish military behavior in America was detectable as a consequence of the rise of the liberals in Spain. "Under the (restored 1812) Constitution they have been more violent and more double-dealing (if it is possible to be more), than in times past," Sucre wrote. He placed his observations in the same vein a few days later when he spoke of new barbarisms being practiced by "these constitutionalists." Here was a glimmer of the larger view that Sucre would develop: The Spanish-American independence process should be shaped in America, not Europe. He was particularly skeptical of any attempt to involve the independence enterprise in European politics. This became an outstanding trait of the policy he later developed to block the efforts of Britain to mediate the war in the Eastern Bank.[30]

One particular exchange between Sucre and Bolívar exemplifies their different outlooks. Bolívar resented the fact that the United States had recognized Colombia in March 1822, while no European country had yet taken that step. Sucre, en route to his assignment in Ecuador, wrote Santander that "it is better that the United States be the first to recognize Colombia. We are all Americans and we had better adjust to each other."[31]

Sucre's disdain of Europeans was focused on those in America. In 1820, the Braganzas in Brazil were still on the distant horizon as far as Sucre was concerned. Yet even so, Sucre was dubious. The salient fact for him was that they were European royalty. The only policy to be expected from the Braganzas, was that of using the disarray of the Spanish Americans to pursue a policy of territorial aggrandizement. Sucre saw the occupation of Montevideo by Lecór's army in this light. The only thing it meant, he observed dryly, was that "the government of Brazil will want to expand its possessions or annex the Eastern Bank and declare war against the republic of the Plata since the only one it has had until now has been with Artigas."[32]

A suspicion and dislike of Europeans permeates much of Sucre's correspondence. It was particularly evident in many of his asides. He was particularly barbed toward the French and English. By 1821, the most revolutionary of the European states, France, had become the most legitimist, and part of its new role was to represent the interests of the Holy Alliance in connection with the fate of Spain's empire in America. The French "have men for all principles," Sucre wrote. If French emissaries came over from Europe they would likely be "aristocratic commissioners, who will bring a Napoleonic apparatus—that is to say negotiators with force." Some years later, when the British seemed to be taking over the mediation of the war in the Eastern Bank, Sucre opened his conversations about that war with an Argentine envoy this way: "We will negotiate, Mister Ambassador, without the fastidious ceremony of the

Europeans, with an American candor devoid of deceit." For Sucre, European leaders were all elitists who still looked at the South Americans as "Indians."[33]

Sucre felt that European systems were too aristocratic and monarchic to suit American purposes. He preferred the simple model of government presented in this statement by James Harrington, a copy of whose *Political Aphorisms* Sucre had obtained and evidently read in the French translation: "The greatest happiness which a people can aspire to on this earth, and which Divinity can give them, is a Republic well ordered and founded in equality." He signed his name by this passage.[34]

He conceded that Britain might have a less reactionary political system than the rest of Europe, but it was still a European power and, therefore, likely to seek control over the South Americans for its own convenience. At one point, Sucre told Daniel O'Leary (who advocated the stabilizing value of British diplomatic good offices in Spanish America) that he had "a repugnance for any interference by European governments in our (American) affairs. ... The interests of our governments and theirs are contrary." Attempts by Europe to mediate American conflicts will lead them to "one day impose themselves by force on us. You will see that this is an ingenuous confession that we are small and for this reason caution is necessary, since to our disgrace the colonial education that we had (under the Spanish) has made us very inexpert in the science of government." O'Leary was left with no doubt that Great Britain was included in this stricture.[35]

Sucre's distinct distrust of Europeans was due originally to his provincialism. Eventually, he became convinced that European influence would retard the growth of responsible political and diplomatic relations among the Spanish Americans, as well as their republican growth. This attitude put Sucre's thinking at odds with Bolívar's in determining the political goals that would drive Colombia's military expansion in seeking Spanish-American independence. This included the ultimate question of whether the European-backed monarchy in Brazil should be challenged as a way of firming up the republican structure of Spanish-American independence. But that bridge was far down the road. The immediate challenges lay in Ecuador and Peru; it was there that different political outlooks of these two great liberators became evident.

The Conflict over Ecuador

Bolívar's orders to Sucre concerning Ecuador provided no basis for encouraging a self-determination process there or for inviting San Martín to participate in the campaign. The orders envisioned an exclusively

Colombian campaign leading, after victory, to the forced annexation of Ecuador to Colombia. In particular, they left no room for the accommodation of long-standing Peruvian rights to the Ecuadorean port of Guayaquil. Bolívar ordered Sucre to sign a treaty with the *junta* (committee) of elected local authorities in Guayaquil, incorporating that province into the Colombian state. He was not prepared to tolerate resistance on this point. He told Sucre that his "intentions are to liberate Colombia from Túmbes (a coastal town located in northern Peru on the boundary between the viceroyalties of New Granada and Peru) to the mouth of the Orinoco" and that he would not be stopped in that endeavor "by any human power in America," including any recalcitrance on the part of the local authorities in Guayaquil or any interference from San Martín. In his own communications to the authorities in Guayaquil, he said that the matter was not negotiable: His appearance in their midst would be delayed "until Colombian flags were fluttering" over the port city.[36]

Despite the tenor of his orders, Sucre sought to preserve some margin for Ecuadorean self-determination, particularly in Guayaquil, as well as a margin for cooperation between the Colombians, the Argentines and the Peruvians under San Martín's command, in the overall campaign against Quito, the basis for freeing Ecuador from Spanish control. His initial approach to structuring the campaign, politically and militarily, contrasted sharply with the narrower, more chauvinistic approach that was prescribed in his orders from Bolívar. Sucre was thinking of liberating Ecuador; Bolívar was thinking of occupying it.

Sucre arrived in Guayaquil with several hundred Colombian troops in May 1821, after an excruciatingly slow passage on overcrowded ships from the Colombian port of Buenaventura. He found political opinion divided. The people apparently supported a union with Colombia, but the *junta* harbored separatist feelings toward Quito and evinced a partiality toward Lima, with which the port had more of a historic and economic relationship than with Bogotá. A distinct pro-Peruvian party existed with links to San Martín.

Sucre failed to achieve a treaty of incorporation and settled for a resolution that effectively postponed that decision until a provincial assembly met. He defended this decision on the grounds that to push the *junta* harder, or to go around it and call for a plebiscite of the people, would interfere with getting the cooperation of the *guayaquileños* in the campaign to liberate Quito and would arouse anti-Colombian sentiments. He informed Bolívar that he "had given up nothing" in order to gain larger advantages. He had "taken the road which (he) believed would lead to us obtaining this province, which is that of the prestige that our government has among the people of the province and that which our troops and officers will eventually gain" from the campaign. He predicted that the provincial assembly, when it met, would approve incorporation of the province to Colombia unanimously. Sucre proposed "linking the interests of Guayaquil to Colombia (by having) the province recognize that by right, and in some degree *de facto* (it) belongs to Colombia."[37]

The phrasing "in some degree *de facto*" betrayed a tension between Sucre's policy and his orders, with their emphasis on creating Colombian control of Ecuador's liberation. He took an outright step toward rejecting the *de facto* approach, when he made an effort to involve San Martín in the Ecuadorean campaign. This was not strictly a matter of choice. The lateness in the arrival of Colombian reinforcements from Buenaventura made Sucre delay the timetable of the Colombian campaign. He, therefore, began to negotiate with San Martín's protectorate for help from Argentine and Peruvian forces located in the northern Peruvian province of Piura. Sucre's first idea was for them to attack Cuenca, in southern Ecuador, while Sucre's Colombians and the *guayaquileños* attacked the capital of Quito. Then Sucre went even further. He requested that San Martín's forces be dispatched to Guayaquil, where they could be formalized as auxiliaries of the *junta* and then they could mount the assault on Quito, while Sucre's forces attacked Cuenca. Sucre promised that he would widen the collaboration arising from Ecuador's liberation by taking several thousand Colombian soldiers himself to serve in Peru under San Martín's orders. "The identity of our cause moves me," he wrote to San Martín, "to propose these measures which you can consider to be in the reciprocal interests of America."[38]

In the end, Sucre's policy in Ecuador was overshadowed by Bolívar's purposes due to, ironically, San Martín's refusal of Sucre's offer of cooperation. San Martín attempted to structure his offers of military assistance to Sucre in such a way as to leave Peruvian and Argentine forces in control of Guayaquil. Hoping to displace Sucre as commander, San Martín had considered sending senior Peruvian officers, to join a column of Peruvian troops under the command of Andrés Santa Cruz which had been sent from Lima to participate in the Quito campaign. Santa Cruz's orders were then changed in Lima in order for him to split off from Sucre's campaign and undertake a Peruvian occupation of Guayaquil. At the same time, San Martín attempted to foment pro-Peruvian sentiment in Guayaquil by sending his agents there, including José La Mar, a *creole* officer born in Cuenca, Ecuador. These maneuvers brought San Martín into direct and ironic conflict with Sucre and simply opened the way for Bolívar's plan to establish *de facto* Colombian control of all of Ecuador.[39]

This narrowness of outlook in Lima got in the way of Sucre's efforts to form American relations around the liberation of Ecuador. He felt that the Peruvian government's motives were Machiavellian, the product of a relationship between San Martín's clique and its Peruvian stooges, which was driven by a growing fear of Bolívar's power. Peru's "conduct of policy begins where that of other governments ends (and is based on) intrigue and malignity, without any rules over them." Sucre felt that Peru, in its present condition, was blind to the American opportunity he had offered it with the liberation of Ecuador. It deserved whatever results in Ecuador that Bolívar chose to impose. Sucre ruefully expressed the hope that Bolívar would beat him to Quito. That way "only the troops of Colombia would take" it and teach the Peruvians a lesson.[40]

In the event, it was Sucre who liberated Ecuador. He forced Santa Cruz to tear up his new orders from Lima and to continue under Sucre's command in the attack on Quito, something that did not endear Sucre to Santa Cruz. Sucre mounted a strategically deft campaign that combined *llanero* fighting tactics with highly orchestrated mountain marches and countermarches. Sucre was a master at fighting wars of position. His campaign culminated in the lofty battle of Pichincha (May 21, 1822), which freed Quito. Bolívar was pleased with Sucre's results in the Quito campaign, even a little jealous. The Liberator had gotten bogged down in his own attack from the north.[41] In a sense, Bolívar and Santa Cruz had one thing in common—they both had been upstaged by Sucre.

Since Bolívar arrived in Quito after Sucre, he was in a hurry to catch up. His operations in Ecuador were necessarily, however, more political and administrative than military; the military liberator of the country was Sucre. That Quito would become part of the Colombian state was never in doubt after Pichincha. But "temporarily," Bolívar created a military government, invoking as his authority to do so the extra-constitutional powers clause that he had written into the Cúcuta Constitution. He made Sucre the *intendente* (administrator) of Quito, pending the creation of a formal military governorship and promoted him to the rank of divisional commander.[42] He then proceeded to smash through Sucre's delicate diplomacy in Guayaquil. As he had predicted, Colombian flags were flying when he showed up on the outskirts of Guayaquil with a sizable army. Bolívar put the *junta* out of business and called for a plebiscite, the outcome of which was never in any doubt. The whole province was added to the Colombian state but placed, along with the rest of Ecuador, under the "temporary" administration of Bolívar's military government.

Now that Ecuador was secured, Bolívar turned to Peru and the matter of Colombian intervention to finish what San Martín had started but evidently could not finish. As he did so, he prepared to extend his external power structure in order to distance himself from the republican system of Colombia.

Bolívar and San Martín were, more or less, equals at that time in terms of prestige. Three factors, however, created barriers between them: (1) San Martín's European-oriented monarchism; (2) the recent stagnation of Argentine power in Peru; (3) the conflict between him and Bolívar over Guayaquil.

The two legendary liberators met finally at Guayaquil from July 25 to July 28, 1822. They disagreed politically, however. Bolívar pressed San Martín to see in Mexico the model for Spanish America—a national monarchy under Iturbide that might yet get back on track and re-establish its popular base. San Martín insisted, however, on the need for European royalty in the Spanish-American states. He pressed Bolívar to form a federation between Argentina and Colombia as the basis for regulating the South American system. Bolívar was not interested. He was looking for more powerful grounding than either San Martín or Argentina could offer him. San Martín arrived at the conference at Guayaquil with a large chip on his shoulder because of Bolívar's peremptory actions in Guayaquil. He was prepared to dislike Bolívar and he did. His offer to cooperate with Bolívar in the liberation of Peru was perfunctory. Bolívar's magnetism was not evident on this occasion. He was half-hearted about cooperating with San Martín as equals in the liberation of Peru. At bottom, San Martín was in a weaker position than Bolívar and both knew it. Bolívar therefore preferred to talk just about getting more Colombians into Peru. At Guayaquil, the chemistry was lacking between the tall, white, aloof Argentine and the small, mercurial mulatto from the tropics. What was clear already, however, was that Argentine military power was ready to cede its role to Colombia in the vanguard of South America's emancipation. Before San Martín left Guayaquil, he made up his mind to quit Peru and leave the field of combat against the Spanish open to Bolívar.[43]

The Conflict over Peru

The form of the Colombian intervention in Peru is instructive when examining whether Colombian power could be instrumental in advancing the republican cause of South America's independence—and eventually be used against the monarchy in Brazil. The Peruvian intervention resulted in Bolívar's dictatorship in that country. This suggested an anti-republican agenda behind Colombian power in Peru. The intervention also sparked a visceral fear and jealousy of Colombian power, which in turn caused resistance to Colombian hegemony. These two aspects of Colombia's power in Peru—its political authoritarianism and the anti-Colombian nationalism that this caused—overshadowed Peru's fragile republican politics and prevented Colombia from fully taking up the republican cause in South America's independence. What the Colombian intervention in Peru makes clear is that the Spanish American societies were more likely to respond to nationalistic fears and resentments against "outsiders," than to unite as republics against the Brazilian monarchy.

━━◈━━

San Martín had left Peru in 1823, several months before Sucre arrived in Lima as Bolívar's personal envoy. San Martín decided to turn his governing power in Peru over to a triumvirate of Peruvians. He, more or less, gave his blessing to a campaign plan that was designed to score a major victory over the Spanish before the Colombians arrived in force. He left remnants of his Army of the Andes behind in Peru. Under the approval of the triumvirate, these forces and the Peruvian army attempted to flank the Spanish forces encircling Lima by sailing south to the port of Intermedios and opening a campaign from there. It ended in a total rout for the Argentine, Chilean, and Peruvian forces involved. In the aftermath of the disaster at Intermedios, the triumvirate was overthrown by a Peruvian military coup, which installed José de la Riva Aguero, a vigorous, nationalist civilian politician in the newly created office of president.[44]

Riva Aguero ordered Santa Cruz to form an entirely Peruvian army to try its hand against the Spanish in the south, and reduce the need for Colombian auxiliaries. Santa Cruz had returned to Peru from the Ecuadorean campaign a military hero, much to Sucre's chagrin. He confided to Santander that Santa Cruz deserted the field of battle at Pichincha only to reappear in time for the imminent victory of Colombian forces over the Spanish.[45] Santa Cruz, however, become an important, nationalist leader of the Peruvian military. In fact, he engineered the coup that placed Riva Aguero in power. Santa Cruz believed that the first Intermedios campaign failed because it did not have the vigorous support of the triumvirate, and it was led not by Peruvian officers, but by Argentine officers. He castigated the mercenary behavior of the Chileans and the Argentines toward the Peruvians. He was convinced that they had a vested interest in keeping the Peruvian army weak in order to justify their own continued presence and parasitical existence. If the body politic of Peru were to be invigorated, a "violent revolution in the atmosphere, produced by a Peruvian military victory" was needed.[46]

That victory was expected from the second Intermedios campaign. Santa Cruz's vaunted army, however, was routed by the Spanish in that campaign. Prior to this event, Spanish forces descended from the mountains and occupied Lima forcing the government to retreat to the fort at Callao, where Sucre had narrowly prevented a move by the congress to overthrow Riva Aguero. Riva Aguero proceeded to sail north to Trujillo, where he established a rump Peruvian government, recruited an army, and prepared to openly challenge Bolívar. In the months before Bolívar's arrival in Lima (September 1, 1823), Sucre undertook a valiant but tardy effort to rescue Santa Cruz's forces in the south.[47]

For Peru, the year 1823 represented a transition from the mercenary regime established by San Martín's Army of the Andes to the auxiliary regime put into place by the Colombians. This represented a basic change in the politics of the liberation of Peru, one that defined Peruvian nationalism in anti-Colombian terms and defined Bolívar's interest in Peru in authoritarian terms.

When San Martín left Peru in 1823 to make way for Bolívar, his Army of the Andes was widely perceived by Peruvian supporters of independence, Santa Cruz among them, as consisting of arrogant mercenaries who, like "sultans," engaged in speculative and extortionary activities, using their troops and position for private gain and humiliating native Peruvians.[48] It was likely to be different in the case of the Colombians; they were explicitly oriented toward an auxiliary role in Peru. They were, in contrast to the freelancing Army of the Andes, proud to be Colombians fighting for freedom. With their tight organization and high morale, they stood a much better chance of defeating the Spanish forces. Their loyalty to Bolívar was enormous. In turn, Bolívar was powerfully identified with the Colombian state, even if he was alienated from the politicians in Bogotá. It was therefore possible that he would try to impose Colombian political dominance over Peru as the price for defeating the Spanish or at least his version of Colombian political dominance. Much of the Peruvian public opinion that supported independence, and which even recognized that the Peruvians needed help if the Spanish were going to be defeated, was nevertheless ambivalent toward the prospect of Colombia's full scale entry into the war, especially if this meant Bolívar coming to Peru to direct the war. Having to endure the mercenary behavior of the Chileans and the Argentines was bad enough. But the "cure" of Colombian auxiliaries, especially if they were united under Bolívar's command, might prove worse than the disease. The Argentines and Chileans, could not, as mercenaries, organize enough authority to be politically dangerous to the Peruvians. The Colombians, as auxiliaries, could.

Notwithstanding the hedge of Santa Cruz's operations in the south, there was never any doubt in the minds of the Argentine, Chilean, Peruvian, or Colombian officers in Peru that Bolívar would take command of the military effort against the Spanish once he was in the country. Nor was this doubted by Peruvian politicians and government leaders. What was in doubt was how much *political* authority he would take. In fact, the transformation of his military leadership into a political dictatorship occurred in the space of just seven months following his arrival in Peru; the process was complete as of early February 1824.

The main obstacle to Bolívar's takeover in Peru was Riva Aguero. Soon after his arrival in Peru on September 1, 1823, Bolívar had begun a political campaign to prevent Riva Aguero from becoming a martyr among Peruvians. He capitalized heavily on the secret negotiations that Riva Aguero had been conducting with the viceroy. As Riva Aguero's position collapsed, Bolívar sought to cultivate Peruvian opinion. There were basically three segments of opinion he had to deal with.

The first consisted of the republican-minded politicians in the congress who bore a grudge against Riva Aguero because of his complicity in the coup that ousted the triumvirate and effectively reduced the political authority of the congress. Francisco Javier Luna Pizarro, a revolutionary priest from Arequipa, provided a strident leadership and an inflammatory rhetoric for this wing. Although his supporters bid a good riddance to Riva Aguero, they were far from enthusiastic about the resulting accretion of Bolívar's political power. Luna Pizarro had sounded the alarm during the time of the triumvirate, when offers of Colombian help began to arrive from Bolívar. He had predicted dire results if the congress failed to create order. "If we permit anarchy to reign," he warned in one congressional session, "Bolívar will have a pretext to introduce himself and, the formidable warrior that he is, he could conquer our independence for us but in exchange he would aspire to make himself a despot and dominate us like slaves. Events will prove the exactitude of my prognosis." What this group came to want, as Bolívar's dictatorship took hold, was the return of political authority to the congress and the opportunity to draft a republican constitution for Peru. In the eyes of this group, Bolívar's dictatorship in Peru was more illegitimate than Riva Aguero's coup-based presidency and ultimately more threatening to Peru's republican prospects.[49]

A second group consisted of some officers and politicians who refused to believe that Riva Aguero was a traitor and saw him rather as a martyr and victim of Bolívar's power aspirations. The commander of Peru's naval forces, Vice-Admiral Martín George Guisse came to the forefront of this group. Both of the groups led by Guisse and Luna Pizarro were highly nationalistic and hostile toward Bolívar. The third group, however, consisted of those individuals who believed in Bolívar and saw him as the only means of Peru's salvation. Sanchez Carrión, one of the leading deputies in the congress and a prominent figure in the Callao decrees that sought to overthrow Riva Aguero, and La Mar, who had himself been a member of the triumvirate, came to the forefront of this third group. It formed the basis of what came to be called the Bolivarian party in Peru. Manuel Pando, one of the delegates later sent by Bolívar to represent Peru at the assembly in Panama, was the most prominent member of this group after Carrión. The other key figure among the Bolivarians was Santa Cruz.

Originally, Santa Cruz had confidence in the fighting capacity of the Peruvian army and in the political system of Riva Aguero. He wanted to keep the Peruvian army and the Colombians apart in order to show what the Peruvians could accomplish on their own and to give them the confidence that they could deal with the Colombians as equals. This was what he hoped to accomplish in the second Intermedios campaign. However, Colombian help was needed by Peru. Since the Colombian force was larger than the Argentine and Chilean forces, it could be used as the basis to "impose order even on those who believe it is in their interest that the army of Peru be destroyed" at Intermedios. Santa Cruz believed that the Peruvian nationalist cause, conceived in nation-building terms and not in terms of xenophobic anti-Colombianism, could be strengthened if the vested interests of mercenaries were displaced by the greater authority structure and more disinterested purposes of the Colombian auxiliaries. Bolívar would grant the Peruvians the respect they deserved; the mercenaries would not give them the chance. Fearful that the "allies" at Lima would not do their part, thus repeating the result of the first Intermedios campaign, Santa Cruz appealed to Bolívar to come to Peru and take command of the allied armies in Lima in order to guarantee the success of the Intermedios invasion.[50]

Even before the loss of his army in the south, he defied Riva Aguero's attempts to get him to save his position at Trujillo and advised him to repair his relations with Bolívar. After the debacle in the south, Santa Cruz broke off relations with Riva Aguero and joined Bolívar. Many of Santa Cruz's officers, including his second in command, Agustín Gamarra, followed Santa Cruz into the Bolivarian camp.[51]

Within this configuration, the lines between the three groups were fluid. Certain individuals acted as brokers between the groups, and others pursued a more dynamic strategy of influence-seeking by positioning themselves to shift from one group to another at opportune moments. Others tried to straddle the groups. La Mar, for example, was an anti-Bolivarian in Guayaquil but a Bolivarian in Lima. His relations with Luna Pizarro were much better than Carrión's, who was a pure Bolivarian. Manuel Vidaurre, another of the Peruvian delegates to Panama, based his political career on positioning himself prominently among the Bolivarians but poised himself to join the Luna Pizarro's party at the first sign of cracks in Bolívar's dictatorship. Gamarra followed a similar strategy to Vidaurre's but from his base in the Peruvian military. The key question in all of this concerned the particular interplay between the

Bolivarians and the nationalists in Guisse's and Luna Pizarro's groups. Were these two groups mutually exclusive or could common ground be established between the moderates in each group? This was the key issue in Peruvian politics from the time Bolívar landed in Lima until six months after he left the country, in August of 1826.

Over this potpourri of factions, Bolívar spread favors around in a strategy of cooptation. To the politicians and opinion-makers went patronage, offices in the dictatorship, and his personal solicitude. To the military officers went promotions and the prospect of basking in Colombia's military prestige. He re-established the Peruvian army and gave it divisional status, which put it theoretically on a par with the Colombian forces in Peru. Bolívar put La Mar at the head of this army with Santa Cruz as his second-in-command. He studiously avoided placing Peruvians under Colombian officers, even though in the upcoming campaigns he always made sure that his Colombians were behind the Peruvians as well as in front of them.[52]

The latent conflict between Sucre and Bolívar came to the surface in Peru over the matter of Riva Aguero. Immediately after his arrival in Lima, Bolívar insisted that Sucre lead Colombian troops north in preparation to attack Riva Aguero's forces at Trujillo. Sucre, already aware of allegations that he had contributed to Riva Aguero's isolation, absolutely refused. He said that it was an internal affair among Peruvians in which Colombia should not interfere. Some bitter conversations ensued between Sucre and Bolívar. Bolívar felt that Sucre had created the problem of Riva Aguero by not siding more decisively with the congress at Callao and getting rid of him there. He was now giving Sucre a chance to redeem himself but Sucre would have none of it. The more Bolívar fulminated, the more immovable Sucre became. Sucre's attitude toward Bolívar's plan for eliminating Riva Aguero bordered on "contempt" according to Bolívar. The most Bolívar could get out of him was his consent to accompany, in the role of "observer," an army to be led by Bolívar against Riva Aguero. Bolívar attributed Sucre's reluctance to delicacy. Actually his motive was political.[53]

Sucre was dubious of Bolívar's attempts to flatter Peruvian politicians and military leaders and get them to acquiesce in the plan to eliminate Riva Aguero. He was particularly barbed toward Bolívar's patronizing of Peruvian military officers. Sucre had described La Mar earlier to Bolívar as having good relations with Luna Pizarro and being "not a friend of your's," whatever his protestations currently might be. As for Santa Cruz, Sucre despised him as a result of their experiences in the Quito and Intermedios campaigns. He was distrustful of the rapport that had developed between Santa Cruz and Bolívar. Sucre warned Bolívar repeatedly about trusting the Peruvians. He sprinkled his caveats generously over Peruvian personalities and was fond of describing known enemies of Bolívar as "particular friend(s) of Santa Cruz." As for Riva Aguero, in Sucre's mind, he was totally discredited and therefore to be pitied. Sucre even said that Riva-Aguero had always been "friendly" toward him personally. The more dangerous Peruvians, Sucre implied, were the ones that actively professed friendship for Bolívar and offered him their collaboration.[54]

The crux of the disagreement between Sucre and Bolívar was this: Bolívar felt that it was necessary to discredit and eliminate Riva Aguero in order to gain control over Peru. He wanted to eliminate him in order to remove an obstacle to the expansion of his dictatorship. Sucre was fearful that the elimination of Riva Aguero would have precisely that effect.

Sucre was also extremely concerned that Bolívar's political activities in Peru were alienating him from the republican structure of Colombia. Indeed, this was true. The political polarization that was caused in Peru by Bolívar's dictatorship was paralleled by a polarization that occurred between the dictatorship and the Colombian government at Bogotá. That conflict with Bogotá drove Bolívar further politically into Peru.

Bolívar's difficulties with Bogotá had started when he was in Ecuador, where, as we know, he had set up a military government by using the extra-constitutional powers that he had extracted from the Cúcuta Congress. The congress at Bogotá resented the fact that Ecuador continued to function under Bolívar's military government long after the fighting had ceased and the area had been annexed to the Colombian state. There was also some anxiety caused by the strong-arm tactics that Bolívar had used in Guayaquil. The issue was exacerbated when Bolívar continued to give orders to the persons he left in charge in Quito even after he left for Peru and had begun exercising his dictatorship there. Santander had initiated a congressional debate on this issue by raising the question of whether orders issued by Bolívar as dictator of Peru were enforceable within Colombian territory. He asked, furthermore, whether the field promotions Bolívar had given to the Colombian army in Peru were valid since the constitution vested the power to grant military promotions in the president of Colombia, and he (Santander) was the acting president of Colombia in Bolívar's absence. Santander's inquiry raised these and other "anomalies" created by the "peculiar circumstance" of Bolívar exercising his dictatorship in Peru while he was still legally president of Colombia.[55]

Considerable friction between Bolívar and Santander had been caused by the matter of the recruitment of Colombian troops for the war in Peru. Bolívar expected Santander to raise new armies for him regardless of the requirement of prior congressional authorization for any military draft. For a time, Santander got around this problem by sending recruits to Guayaquil, where they could be shipped to Peru under authority of Bolívar's military government in Ecuador. This represented only a temporary expedient of dubious legality.[56] The constitutional problem created by Bolívar ordering a draft in Colombia as dictator of Peru, bothered the increasingly legalistic Santander. For Santander, there was an inherent gap between the place where Bolívar's authority in Peru left off and his own in Colombia began. Bolívar was insisting on a *de facto* fusion of the two authorities. Santander pressed his objections. Colombia was ruled by its own laws, he said, and not the exigencies of any foreign state, even one that was hosting a large portion of Colombia's fighting men as well as Colombia's peripatetic leader.

> I am an official of Colombia and not of Peru and the laws which have been given to me to govern Colombia have nothing to do with Peru and their nature has not changed because the President of Colombia is commanding an army of Colombia in a foreign country. I do too much even to send some troops to Guayaquil. I have no law authorizing me to do it; nor any law putting me under your orders nor any law authorizing me to send to Peru what you need and you ask for. Either there are laws or there are not.[57]

Exasperated over what he saw as the constitutional prevarications of Santander, Bolívar sent personal envoys to make direct contact with military officers in Colombia for the purpose of raising recruits for Peru. He also dispatched to Colombia his aide, Diego Ibarra, to put pressure on Santander and the congress. Ibarra, with considerable difficulty, worked out an arrangement in Bogotá under which he would raise an army for Peru in Venezuela, while Santander and the congress would raise one in New Granada. Ibarra's comments on his protracted negotiations were calculated to amuse Bolívar. "The worst part was the constitution since this damned book they pull out for everything. You cannot even say good morning here without first finding the authority for it in the constitution."[58]

The Bogotá Congress was lukewarm about sending more Colombian troops to Peru. It was willing to do so, however, provided it was clear that any such recruitment was done on the authority of the congress and not Bolívar's fiat from Peru. The implication, and this was operationally clearer in the case of the army recruited in New Granada, was that the congress would exercise more authority over the new forces arriving in Peru than it had over the earlier ones, which were raised under treaties made between Bolívar and the Peruvian governments of San Martín and Riva Aguero. It was to reinforce this point that the congress had pro- ceeded, with Santander's tacit consent, to relieve Bolívar of his com- mand authority over Colombian forces in Peru. In addition, the congress revoked the extraordinary powers clause that enabled Bolívar to operate a military government in Ecuador. These steps were taken in the belief that the congress had to assert its own authority and that of the constitu- tion, vis-à-vis Bolívar lest they both be overshadowed by him. Santander was an accomplice in these actions by his own admission. Bolívar's mili- tary government in Ecuador began to be dismantled by Bogotá, while the chief executive authority in the area was vested in Santander as the acting president of the nation.[59]

Bolívar was advised of these peremptory actions in June 1824, when he was campaigning high in the Peruvian *sierra*. He promptly designated Sucre as commander-in-chief of the Colombian army in Peru, subject to Bogotá's approval. He told Sucre that from then on he would not involve himself in the internal matters of the Colombian army. Rather, he would limit himself to giving orders by virtue of his role as "dictator of the coun- try in which the Colombian army is serving as auxiliaries." He indicated that his role as president of Colombia had been virtually rescinded by Bogotá for the duration of his activities outside of Colombia. This further distancing of Bolívar's power in Peru from the republican system of Colombia was worrisome to Sucre.[60] In addition to this tense situation, there was the matter of Bolívar's tendency to put European politics ahead of American politics. The split between Sucre and Bolívar on this issue occurred high in the Peruvian mountains where both men were attempting to position patriot forces to withstand an expected attack by the much larger Spanish army.

<hr />

The Holy Alliance's invasion of Spain occurred during the two months prior to Bolívar's arrival in Peru on September 1, 1823. Rumors of the French proposals made to Ferdinand began reaching American capitals, including Lima, by the end of 1823. Both Sucre and Bolívar tried to cal- culate the implications of these events in Spain for Colombia's objectives in Peru.

On the face of it, these implications were grave indeed, not only for Peruvian independence but for all of the Spanish-American indepen- dence movements. Yet Bolívar saw the downfall of the liberals in Spain as a blessing in disguise. The keys to Bolívar's thinking lay in the expecta- tions he had concerning Canning's policy. He perceived Castlereagh as too much of a monarchist to manage a British break with the Holy Alliance. Canning, however, was more liberal and, therefore, more willing to risk a showdown with the Holy Alliance. Bolívar reasoned that the absorption of Spain into the Holy Alliance would put Europe beyond the ability of Britain to "balance" unless Spain went in *without* the American colonies. On the other hand, the colonies, made a part of Europe's system as independent states, could be used to restore Britain's capacity to balance Europe by providing weight against the Holy Alliance. He believed that the downfall of the liberals in Spain, by opening up the prospect of a Holy Alliance intervention in America, would force the British hand. "Britain wants our independence more than ever," he wrote to the Colombian envoy in London. Events in Spain would increase the threat of a Holy Alliance intervention in America, but at the same time, they "would speed up the wheels of the coach carrying our revolutions" by accelerating British protection.[61]

In this perspective, Bolívar felt that in Peru time was on Colombia's side; the army should not be rushed into a large battle if victory were not certain. It was better to await more reinforcements from Colombia and to, above all, give British policy a chance to crystallize in the wake of the Holy Alliance intervention in Spain. The purpose of Colombian power in Peru should be seen in these terms. Bolívar wanted to demonstrate to Canning the stabilizing role that Colombia's military under Bolívar's guidance could play. Bolívar, therefore, saw the Colombian army's mission in Peru in broader terms than simply beating the Spanish militarily. Its purpose was to provide an anchor for the Spanish-American revolutions on the whole continent. "The Colombian army is simultaneously," he told Sucre, "the safeguard of Peruvian independence, the vanguard of Colombia, and the military guarantor of all of South America." Its purpose was not only to fight in Peru but to stay there "for all the world to see." British diplomacy would do the rest. If Great Britain wanted assistance from the Spanish Americans to carry on a struggle against the Holy Alliance on a global scale, they would be ready and organized for that role.[62]

Sucre rejected Bolívar's whole analysis. On February 25, 1824, after a period of shadowing the movements of the Spanish army, he arrived in the small hamlet of Yungay. Like Bolívar, he was troubled by the turn of events in Spain but the inferences he drew were diametrically opposite. Their premises were different: Sucre did not trust the British any more than the Holy Alliance. He decided to give Bolívar the benefit of his own analysis and composed his controversial "Yungay letter." It remains the best evidence of Sucre's view of international politics in general, and the Colombian role in Peru in particular.[63]

Ostensibly, the Yungay letter advances an argument for Colombia to cut its losses in Peru and look to its own defenses. It appears to be parochially Colombian in that sense. The reason for this is that at the time Sucre gave his recommendations to Bolívar, the evacuation of Colombian troops from Peru seemed warranted by the deteriorating military situation. The Spanish army in the Peruvian mountains, backed up by an army of occupation in Upper Peru, was highly mobile and superior in numbers to the allied forces. Sucre had been placed in command of the allied army, which had been assembled as an observation army along a northern perimeter around the Spanish army. If the Spanish attacked, it was uncertain that the line could be held, and it was necessary to consider fall-back scenarios.

It was not only the military advantage that the Spanish had that caused the pessimism of Sucre's Yungay letter. Rather, Sucre was fearful that Colombia's "allies" would get in the way. He saw the Peruvian army as Bolívar's sop for national feelings. It remained necessary to keep a Colombian division behind it to prevent desertions. He was equally disillusioned with the remnants of San Martín's forces. As far as numbers went, Sucre said that he would rather "risk a battle with forces more or less equal to the enemy, in which we have a majority of Colombians, than to risk one in which, although we have numerical supremacy, our army consists of a majority of Peruvians, Chileans, and Argentines."[64]

Sucre argued in his letter that the war might not be winnable against the Spanish in Peru and that Colombia should look to protect itself against what might be new threats from the Holy Alliance. The Spanish in Peru, if they were allowed to stay there in control, even as enemies of Colombia, could only threaten Quito, while the Holy Alliance could strike at the heart of Colombia and "destroy everything." Sucre pragmatically urged Bolívar to repatriate Colombian forces and protect what had been won already rather than risk losing everything.

> We have arrived at the crisis of the revolution and I believe that we should be less stubborn than these Spanish (liberals) in order to conserve the most precious part of our sacrifices, since destiny does not want to leave us with all of it. The Spanish liberals, trying to retain their Constitution at all costs, lost it. ... Although we should all prefer to die rather than to return to being colonies of Spain, we do not want to make such a choice if by other means (Colombia) can preserve itself for itself.[65]

Sucre started his letter by agreeing with Bolívar that events in Europe arising from the Holy Alliance's intervention in Spain would have critical implications for the American revolutions. But it was not to British policy that Colombia should look in order to define its objectives in Peru. He conceded that "(e)very Colombian" should keep one eye on Peru and the other on the Holy Alliance." But Sucre's "eye" on the Holy Alliance's occupation of Spain perceived things other than the new resoluteness in British policy on behalf of American independence that Bolívar's "eye" perceived. For the pragmatic Sucre, the two salient aspects of the Holy Alliance action in Spain were, first, the stubbornness of the liberals in not agreeing to some widening of Ferdinand's powers in order to buy their way out of an intervention and, second, the failure of the British to stop the intervention. Sucre saw no essential reason why the British would do any more for the Spanish Americans than they had for the Spanish liberals. He thought that Bolívar placed far too much emphasis on the efficacy of British protection of Spanish America. Although it might be less reactionary than the Holy Alliance sovereigns, Britain was still a European power and, as far as Sucre was concerned, it would measure its relations with the American states according to its "own convenience." In particular, he was convinced that Britain would not risk war with the Holy Alliance over America. Sucre felt that the safety of the American revolutions lay in their mutual efforts to head off a legitimist intervention rather than counting on a speculative British policy.

Whereas Bolívar saw the intervention as increasing Britain's intention to not allow Spain to hold onto its American colonies, Sucre saw new *American* opportunities to force Spain into acceptance of independence. Sucre saw the Holy Alliance's intervention in Spain as producing a conflict between Ferdinand and his new alliance patrons, on the one hand, and, on the other, between Ferdinand and the Spanish commanders in Peru, many of whom were supporters of the constitutionalist movement in Spain. Much of the local loyalist opinion in Peru was premised on the concept that Spain was undergoing a transition from absolutism to liberalism and that Peru had more to gain, politically, from not breaking with Spain than from independence. The resurgence of absolutism in Spain was a result of the Holy Alliance's intervention. This might, Sucre reasoned, weaken the premise of loyalist opinion in Peru and even prompt the Spanish commanders to declare the independence of Peru from the mother country in order to save their own careers. What was needed was for Colombia to provide encouragement for them to take this step and thus allow Peru to become an American state with an interest in resisting any efforts by the Holy Alliance to extend its intervention in Spain to the New World.

Sucre therefore proposed in the Yungay letter that a nonaggression pact be signed between Colombia and the Spanish commanders in Peru. Common cause should furthermore be made with them against the Holy Alliance and Ferdinand. The promise of a Colombian evacuation of Peru would be enough of an incentive, combined with the destruction of the liberal, constitutional cause in Spain, to bring them around. He reasoned that the rumored plans for leaving Spanish royalty in possession of only part of Spanish America (not necessarily Peru), while other European royalty took over the rest, would further diminish the Spanish commanders' loyalty to Spain. Sucre argued that an anti-Spanish/Holy Alliance treaty between Colombia and the other Spanish-American states adjacent to Peru one the one hand and the Spanish commanders in Peru, on the other, would serve simultaneously the interests of all parties. It was thus an Americanist proposition.

> These leaders (the Spanish commanders in Peru) are enemies of Ferdinand and, flattering their pride and their own victories (the two Intermedios campaigns), they will perhaps give in. I do not doubt that they are close to declaring themselves independent (of Spain) and if to this design can be added the support of neighboring states, they would be less distant from committing themselves (to independence) … (B)eing themselves the most powerful influence in the government (of Peru), they could count on always being the political leaders (of Peru).[66]

The main task for Sucre was to press Bolívar to trade the Colombian evacuation for political concessions from the Spanish commanders. The key inference from his letter was that Peru's capacity to form relations against Europe with neighboring American states would be enhanced by withdrawal of the Colombian army from Peru and the dismantling of the dictatorship that Bolívar was trying to establish. Thus, in the final analysis, Sucre was convinced that Peruvian independence might be established on a more American basis if it were inherited by the Spanish constitutionalists in Peru, relying on the act of secession from Spain, rather than by the Peruvian Bolivarians, relying on their subservience to the dictatorship. The Spanish commanders would make more reliable allies because they would be less jealous of Colombia. Colombia could enter into relations with Peru as a coalitional state as opposed to being compromised by bringing Peru under its hegemony through the dictatorship. For Sucre, the Bolivarians were simply creatures of Bolívar's dictatorship. The more popular party in Peru answered to Luna Pizarro, and in it a dangerous anti-Colombianism prevailed. It would only become more so, if Colombian arms succeeded in defeating the Spanish and the dictatorship deepened, as it likely would.

The Yungay letter reflected Sucre's disenchantment with the Peruvian nationalists and their disenchantment with him. Rumors spread in Peruvian circles that Sucre had deliberately contributed to the annihilation of Santa Cruz's army by delaying his attempt to join up with him. That was the version that Santa Cruz chose to believe. This view, coupled with a widespread belief that Sucre had incited the congress to revolt against Riva Aguero by publicly pledging to it the support of the Colombian army, made Sucre a highly suspect figure in the eyes of many Peruvians in both the Bolivarian and the nationalist camps.[67]

Bolívar had told Sucre that he approved of his actions in the Intermedios campaign. But in Sucre's view, the Liberator still had to learn "how right I am" about not trusting Santa Cruz and the Peruvians and about how sound the strategy of the Yungay letter was. "I have always believed it," Sucre wrote a friend in early 1824 in reference to the letter. "This view may be mistaken but time will prove if it was, or was not right."[68]

Events in mid-1824, however, changed the whole military picture in Peru. Emboldened by the Holy Alliance's intervention in Spain, the commander of the Spanish forces in Upper Peru, Pedro Olañeta, sided with Ferdinand against the liberal Spanish commanders in Peru. He defied the authority of the Peruvian viceroy, who was forced to send an army to Upper Peru to try to subordinate him. This action shifted, temporarily, the numerical balance in Peru in favor of the allied forces and prevented the Spanish from taking the offensive. At Sucre's urging, Bolívar took the offensive without waiting for more reinforcements from Colombia. In the late afternoon of August 6, 1824, on the lofty plain of Junín, the Colombian and Peruvian cavalry decimated the Spanish cavalry and caused their infantry to reel back in retreat. Junín was a battle fought without musket fire or artillery. Lance was pitted against lance, sword against sword. The margin of difference was the extraordinary horsemanship of the Venezuelan *llaneros*, and the ferocious use of their long lances.

After he had given command over the Colombian forces to Sucre, in response to the actions of the Bogotá government, Bolívar decided to go to Lima to oversee the arrival of more reinforcements from Colombia and to make some political capital out of the victory at Junín. He left Sucre in command with orders to wage a war of positions against the enemy. He did, however, leave Sucre with a carefully guarded option of committing his forces to a battle if the circumstances were overwhelmingly favorable. That was all Sucre needed.[69]

The Spanish army returning from Upper Peru had been able to rejoin the viceroy's army, thereby achieving a large numerical superiority over Sucre's forces and supplying new cavalry to fill the losses sustained at Junín. But the skill with which Sucre maneuvered his army, combined with the superior morale of his Colombian troops, made the difference when the two armies met on the slope of a mountain adjacent to the plains of Ayacucho on December 9, 1824. Unlike Junín, the battle of Ayacucho was essentially a battle of infantry. It was decided by key charges made by the Colombians and the Peruvians. The hero of the battle was José María de Córdoba, a Cundinamarcan. The Spanish lost over 1,000 men and the bulk of the rest were taken prisoner, including the viceroy and his whole staff. For the Inca, whose armies had won a savage victory there, Ayacucho meant the "corner of death." That is what it represented for the Spanish empire in South America.

The campaign was not however without friction between Sucre and the Peruvians. Sucre's temper got the best of him in one particular incident in which he humiliated La Mar in front of his own troops. La Mar did not forgive or forget. It did not go unnoticed by Peruvian officers that Sucre was sparse with his field promotions to the Peruvians who fought at Ayacucho and that his rhetoric pictured the victory as essentially a Colombian one. They criticized La Mar for tolerating Sucre's perceived arrogance, and they complained to Bolívar, even as they conspired with the anti-Colombian nationalists. One of these officers, the sometime Bolivarian, Agustín Gamarra, was destined to play a large role in overthrowing Colombian "hegemony" in the name of Peruvian nationalism. Three years later when Sucre labeled Gamarra's political career an insult to Ayacucho, Gamarra reminded him that Peruvians also did their duty there.[70]

After Ayacucho, Olañeta's army in Upper Peru needed to be dealt with. The army sent by the viceroy to subordinate Olañeta had fallen short of success. Under pressure to return to the theater in Peru, its commanders had to settle for what amounted to an armistice with Olañeta. His army remained intact and under his command. Olañeta coyly congratulated both Sucre and Bolívar on their victories over the viceroy in Peru. He said that the viceroy was his enemy too. The point had to be conceded, that Olañeta had made those victories possible by drawing off the viceroy's forces into Upper Peru. Yet Olañeta, despite his overtures of friendship to Bolívar, continued to profess loyalty to Ferdinand and to refuse to accept independence from Spain. Bolívar, after toying with the possibility of making a political arrangement with Olañeta, ordered Sucre to attack him.[71]

Notes

1. Encyclopedia Britannica: *Colombia.* Trans. by Lorenzo Lerras. Bogotá, 1837. Jerónimo Becker and José María Rivas Groot, *El Nuevo Reino de Granada en el Siglo XVIII.* Madrid, n.d. Jesus Henac, and Gerardo Arrubla, *History of Colombia.* Trans. and ed. by J. Fred Rippy. Chapel Hill: North Carolina Press,

1938. L. Lopez de Mesa, *Escrutinio Sociológico de la Colombia.* Medellin, Colombia, 1970. Allan J. Keuthe, *Military Reform and Society in New Granada, 1773–1808.* Gainesville: University Presses of Florida, 1978.

2. Carlos Irazabel, *Venezuela Esclavo y Feudal,* Caracas, 1964. Guillermo Morón, *Historia de Venezuela,* 3rd. ed. Caracas, 1961. Vicente Lecuna, *Crónica Razonada de las Guerras de Bolívar.* 4 vols. New York: Colonial Press, 1950.

3. Vallenilla Lanz, *La Guerra de Nuestra Independencia Fue Una Guerra Civil.* Caracas, 1959; Vicente Lecuna, *Crónica,* I. Overthrow of white, "populist" leadership in Venezuela: Carlos O. Stoetzer, *The Scholastic Roots of the Spanish American Revolution.* New York: Fordham University Press, 1979, 227–29. Links between returning whites and Páez: Laureano Vallenilla-Lanz, *Cesarismo Democrático.* Caracas, 1961, and by the same author, *Desgregación y Integración,* 2nd ed. Madrid, 1962. A contemporary on the scene analysis: Briceño Mendez to Bolívar, December 23, 1825, in Lecuna, *Cartas del Libertador,* V: 244–47.

4. David Bushnell, *The Santander Regime in Gran Colombia.* Newark: University of Delaware Press, 1954, 14–22.

5. Stoetzer, 89–92, 123–25, 168–72, 237–38. Torres's career: Rafael Gómez Hoyos, *Revolución Granadino de 1810.* Bogotá, 1962. II: 7–44, especially 14–18. See also Manuel José Forero, *Camilio Torres.* Bogotá, 1960. Tax revolt as precursor of independence revolution: Stoetzer, 144; Gómez Hoyos, II: 155–202.

6. Lecuna, *Crónica.*

7. Complexion of Cúcuta Congress: Restrepo, *Historia,* III: 143–56. Vicente Azuero to Santander, June 6, 1821 in Cortazar, *Corespondencia,* I: 302–06.

8. Restrepo, Historia, III: 143–56.

9. Cúcuta Congress: Gil Fortoul, *Obras Completas.* Caracas, 1953, 455–73; Bushnell, 14–22.

10. Páez to Bolívar, October 1, 1825, in O'Leary, *Memorias,* 57–60; Santander to Páez, July 14, 1826 in Roberto Cortazar, ed., *Cartas y Mensajes de Santander.* Bogotá, 1953, 367–68. For Santander's earlier statements to Páez that "might does not make right," Santander to Páez, n.d. (1817, in Gilberto Salazar Prado, *Pensamiento Político de Santander.* Bogotá, 1969, I: 11–17). See also Ernesto Restrepo, ed., *Archivo Santander,* Bogotá, 1918–1932, XIV, for the challenges to Santander's political principles that were posed by the occurrence of the Páez revolt.

11. Bolívar to Santander, *Obras,* May 25, 1821, I: 563–64.

12. Bolívar to Francisco Peñalver, April 21, 1821, in ibid., 552–54.

13. Briceño Mendez to Bolívar, December 23, 1825, in Lecuna, *Cartas,* V: 244–47. Páez to Bolívar, October 1, 1825, in O'Leary, II: 57–60.

14. Santander to Bolívar, June 15, 1826, Cortazar, IV: 380–86.

15. Constitutional problems of supplying Bolívar with troops from Colombia: Carlos Cortes Vargas, *Participación del Colombia en la Libertad del Peru.* Bogotá, 1924, II: 60–80. Quotation: Santander to Bolívar, May 10, 1823, Cortazar, IV: 399–401.

16. Harold A. Bierck, *Vida Pública de Don Pedro Gual.* Caracas, 1976.

17. Text of Jamaica Letter: *Selected Writings of Bolívar.* Ed. and trans. by Vicente Lecuna and Harold Bierck. New York: Colonial Press, 1951, I: 103–22.

18. Bolívar's warning to Bernardo O'Higgins, August 29, 1822, ibid., 675–676; instructions to his treaty envoys: Felipe Larrazabal, *Vida de Libertador*, Simón Bolívar, II: 384–86.

19. Bolívar to Pedro Briceño Mendez, August 29, 1822, Lecuna and Nazaris, *Obras Completas*, 674.

20. For the lineage of the Alcalá-Sucre lines: Laureano Villanueva, *Vida de Antonio José de Sucre*. Cacaras, 1945, 8; Gonzales Rumazo, *Sucre: Gran Mariscal de Ayacucho*. Madrid, 1963, 19; J. A. Cova, *Sucre: Ciudadano Americano*. Caracas, 1943, 20–2; Bolívar's defense of Sucre's bloodlines: Nícolas Navarre, ed., *Diario de Bucaramanga por L. Peru Lacroix*, Caracas, 1935, 103. This is a controversial source that needs to be used carefully.

21. Sucre's comment on his mother's death and his uncle's comments are quoted in Cova, 26, 36. See also Villanueva, 15–21 for early life details.

22. Villanueva, 24, 50, 63, for Sucre's loss of family. The first thing that Sucre wrote that still exists is a description of a skirmish lin 1813 in which he was able to save his life only by swimming into the sea: Pedro Grases and Ester Barret de Nazaris, eds. *Archivo de Sucre*. Caracas, 1973–85, I: 5–6.

23. Bolívar's first contact with Sucre: Lecuna I: 240 ff.; John M. Hoover, *Admirable Warrior: Marshal Sucre, Fighter for South American Independence*. Detroit, Mich.: Blaine Ethridge, 1977, 3–5; Juan Domingo Cortés, *Galería de Hombres Célebres de Bolivia*. Santiago, Chile, 1869, 52 .

24. Orinoco encounter: Daniel O'Leary, *Bolívar and the Wars of Independence*. Trans. and ed. by Robert F. McNerney, Jr. University of Texas, 1970, 188; Hoover, 7–8; Promotion of Sucre to brigadier general by Zea, notice to Bolívar: Sucre to Bolívar, September 23, 1819, *Archivo de Sucre*, I: 552. Promotion of Sucre to brigadier general by Bolívar on January 16, 1820, *Archivo de Sucre*, I: 543–4.

25. Bolívar's earliest extant communication to Sucre is dated October 7, 1817, and contains instructions for Sucre's mission to foment loyalty to Bolívar among Marino's troops: *Archivo de Sucre*, I, 547. Sucre's first communication to Bolívar is dated October 17, 1817, and sets forth his progress on this assignment: *Archivo de Sucre*, I: 11. Sucre's military promotions from 1813 to 1820 are documented in *Archivo de Sucre*, I: 542–44.

26. Bolívar's first contact with Sucre: Lecuna, *Crónica*, I: 240 ff.; Hoover, 3–5; Cortes, 52. "Poor rider": O'Leary, *Bolívar*, 188. Sucre's little-known stint as minister of war from September 27, 1820, to November 9: *Archivo de Sucre*, I: 75–76; Promotion to chief of staff on November 16, 1820: *Archivo de Sucre*, I: 558; Instructions from Bolívar to negotiate the armistice treaty: *Archivo de Sucre*, I: 556–57.

27. The most intimate description of Sucre's personal habits is a book written by his secretary from 1823–1828: José María Rey de Castro, *Recuerdos del Tiempo Heróico*. Guayaquil, Ecuador, 1883. For Sucre's abstemiousness, Alfonso Rumazo González, *Sucre: Gran Mariscal de Ayacucho*, Madrid, 1963, 101. His physical appearance is best indicated, in my view, by an oil painting done in 1830 by José Sáez. It currently hangs in the Ecuadorean chancellery. See Angel Grisanti, *Retratos de Bolívar y de Sucre*, Caracas, 1969. For commentaries on Sucre's physical appearance and manners in 1815: Lima de Pombo, *Reminiscencias del Sitio del Cartagena*, 1862, as quoted in Rumazo, 61. Arturo Costa de la Torre, *Romance y Descendencia del Gran Mariscal de Ayacucho en la Ciudad de*

La Paz, La Paz, 1961, contains a useful compilation of verbal sketches of Sucre by contemporaries, 14–18. In English, we have Joseph Barclay Pentland, *Report on Bolivia,* 1827, London, 1974, 246; William Miller, *Memoirs of General Miller,* London, 1829, II: 66; Captain Andrew, *Journey from Buenos Aires to Peru,* London, 1827, II: 96. On Sucre's habit of working right through the night: F. Burdett O'Connor, *Independencia Americana,* Madrid, n.d., 105. Sucre's asceticism: Quevado, 114–15 and Rumazo, 39, 101, 165, 212.

28. Sucre's romantic liaisons and offsprings: Arturo Costa de la Torre and Sosa, *Gestiones Dialecticas,* Caracas, 1967. Bolívar's use of the term *dulzura:* Simon Bolívar, *Resúmen Sucinto de la Vida del General Sucre,* Lima, 1824, reprinted in *Archivo de Sucre,* I: XLVI. The "independence of his ideas": Tomas Héres's marginal notes on a letter to Sucre, Vicente Lecuna, *Documentos Referentes a la Creación de Bolivia,* Caracas, 1975, II: 365. Bolívar's comment on the Sucre's disingenuousness: Nicolas Navarre, ed. *Diario de Bucaramanga por L. Peru de Lacroix,* Caracas, 1935, 235.

29. Bolívar's comment on Spanish liberals: letter to Carlos Soublette, June 19, 1820, Bierck, 234.

30. "These constituionalists": *Archivo de Sucre,* I: 96; "Double-dealing": Ibid., I: 80.

31. Sucre to Santander, October 21, 1822, Julio Cortazar, *Correspondencia al Santander,* Bogotá, 1964–1970, XII: 435–38.

32. Sucre to Santander, October 30, 1820, *Archivo de Sucre,* I: 184–85.

33. Bustos conversation with Sucre, April 10, 1828, in Carlos Savaadra, *El Dean Funes y la Creacíon de Bolivia,* La Paz, 1972, 66. Sucre's comment of obsequiousness of the Frenchman: *Archivo de Sucre,* I: 262; "Men for all principles" and "aristocratic commissioners": Sucre to Bolívar, May 12, 1825, *Archivo de Sucre,* VI: 86–90; "Indians": Sucre to Bolívar, February 25, 1824, *Archivo de Sucre,* IV: 145.

34. Sucre's signature in the Harrington book: Quevedo, 32.; Sucre's study of English: O'Connor, 211.

35. Sucre's disputatious remarks to O'Leary: letter, November 7, 1828 in Daniel O'Leary, *Memorias del General O'Leary,* Caracas, 1880, IV, 490–91; Sucre's provincialism: O'Connor, 105–07.

36. Sucre's instructions: Bolívar to Sucre, January 2, 1822, *Archivo de Sucre* II: 588–89; "No human power" is a phrase of Bolívar's in these instructions; "Colombian flags fluttering": Bolívar to Jose Joaquín de Olmedo, January 2, 1822, Lecuna and Barret de Nazaris, *Obras Completas,* I: 612–13.

37. Sucre to Colombian minister of war, Briceño Mendez, May 15, 1821, *Archivo de Sucre,* I: 331–33.

38. Sucre's entire correspondence to San Martín between May 10, and December 14, 1821: *Archivo de Sucre,* I: 311–507. Quote: Sucre to San Martín, June 12, 1821, *Archivo de Sucre,* 351. Sucre to Briceño Mendez, May 15, 1821, *Archivo de Sucre,* I: 331–33. Standard treatments do not take adequate account of Sucre's invitation to allow San Martín's forces to take Quito, while the Colombians opened a secondary front around Cuenca. They, therefore, do not perceive the divergence between the approaches of Sucre and Bolívar. Hoover, for example, says (84) that Sucre's "mission (to Guayaquil) was to extend Colombian hegemony to the south." It was, in terms of his instructions, but not his actions. Bolívar would have been

horrified at the prospect of the Argentines liberating Quito. Fransisco A. Encina, *Emancipación de la Presidencia de Quito*, 50–54, imputes a similar motive to Sucre's activities in Guayaquil. He portrays him as being even more chauvinistic than Bolívar, a picture he maintains throughout his description of Sucre's activities in Peru. The Chilean ambassador in Lima during Sucre's time there, Joaquín Campino, projected this image of Sucre in his diaries, which have exerted a large influence on Chilean anti-Bolivarian historiography of this period.

39. Sucre's view of Santa Cruz's intentions toward Guayaquil for Peru: Sucre to Bolívar, December 14, 1823 in Daniel F. O'Leary, *Cartas de Sucre al Libertador*, Madrid, 1919, I: 137–38.

40. Sucre to Santander, April 5, 1822, *Archivo de Sucre*, II: 113–15.

41. Bolívar to Santander, June 9, 1922, *Obras*, I: 638–39.

42. Sucre's promotion and appointment to Quito intendant: Sucre to Santander, July 1, 1822, *Archivo de Sucre*, II: 187–88.

43. Bolívar's detailed version of the Guayaquil conference: J. G. Perez to the Colombian Foreign Ministry, July 29, 1822 in Lecuna and Barret de Nazaris, *Obras Completas*, I: 655–59.

44. First Intermedios campaign: Mariano Felipe Paz Soldan, *Historia de Peru Independiente*, II: Chapters 2 and 3. The rationale for the coup was set forth in an address by Santa Cruz to the Congress on January 18, 1823: *Archivo Historico del Mariscal Andrés de Santa Cruz*, La Paz, 1976, 58–61. Coup details and background: Paz Soldan, II: 26–27; Encina, *Emancipación*, 204–05, 224–25.

45. Cova, 94, note no. 5. Sucre to Santander, January 30, 1822, in Cortazar, *Corespondencia*, XII: 444–52.

46 Andrés Santa Cruz to Tomás Héres, December 8, 1822, *Archivo Histórico*. La Paz, 1976, I: 56.

47. Sucre to Bolívar, May 31, 1823 and June 19, 1823, in O'Leary, *Cartas*, I: 57–60 and 62–73, respectively.

48. Andrés Santa Cruz to Tomás Héres, December 8, 1822, *Archivo Histórico*, I: 56.

49. "Formidable warrior": as quoted in Paz Soldan, II: 1143; Ibid., 136.

50. Santa Cruz to Bolívar, May 24, 1823, *Archivo Histórico*, I: 73–74; same to Paz de Castillo, May 24, 1823, Ibid., 74–75; same to Bolívar, June 20, 1823, Ibid., 76–77.

51. Shaping up of the political environment consequent to Bolívar's arrival in Lima: Gonzálo Bulnes, *Bolívar en el Peru; Ultimas Campañas de la Independencia*, Madrid, 1919, I: 231 ff.

52. Vargas, II: 208–10.

53. Larrazabal, II: 217; Rumazo, 161–65.

54. "Not a friend": Sucre to Bolívar, May 27, 1823 in O'Leary, *Cartas*, I: 44; "particular friends of Santa Cruz": Sucre to Bolívar, April 15, 1824 in ibid., 210; Sucre to Bolívar, April 18, 1824, ibid., 211–213; Riva Aguero less dangerous than Peruvian "friends of Bolívar": Sucre to Bolívar, July 19, 1823 in O'Leary, ibid., 98–100.

55. Santander to the Congress, May 17, 1824, in Cortazar, *Cartas*, IV: 425–26; Bolívar to Bartólome Salom, January 1824, in R. Blanco Fombona ed., *Cartas de Bolívar*, Madrid, 1921, 143–47.

56. Constitutional problems of using Guayaquil as a staging area: Vargas, II: 60–80.

57. "Either there are laws or there are not": Santander to Bolívar, May 10, 1823, in Cortazar, IV: 399–491.

58. Diego Ibarra to Bolívar, May 31, 1824, in O'Leary, *Memorias,* II: 419–20.

59. Effects of the repeal of the extra-constitutional powers: Vargas, II: 81–100. Santander admitted to Bolívar that the congress's action stemmed from his request that it examine the relationship between Bolívar's presidency of Colombia and his Peruvian dictatorship. Santander to Bolívar, May 21, 1824 in Vicente Lecuna, *Cartas de Santander,* Caracas, 1942, I: 293–95.

60. Bolívar to Santander, November 10, 1824, is Lecuna, *Obras Completas.* II: 39.

61. Bolívar to Colombian secretary of state (Restrepo), January 24, 1824, in Blanco-Fombona, 143–44.

62. Bolívar to Sucre, May 26, 1823, in ibid., 18–25; Bolívar to Salom, January 24, 1824, in ibid., 143–47; Bolívar to Sucre, February 4, 1824, in ibid., 159–63 and note on 159; Bolívar to Sucre, February 16, 1824, in ibid., 179–81.

63. Text of Sucre's "Yungay letter," February 25, 1824, is in O'Leary, *Cartas,* 173–8 and in *Archivo de Sucre,* IV: 143–47. On the difference between Sucre's Yungay letter and Bolívar's own analysis of the significance of the Holy Alliance's intervention in Spain, see the editor's extensive footnote in Blanco-Fombona, 143–45.

64. Sucre to Bolívar, January 4, 1824, in O'Leary, *Cartas,* I: 140–48.

65. Sucre to Bolívar, February 25, 1824, *Archivo de Sucre,* IV: 147.

66. Ibid., 146.

67. Santa Cruz to Bolívar, October 28, 1824, *Archivo Histórico,* I: 119; Santa Cruz to José María Perez de Urdininea (Upper Peruvian guerrilla), October 31, 1823, in ibid., 124.

68. Sucre to Diego Ibarra, December 22, 1823, in O'Leary, *Cartas,* II: 359–60; Sucre to Gabriel Paz (Colombian officer), March 24, 1824, in ibid., 361–63.

69. Bolívar to Sucre, November 26, 1824 in Lecuna and Barret de Nazaris, *Obras Completas,* II: 46–49. For Bolívar's assessment of Sucre's military genius, Navarre, 214.

70. Sucre's berating of La Mar: O'Connor, 138–39; "Peruvians did their duty at Ayacucho": Agustín Gamarra to Sucre, July 17, 1828, in Alberto Tauro, ed., *Epistolario del Gran Mariscal Agustín Gamarra,* Lima, 1952, 110–11. Bolívar to Sucre, October 25, 1824, in O'Leary, *Memorias,* II: 292.

71. Bolívar to Santander, February 23, 1824, in Lecuna, *Cartas,* IV: 266–73.

3

Relations Between the Monarchy and the Republics

THE EXPANSION OF COLOMBIA'S MILITARY POWER on the continent provided a new perspective (the old one was confined to Argentina's relations with the monarchy) from which to view the monarchy's position in South America. A new order of questions arose. Did the military expansion of Colombia serve to make the monarchy in Brazil less acceptable to Spanish America because it was more vulnerable to Colombia's military might? Or, did Colombia's military expansion tend to make the monarchy more acceptable to Spanish America because Bolívar's power represented more of an intrusive threat to the republican possibilities of the Spanish-American states than Pedro's monarchy did?

Simultaneously, the new Colombian element was being incorporated into the relations between the monarchy and the republics in three areas: (1) a new policy initiated by Argentine president, Bernardino Rivadavia, was laying the groundwork for diplomatically settling the Eastern Bank question before the possibility of a military challenge to the monarchy, involving perhaps Colombian power, could materialize; (2) Canning was pursuing his efforts to forestall a military confrontation between Pedro and Bolívar; and (3) Pedro, to some extent emboldened by his feeling that Canning would hold Bolívar in check, was laying the groundwork for undertaking a major military campaign in the Eastern Bank. A fourth area was internal to the Colombian factor. It concerned the differences of opinion that had arisen between Sucre and Bolívar in the course of defining the purpose of Colombian power in Ecuador and Peru. These differences came to a head during the liberation of Upper Peru, precisely where the question of the monarchy first appeared on the horizon of Colombia's military power. This key process will concern us in the next chapter.

Rivadavian Politics in Argentina: A Move Toward the Brazilian Monarchy

Until 1820, the predominant Argentine pattern of seeking accommodation with the first Brazilian monarchy took the form of active attempts by the centralists in Buenos Aires, instigated largely by Pueyrredón, to collaborate with the Braganzas in Brazil. The failures of their armies, the departure of San Martín, and the ascendancy of Artigas in the Eastern Bank combined to cause the centralists to lose faith in their ability to militarily impose their control on the provinces. As a result, the centralists began to explore collaboration with the Braganzas as a means of strengthening their position in Argentine politics. They began to consider the idea of adopting a European-based monarchy—Portuguese (as John was offering), or French, or even Spanish—in Argentina as a means to establish centralist rule and to arrange European acceptance of Argentine independence. It was a foregone conclusion that if a Braganza took a throne in Argentina, either the Eastern Bank would be ceded to Brazil, or it would become part of a new imperial state that linked John's throne in Rio with the projected one in Buenos Aires. In either case, Artigas's attempt to create a federal league of the provinces to oppose Buenos Aires would lose its effect; his challenge to the Argentine centralist authority would be neutralized, and the centralist political organization of the Argentine state would be accomplished. The centralists initiated negotiations in 1815 with John and his advisers, with this purpose in mind. They secretly encouraged the invasion of the Eastern Bank by imperial forces under the command of Lecór in 1817. This invasion destroyed Artigas's military position and threatened his league. The centralists withheld assistance to Artigas and, in effect, encouraged the Portuguese to destroy him.[1]

The events of 1820, however, forced the centralists to modify their strategy. A less conspiratorial and less approach seemed to be called for. Rivadavia was the bearer of the new tactic.

The year 1820 witnessed a massive escalation of the *caudillo* opposition to the government at Buenos Aires. Although Artigas did not participate himself, being forced by Lecór into a terminal exile in Paraguay, his lieutenants in Santa Fe and Entre Ríos led a military attack in this crucial year against Buenos Aires in the name of Artigas's federal league. Just days before Buenos Aires's Army of the North was about to engage the league forces, a mutiny in its ranks broke out against Buenos Aires. It was instigated by Juan Bautista Bustos, an officer from the province of Córdoba. Most of the officers who supported the defection from the centralist cause, in fact, were men of the provinces. They proceeded to take contingents of the defunct Army of the North with them in order to establish systems of *caudillo* rule within their respective provinces.[2]

The defection of the Army of the North left Buenos Aires at the mercy of the *caudillo* armies of the league. Hastily mustered centralist forces commanded by General Juan Ramón Balcarce were destroyed in the battle of Cepeda on February 1, 1820, leaving the way to the port city open to the invaders. The Director, José Rondeau, and members of the congress fled or hid out as the *cabildo* assumed authority in the city and sent emissaries to seek an arrangement with Francisco Ramírez, a *caudillo* in Entre Ríos. These negotiations produced the Treaty of Pilar, which created a league of Santa Fe, Entre Ríos, and Buenos Aires provinces. Buenos Aires was required to pay stiff reparations to the other two provinces, cease collaboration with the Braganzas in the Eastern Bank, and try on criminal charges the members of the centralist congress who engaged in the secret negotiations with the court at Rio.

Between 1820 and 1824, there were no national institutions in existence in Argentina. The only semblance of "national" activities were some interprovincial pacts, such as the Quadripartite Pact signed between the province of Buenos Aires and the littoral provinces. During this period, each of the provinces was run by *caudillo* fiat. The notable exception was the province of Buenos Aires. During the years from 1821 to 1824, under the governorship of Martín Rodríguez, the centralists were busily consolidating civilian, republican government and undertaking concerted liberal reforms. Bernardino Rivadavia, Rodríguez's minister of government, became the driving force behind the new centralist program. The shock of 1820 had done its work.

The new centralist policy for defeating the *caudillo*s reflected less of the "hankering for monarchy," in John Q. Adam's words, that colored the previous strategy. It took, rather, the form of demonstrating the superiority of liberal, republican government in the province of Buenos Aires over *caudillo* rule in the interior. Concomitantly, contacts were initiated by Rivadavia with John and then with Pedro, with the purpose of a negotiated solution in the Eastern Bank. Rivadavia especially wanted to prevent a patriotic war initiated by the *caudillo*s in the interior to liberate the Eastern Bank from its foreign occupiers, whether Portuguese or Brazilian.

By 1820, Rivadavia had gotten over his earlier, monarchist phase, during which he had actively solicited support from the Holy Alliance and Britain for the construction of a constitutional monarchy in Argentina based on European royalty.[3] He had been transformed into a doctrinaire liberal republican. While in Britain during his European tour, he had formed a close friendship with Jeremy Bentham. Once back in government in Buenos Aires, he began implementing a range of public policy reforms effecting the funding of the debt, freedom of the press, electoral reform, penal reform, reduction of ecclesiastic influence on politics, subordination of the military to civilian authority, social welfare, aesthetics of the city, and university reform. Many of these were modeled after Bentham's legislative codes. Rivadavia believed that on the basis of his record in Buenos Aires the provinces would yield to Buenos Aires peacefully and without the need for conspiracy or coercion. According to the American consul, John M. Forbes, Rivadavia was

> firm to his principles, professing his sole and entire reliance on the growth of moral influences in his country ... (Rivadavia) did not deem it necessary to hasten the forms of a diplomatic intercourse, repeating the opinion ... that he looked steadily for the best foundations of political character and security to the progress of internal civilization and illustration and to the wise institutions which would result—that he hoped that the gradual operation of these causes, exemplified in the progress of Buenos Ayres, would shed their influence over the other Provinces, promote a perfect harmony of political views and at no distant period induce a Confederation much more permanent than that which had been formerly established under the odious influence of intrigue and force.[4]

Rivadavia believed that it was from Europe, especially northern Europe and Britain, that Argentina could draw the resources it needed—political, cultural, human, economic—to develop into an integrated, civilized nation. Although a Europeanist, Rivadavia did not reject totally the possibility of an American political system arising out of independence, even one staked on excluding the Braganzas in Brazil on republican grounds. He was, however, deeply skeptical of this possibility. Artigas's power and the power of the *caudillos* in the interior had made it necessary, in Rivadavia's view, for the centralists to rely on European political influence, and hopefully, a diplomatic solution of the Eastern Bank problem, in order to blunt the *caudillos'* disruptiveness.

Ultimately, Rivadavia's purpose was to strengthen the experiment in Buenos Aires to ensure that if Brazil had to be attacked in the Eastern Bank, it would be in the name of the liberal-republican-civilian principles that Buenos Aires stood for and would not be a military adventure that would give the *caudillos* an excuse to shunt those principles aside. In the meantime, he wanted the independence process to be completed by soliciting European approval as opposed to seeking victories on American battlefields. This was clearly the thinking that lay behind a treaty that he signed with Spanish emissaries in Buenos Aires in 1823. It called for an armistice on all battlefronts in Peru, pending separate negotiations by the concerned Spanish-American states with Spain on the independence question.

For these reasons, Rivadavia was intent on pursuing a diplomatic accommodation with Pedro in the Eastern Bank; he was not looking for an American battlefield. He believed that he should try to gain acceptance of the monarchy by his countrymen by showing that a favorable resolution of the conflict in the Eastern Bank, could be achieved without recourse to military methods; instead, British mediation would do the trick. He believed that this would also set an example for other Spanish-American populations that were wrestling with their own versions of *caudillo* rule. He feared that any military challenge to the monarchy would only serve to give the *caudillo*s an excuse to crush his government in Buenos Aires.

It was through accommodation with Pedro, and not challenge, that Rivadavia believed he could secure his centralist, liberal experiment in Buenos Aires against the forces of militarism. Although his government was republican, it was not the principle of republican politics per se that he sought to vindicate through his rapprochement with the Brazilian monarchy. Rather, what he sought to vindicate was his liberal centralism, as an alternative to *caudillo* militarism.

John M. Forbes, the U.S. chargé in Buenos Aires, wondered whether it would be a good thing if the Argentine provinces came together to wage a patriotic war against Lecór's army in the Eastern Bank in order to liberate a sister province. The *caudillo*s of the interior appeared intent on using "immediate and unqualified force" to emancipate the Eastern Bank "from the Brazilian lake." He reported that a strong military force was capable of being assembled in the provinces of Santa Fe, Córdoba, Entre Ríos, and Corrientes with which to attack Lecór's army. He noted sympathetically the efforts of Rivadavia to cool the "patriotic ardor" of the provinces and to "temper the threat of military coercion with diplomatic efforts." He gave credence to the fact that the ostensible purpose was to attack the Portuguese but the real object was to create a new Argentine union "under the protection of military force" combined with the dictatorship of General San Martín "a lion who has been sleeping for more that six months at Mendoza, under pretext of bodily indisposition." Forbes doubted that posing a military challenge to Lecór in the Eastern Bank would assist the republican process in the Argentine state. Rather, he felt that the "the spirit of this new Coalition is to be found in the restless ambition of a few Military Chiefs."[5]

Clearly, these military energies focused on regaining the Eastern Bank from the Portuguese were not wedded to republican principles. In 1822 and 1823, the Brazilian forces in the Eastern Bank under Lecór were mainly Portuguese, not Brazilian. The drive to rid the Eastern Bank of them therefore was seen as an American struggle against European interference. The empire declared by Pedro had not yet come into focus in the Eastern Bank. As this did begin to happen, and as Pedro appeared to become more authoritarian by dissolving his Constituent Assembly and building up his imperial army with the apparent intent to invade the Eastern Bank anew and force it into the empire, the basis for opposing him on republican principles as an arbitrary, despotic monarchic became more plausible.

The U.S. secretary of state at the time, John Q. Adams, believed that the appearance of imperial forces under Pedro's authority in the Eastern Bank would give Buenos Aires the privilege of delivering the final republican *coup d'grace* to monarchy in the New World.

> Brazil has declared its own independence of Portugal, and constituted itself into an empire, with an Emperor at its head. General Lecór has lost the real command of his own army, and has been, or cannot fail shortly to be, compelled to embark, with all his Portuguese troops, for Lisbon. Then will come the question between Buenos Ayres and Brazil, for Montevideo and the Oriental Band (Eastern Bank) of the La Plata, and then will soon be seen that the Republican Hemisphere will endure neither Emperor nor King upon its shores.[6]

Adams was predicting, as a matter of republican principle, that Buenos Aires would lead Argentina to stand behind the Eastern Bank's right not to be forced into the empire.

> From the time (Lecór's army departs from the Eastern Bank) the inhabitants of the Oriental Band themselves will prefer their old and natural connection with Buenos Ayres to a forced Union with the Empire of Brazil. It will certainly be the favorable moment for Buenos Ayres to recover the Eastern shore of the River, and with it the means of re-uniting under one free and Republican Government the scattered fragments of the old Vice-royalty. ... There will be then much less of incentive for a Buenos Ayrean Government to (experience) the contamination of dark intrigues with Portuguese Princesses or the degrading purchase of a (Spanish) Prince ... to rule over them as a King ... that have pervaded the short history of Buenos Ayres from the first assertions of its Independence. ... It is hoped that you will find little of this spirit remaining to contend with. ... The principles always avowed by Mr. Rivadavia ... are emphatically American. A Government by popular Representation and periodic election, the subordination of the Mil-

itary to the Civil Authority, the suppression of ecclesiastical supremacy, the freedom of the press, and the security of personal liberty ... with these principles, no preference for European connections, much less predilections for European princes, can be entertained.[7]

Yet this analysis was highly problematic. Indeed, Argentina was provided with a strong, republican-liberal impetus by Rivadavia's government in Buenos Aires. But Rivadavia, despite Adams's hopes, was decidedly European in his outlook and inclined to a diplomatic resolution of the conflict in the Eastern Bank, instead of mounting a military effort there. It was by no means clear that attacking Pedro in the bank instead of Lecór would make the military option any more republican in its basis, especially if Rivadavia was right that it was the spirit of military adventurism and instinctive hatred of Buenos Aires, not political principles, that motivated the interior *caudillo*s to clamor for war against the monarchy. In this perspective, a military attack on Pedro in the Eastern Bank would not necessarily spell a republican challenge to the monarchy in Brazil, but rather a *caudillo* challenge to Rivadavia; not a republican coalition but an alliance of *caudillo*s. Was it possible to coordinate a military attack on Pedro in such a way as to strengthen republican principles against the *caudillo*s that threatened them? On balance, Rivadavia doubted that it was. Therefore, his policy was strongly tilted toward defusing such a challenge by pushing his diplomatic contacts with Rio.

We have here a microversion of a macroquestion: Could a military coalition formed by the separate Spanish-American states to attack Pedro's monarchy ever be of republican benefit, given that all of the fledgling republican governments were under the shadow of their own military *caudillo*s? This question was posed to Rivadavia in the form of an emissary from Bolívar, who proposed a defensive military alliance between Colombia and Argentina against Spain and also the formation of a league of Spanish-American states to coordinate policy and serve as a diplomatic forum. Rivadavia had to ask himself how committed to republican principles would such arrangements be? Just as the alliance of the *caudillo*s was a mask for vesting supreme power in the super *caudillo* San Martín, so the new alliance-league proposals were masks for increasing the adherents to the cause of Bolívar's power. Whether it was a league among the Argentine *caudillo*s or a league of American states, as per Bolívar's proposal, they were part and parcel of what Rivadavia referred to as "family alliances among *caudillo*s." Their followings were created during the military fighting that went along with the destruction of the colonial order. They were trying to camouflage the *de facto* basis of their power structures by appealing to military struggles to achieve independence; to personalistic *caudillo* leadership instead of normative commitment to the principles of liberal, republican government.[8]

On March 11, 1823, Forbes expressed the hope to Rivadavia that Bolívar's proposals might be the first step toward building up a "firm system of American policy wholly independent of European interests and influence." Rivadavia was polite but noncommittal. He sent Bolívar's envoy home virtually empty handed.[9]

Three years later, Rivadavia had to reconsider this question: Could Buenos Aires's experiment with liberal, civilian, republican government survive its entrance into a military alliance with Colombia? This time, however, the question was colored by the enormous expansion of Colombia' military power, which brought it to Argentine borders. The alliance in question was no longer aimed against Spain—whose power by that time had been defeated in South America by Colombia's armies—but rather against Pedro's imperial forces which were moving fast into the Eastern Bank. Thus, by 1825 the Colombian invasion of South America was well advanced and became a crucial factor in determining the framework of the monarchy's relations with the Spanish-American republics. Given the "price" that the Peruvians were perceived to have paid for Colombian liberation of Peru, the Argentines supporting Rivadavia could understandably question the utility of Colombian power to the republican cause. The question, however, would become not only whether Rivadavia and his adherents could afford to join forces with Bolívar against the monarchy, but whether Bolívar's forces would join Argentina in a war against the monarchy.

Canning's Progress

Canning's objective was to defeat the formation of any alliance of Spanish-American republics against the monarchy. He feared that such an alliance would encourage the formation of a larger, anti-European coalition of American states. Instead, he wanted to create a balance of power in South America that included Brazil and allowed Britain to play mediator among the states and between them and Europe—all the while garnering the benefits of free trade for Britain and marginalizing the U.S. influence in Latin America. Two key diplomatic missions worked toward these goals: that of Sir Charles Stuart to Lisbon and then to Rio, and that of Lord John Ponsonby to Buenos Aires and Rio. The Stuart mission was a brilliant success for Canning; it legitimated the independent Brazilian monarchy among the thrones in Europe and, Canning hoped, among the Spanish Americans on the South American continent as well.

Stuart succeeded in extracting from John, in Lisbon in early 1825, a commitment to sign a treaty with Pedro recognizing Brazil's independence. Having engineered Portugal's concession of Brazilian independence, Britain had established itself, instead of the Holy Alliance, as Pedro's chief sponsor. "The Emperor has good reason to be proud, and to expect much from the British," Bolívar commented in a letter to Santander, referring to optimistic reports he had received from Lisbon concerning Stuart's mission.[10] By mid-1825, Stuart was en route to Rio with a draft treaty signed by John and stipulating the independence of Brazil from Portugal. That treaty was initialed in Rio on August 29, 1825, after several conferences between him and Stuart. Canning felt that the Spanish Americans should be grateful because he had blunted the threat of a Holy Alliance appropriation of the Brazilian monarchy for its purposes in the New World. It was now up to the Spanish Americans to make their peace with the monarchy.[11]

As the Stuart mission was developing, Canning resolved to end the conflict in the Eastern Bank and remove this impediment to the further normalization of relations between the Brazilian monarchy and the Spanish-American republics. Yet in mid-1825, he was not ready for active mediation or for recognition of Argentina. Canning wanted to put off both until he could be certain that the Holy Alliance would not respond by intervening in the Eastern Bank conflict. In this state of mind, Canning snubbed Rivadavia when he was in London in mid-1825. Under the guise of being a diplomatic envoy, Canning accused Rivadavia of fomenting commercial ventures for his own personal gain. Canning used Rivadavia's letter of diplomatic appointment, which was addressed to Canning instead of, as customary, to the king, as a pretext for not treating with Rivadavia on the twin subjects of British recognition and mediation in the bank, both of which Rivadavia was pressing.[12]

Canning was, however, almost certain that the Holy Alliance did not present a problem for a more active British role in the Argentine-Brazilian dispute. Through the Polignac Memorandum, he succeeded in extracting a commitment from the French not to intervene militarily in America on any pretext. (This is one reason why he lost interest in pursuing negotiations with the United States for common action against the threat of a Holy Alliance intervention in the New World.) By refusing to attend a Holy Alliance meeting, planned for mid-1826 to discuss American affairs, Canning further disconcerted the interventionist aspirations of the alliance and prepared the ground for British recognition of the Spanish-American states. Then, Canning decided to capitalize on the looming success of the Stuart mission by encouraging diplomatic negotiations between Argentina and Brazil in order to settle the conflict in the Eastern Bank. Argentina should be given the opportunity to express its appreciation to the British for Stuart's diplomatic coup in Lisbon, which freed the Brazilian monarchy from the clutches of the Holy Alliance and made it worthy of Spanish-American acceptance. That appreciation should be expressed by Buenos Aires's cooperation in negotiations over the Eastern Bank question. This was the general tenor of instructions that Canning drafted for Lord Ponsonby.[13]

For a brief time in 1825, Canning had been in favor of the adjudication of the Eastern Bank war by the Panama Assembly. By early 1826, however, he was solidly against this. Consideration of the issue in Panama, he felt, would risk causing the republican states to close ranks against Brazil as a common enemy. At best, Canning felt, if the war were not settled and it surfaced as an issue in Panama, "there could be little doubt ... in an assembly so composed ... that any decision would be unfavorable to the Emperor." British mediation was the proper alternative.[14]

Ponsonby was instructed by Canning to pull Pedro back from the brink of war in the Eastern Bank. Pedro was to be warned that any attempt to assert rights of conquest in the bank "would furnish an inducement to the states of Spanish America to unite themselves sooner or later in a common cause against Brazil."[15]

Canning later instructed Ponsonby to push the idea of Argentina paying indemnification to Pedro in exchange for the withdrawal of imperial forces. Too much stubbornness from Pedro was not to be tolerated. Bolívar was prepared to accept the monarchy as part of the South American system, judging from the dispatches from the British envoy in Lima. But Bolívar's forbearance had its limits. The achievement of Pedro's independence from Portugal should make him acceptable to the Spanish-American states, if Pedro played his cards right. To be bellicose in the Eastern Bank would undo all the gains that had been made toward establishing the legitimacy of his monarchy on the South American continent, as the "strongest connecting link between the New World and the Old."[16]

On the Argentine side, Canning was attentive to the tensions between the *caudillos* in the interior provinces and the authorities at Buenos Aires. Buenos Aires's fear that a military escalation in the Eastern Bank would play into the hands of the *caudillos* made Canning think that the *porteños* (inhabitants of the "port" of Buenos Aires) would make concessions in the Eastern Bank and thereby facilitate British mediation of the war. But, by the same token, it was likely that Buenos Aires would lose support in the interior for those concessions. Canning followed the activities of Bustos and Quiroga very closely through the reports of Woodbine Parish, the British consul-general in Buenos Aires, and through the Buenos Aires press.

Rivadavia's agent in London, Frederico Gil, had tried to convince Canning that Sucre was acting as a cat's paw for Bolívar in the liberation of Upper Peru; that Bolívar was angling for a way to get into a war with Pedro so he could overthrow the monarchy and add it to his military laurels. Gil warned Canning that Argentina, despite its better judgment, might have to wage a war of principles (republic vs. monarchy, Europe vs. America) against Brazil if Bolívar and Sucre forced their hand. Canning was aware that the *porteños* might lose control of the Eastern Bank issue. A successful revolt by the *caudillo*s against Buenos Aires would ultimately threaten the stability of the Brazilian monarchy if it encompassed, as was likely, an effort to turn the conflict in the Eastern Bank into a patriotic struggle for the Argentines, backed possibly by the Colombians.[17]

Regarding the payment of an Argentine indemnification to Brazil, Canning was informed by Parish in late 1825 that Buenos Aires was receptive because of its fears that the alternative course—of seeking a military victory over Pedro in the Eastern Bank—would incite the rise of *caudillismo* in the Argentine body politic. "As between the payment of a sum of money to the Emperor and the success of their arms, (Buenos Aires) should without hesitation prefer the former."[18] Canning instructed Ponsonby to push the indemnification proposal to Pedro but to allude to the creation of an independent buffer state in the bank, backed by a British guarantee of free navigation of the Plata River, if Pedro would not agree to restoration of the bank to Argentina. Here was the concept of the future nation of Uruguay.[19]

Pedro's War Plan

The triumph of Colombia's army at Ayacucho and the invasion of Upper Peru added an external dimension to Pedro's growing domestic political difficulties. It created the sense, clearly conveyed in the reports of the U.S. consul in Rio, Condy Raguet, that a Spanish-American noose was being tightened around the neck of Pedro's monarchy.

In July 1823, after the imperial forces had liberated the northern coastal city of Salvador (Bahia) from Portuguese control, Pedro was leaning toward reconciliation with Lisbon and with the local Portuguese community in Brazil, whose property holdings had been confiscated in order to finance the war measures taken against Portugal. The Portuguese who were resident in Brazil, and those other "enemy aliens" who were personal enemies of cabinet ministers, were under constant threat of further confiscation of their property, reprisals of all kinds, and sundry efforts to discredit them. Pedro's chief cabinet Minister, José Bonifácio, had his own share of personal enemies. Like Pedro, he opposed slavery. But whereas Pedro's opposition was emotional in nature, Bonifácio's was based on considerations of political economy.

Bonifácio's "liberal" agenda—including expansion of free trade, increasing European immigration and the mechanization of agriculture to offset slave labor, and elimination of the large landholdings (*latifundio*)—was aimed directly at the interests of two classes which were rooted in the old colonial order: Portuguese merchants and the rural landowning class to which they were linked by intricate family relationships.[20]

In July 1823, Pedro abruptly lifted the emergency war measures that had been taken in response to the possibility of a war with Portugal over Brazilian independence. He halted the confiscation of Portuguese property, much to the chagrin of his cabinet, which was not consulted. At this time, a counterliberal movement in Lisbon toppled the *Cortes* and restored John to royal power—an echo of the Holy Alliance occupation of Spain that restored Ferdinand to power. Portuguese envoys were promptly dispatched to Rio to propose a rapprochement of the two monarchies now that the imperial-minded liberals, Pedro's chosen adversaries, had been toppled in Lisbon. With the threat of war with Portugal now ended, Pedro was receptive. The envoys from Lisbon also sought to stimulate the loyalties of the socially conservative Brazilians, who worried about the liberal reforms on the government's agenda. Bonifácio had come under considerable criticism from this sector. He resigned in July in protest over Pedro's lifting of emergency war measures.

In April 1823, the Constituent Assembly had opened and undertook its charge from Pedro to draft a liberal, monarchic constitution. But a militant, nationalist, republican-minded, anti-Portuguese faction had arisen in the assembly; it became openly critical of Pedro for his softness toward the Portuguese and, in particular, for seeking to incorporate Portuguese troops captured in Bahia into the national army. Pedro's rule began to be perceived by nationalists in the Constituent Assembly as a vehicle for building up dynastic relations with Portugal and at the same time outflanking conservative opinion in Brazil. Delegates in the Constituent Assembly, such as Goncalves Ledo and Januario de Cunha Barbosa, wanted to draft a conservative, republican constitution rather than a liberal, monarchic one. They vilified Bonifácio as the chief architect of a plan for the aggrandizement of the monarchy through liberal reforms.

Pedro's insistence on veto rights over all acts of the assembly heightened tensions to the point that he dissolved it on November 12, 1823, with multiple arrests, jailings, and exiles. In the meantime, he appointed a commission to draft a constitution for a genuinely liberal monarchy. Its work was completed by early 1824. The document was ratified by a majority of the city and town councils and declared to be the official constitution of the empire in April. A national parliament, consisting of a Chamber of Deputies and a Senate was scheduled to be elected under the new constitution in 1826. The prospect, especially in the lower house, of new republican-oriented, nationalist agitation against the monarchy calling, in particular, for emphasis on more cooperative relations with Spanish-American states and less concern with Europe, threatened to revive the earlier conflict between Pedro and the Constituent Assembly.[21]

The political situation in Brazil was especially tense in the north, where republican opposition to the monarchy remained alive. After the victory of Pedro's imperial forces over the Portuguese military around Bahia, a significant regional mobilization broke out in Pernambuco in 1824. The rebels swore loyalty to the Constituent Assembly and repudiated the new constitution prepared by Pedro's commission. But in the meantime, they declared the existence of a separate republic—dubbed the Confederation of Ecuador—which included Pernambuco and various of the surrounding provinces. During 1824, Pedro's land and sea forces eventually surrounded the rebels and crushed their movement. The American consul underscored in his dispatch that a French "sloop of war" accompanied the imperial *flotilla* that sailed for Pernambuco on March 3, 1824. This was a visible sign of the Holy Alliance's interest in the survival of Pedro's monarchy.[22] Despite Pedro's victory over the insurgency in Pernambuco, the situation remained unstable in the north. This, combined with the prospect of contending with a nationalistic opposition in the Chamber of Deputies, influenced Pedro to rally patriotic support for his monarchy and pride in his newly recruited imperial army by scoring a conspicuous military victory against Argentina in the Eastern Bank.

He sought to complete the replacement of the Portuguese garrison by imperial Brazilian forces and to confront a new invader: Eastern Bank expatriates, led by Juan Antonio Lavalleja and supported by Rivadavia's foes in Buenos Aires, were attempting to insurrect the bank population against Brazilian rule and join it to Argentina. A successful Brazilian occupation of the Eastern Bank would not only arouse patriotic support for the imperial army, but it would also demonstrate, perhaps more importantly at least in psychological terms, Pedro's willingness to take the offensive against Argentina even with Bolívar's army approaching his borders.

Although most of the Portuguese units had been replaced by some imperial troops in the Eastern Bank in 1824, the Portuguese commander, Lecór, had stayed on. His situation become precarious because of the insurrectionary activities of Juan Lavalleja. Lecór's situation became critical when Fructuosa Rivera, the head of the Eastern Bank militia, defected to Lavalleja's forces. Lavalleja's plan was to detach the Eastern Bank from the empire and join it to the Argentine provinces.

In early 1825, Pedro began the build-up of imperial forces in the Eastern Bank that would reach a total of 10,000 to 12,000 troops in the field, backed by garrisons of 3,500 in Montevideo and 1,500 in Colonia. Lecór was ordered to use the imperial forces to pacify the countryside, as he did in earlier campaigns against Artigas. In August 1825, Lecór sent a large pacification army into the interior. Pedro hoped that good news from the Eastern Bank would stifle opposition to the war, which was building among his political opponents, and put a damper on the potential opposition that he would have to face in the General Assembly when it convened in May 1826.

Beginning with the news of Sucre's victory at Ayacucho, Raguet reported that "many people began to reflect on the possibility of maintaining a monarchy in the midst of Republiks. ... (In view of Pedro's buildup) all eyes are turned to the Eastern Bank as the next seat of war."[23] Pedro had embarked on a risky enterprise. His military build-up in the Eastern Bank might precipitate Colombian intervention. This would be too much for his fledgling imperial army to contend with, particularly if the republican insurrectionists in the north received support from neighboring Venezuela for their revolt.[24] Further, some of the intelligence that Pedro began to receive about the probable response by what he called the "western republics"—Chile and Peru, which would be joined in mid-1825 by Bolivia—to a Brazilian declaration of war against Argentina in the Eastern Bank was not reassuring. One source informed him, according to Raguet, that "they (Peru, Chile, Bolivia) would make a common cause of it and ... that measures had been adopted (by Sucre) in Upper Peru for a march on Brazil."[25] A naked challenge to Argentina would be too risky in light of this new development. Pedro, therefore, decided to extend an olive branch to Bolívar, while preparing the mailed fist for the Argentines in the Eastern Bank. For the olive branch, he prepared an apology to Bolívar for the confrontation that had developed when units of the Brazilian army had crossed into the Upper Peruvian province of Chiquitos.

Notes

1. John Street, *Artigas and the Emancipation of Uruguay.* New York: Colombia University Press, 1959, 281–88; Bartolomé Mitre, *Historia de San Martín y la Emancipación Sudamericana.* Buenos Aires, 1890, II: 477–562. Secret contacts between the centralists and John's Court: Street, 218–88; Mitre, II: 477–567; Mitre, III: 25; Mariano A. Pelliza, *Dorrego y la Historia de los Partidos Unitarios y Fed-*

erales. Buenos Aires, 1978, 104–11; 118–24. Pueyrredón quotation: Mitre, III: 39. Pueyrredón sellout of Artigas: Street, 287–95.

2. Pelliza, 155–217, esp. 202; Mitre, III: 201–24.

3. Ricardo Piccirilli, *Rivadavia y Su Tiempo*, 2nd ed., Buenos Aires, 1960, I: 219–247; *Comisión de Bernardino Rivadavia ante España y Otras Potencias de Europa, 1814–20*. Edited by E. Ravignani, Buenos Aires, 1933; Mitre, III: 41–71.

4. Forbes to Adams, October 16, 1823. in William Manning, *Diplomatic Correspondence of the United States Concerning the Independence of the Latin American nations*. New York: Oxford University Press, 1925, II: 615–16.

5. Forbes to Adams, April 30, 1823, September 12 and 14, 1823, ibid., I: 620, 625–26, 626 respectively.

6. Adams to Robert C. Anderson, U.S. minister to Colombia, May 27, 1823, in ibid., I: 205.

7. Adams to Cesar Rodney, U.S. minister to Buenos Aires, May 17, 1823, in ibid., I: 190–91.

8. Session of the Buenos Aires Junta, June 9, 1823, as quoted in Larrazabal, *Vida*, II: 398.

9. Forbes to Adams, March 11, 1823, in Manning I: 617–619.

10. Bolívar to Santander, October 11, 1825, in Lecuna and Barret de Nazaris, *Simón Bolívar: Obras Completas*. Havana, Cuba, 1950, II: 227.

11. Canning to Parish, October 19, 1825, in Charles Webster, *Britain and the Independence of Latin America*. London, 1938, II: 130–33.

12. Canning to Parish, May 24, 1825, in Webster, I: 121–22.

13. Canning to Ponsonby, February 28, 1826, and March 18, 1826, in ibid., II: 138–39 and 139–44, respectively.

14. Canning to Ponsonby, March 18, 1826, in ibid., II: 143. For Canning's earlier sentiment "in favor of the adjudication of the Plata war by the Panama Assembly," William W. Kaufman, *British Policy and the Independence of Latin America*. New York: Anchor Books, 1967, 194.

15. Canning to Ponsonby, March 18, 1826, in ibid., II: 141.

16. Canning to Ponsonby, March 18, 1826, in ibid., II: 139–44.

17. Gil's warning to Canning: Federico Gil to Canning, November 20, 1826, Luis Rodríguez, *Ayacucho, la Batalla de la Libertad Americana*. Quito, 1975, II: 193–98. Canning's version of the Gil negotiations and his concern regarding the *caudillo* revolts: Canning to Ponsonby, March 18, 1826, in Webster, I: 139–44.

18. Parish to Canning, December 18, 1826, in Webster, I: 137–38; Dorrego to Bolívar, May 25, 1826, Daniel O'Leary, *Memorias de General O'Leary*. Caracas, 1880, XI: 283–84.

19. Canning to Ponsonby, March 18, 1826, in Webster, I: 139–44.

20. Emilia Viotti da Costa, *The Brazilian Empire; Myths and Histories*. Chicago: University of Chicago Press, 1985, 44–46.

21. Urgings in the Chamber of Deputies that Pedro should stop emphasizing relations with Europe over those with other American states: Ron Seckinger, *The Brazilian Monarchy and the South American Republics, 1822–1831*. Baton Rouge, La.: Louisiana State University Press, 1984, 14.

22. E. Bradford Burns, *History of Brazil,* 2nd ed. Ithaca: Cornell University Press, 1980, 168. French Warship: Raguet to Adams, March 8, 1824, in Manning, II: 777.

23. Raguet to Clay, March 11, 1825, in ibid., 811–12.

24. Raguet to Clay, May 12, 1825, in ibid., 816.

25. Raguet to Clay, March 20, 1826, in ibid., 843–44.

Courtesy of the Foreign Ministry of Ecuador, currently in The Minister of Foreign Affairs Office

Antonio José de Sucre
(1795–1830)

Pedro I of Brazil
(1798–1834)

José de San Martín
(1778–1850)

Courtesy of the Museo Histórico Nacional in Buenos Aires

Bernardino Rivadavia
(1780–1845)

Andrés Santa Cruz
(1792–1865)

Simón Bolívar
(1783–1830)

4

Colombia's Invasion of Upper Peru (Bolivia)

SUCRE SOUGHT TO POSITION Colombian military power in Upper Peru within the tradition of regional patriotism that had developed there. He appropriated an Atlantic strategy that had been developed originally by the judges of the Upper Peruvian *audiencia* to counterbalance the heavy interference by the Peruvian viceroyalty. He sought to pre-empt Peruvian claims to Upper Peru by erecting the separate state of Bolivia and providing it with an Atlantic role defined in terms of an Argentine-Bolivian alliance. Sucre's strategy raised the possibility that Colombia's army in Bolivia could be used to challenge the Brazilian monarchy in support of Argentina as an alternative to spearheading Peruvian expansion under the cover of Bolívar's dictatorship. The conflict between Sucre and Bolívar over Upper Peru may be defined as a conflict between the strategy of republican liberation and the strategy of authoritarian occupation.

Atlantic Basis of Upper Peru's Autonomy

In 1777, the provinces of Upper Peru were transferred from the Viceroyalty of Peru to a new viceroyalty established in the Plata region, with its capital at Buenos Aires. This transfer tended to be viewed favorably by the judges of the *audiencia* of Upper Peru. Generations of judges had contended that the *audiencia* would have more weight in Madrid if it could colonize the Plata area and develop a port at Buenos Aires to replace Lima as the commercial link between Spain and South America. The Atlantic-minded judges in Upper Peru also expected that the formidable tradition of autonomy, which the *audiencia* had already established in relation to the Peruvian viceroys, might even find larger scope with the new rulers in Buenos Aires. The administrative patterns of the new viceroyalty were expected to remain fluid for some time, thereby giving the *audiencia* new opportunities to establish the precedents for regional autonomy. The *audiencia*, therefore, vigorously resisted the extension of the administrative systems of the Plata viceroyalty into

Upper Peru, especially the innovative ones such as the intendancies which replaced the old *corregidor* system as the basis for local district management.[1]

The *audiencia* judges, alleging Napoleon's influence over the Plata viceroy, had already staged a revolt in 1808 in the name of "preserving" the loyalty of Upper Peru to Ferdinand. At the same time, the *audiencia* refused to submit to the authority of the Spanish *Cortes*, which was set up as a resistance government during the French occupation of the peninsula. The American politics of the Braganza Court in Brazil widened the basis for the assertion of the *audiencia's* autonomy and brought it to the verge of claiming territorial sovereignty. The *audiencia* judges had received letters from Carlota proposing her regency over the area of the *audiencia*. It was known to the judges that Pueyrredón and some followers looked favorably on the idea of substituting Carlota's regency over the Spanish-American colonies during Ferdinand's captivity. This collusion was alleged by the *audiencia* to be no less disloyal to Ferdinand than were other proposals in Buenos Aires for joining John in the "Empire of South America." Countering the Braganza proposals of political expansionism, with their apparatus of collusion in Buenos Aires, provided the impetus for *audiencia* activities at establishing the separation of the *audiencia* from the Plata viceroyalty. In reality, the action of the *audiencia* was motivated by creole designs to turn Upper Peru into an independent state.[2]

The Plata viceroy put down the *audiencia's* rebellion in Chuquisaca but was unable to follow through with the pacification of Upper Peru because of a revolutionary movement that broke out in Buenos Aires in late 1808. In the meantime, the Upper Peruvian rebellion had spread from the seat of the *audiencia* in Chuquisaca to the city of La Paz. The viceroy of Peru, Fernando Abascal, decided to step into the revolutionary breach. He was determined to restore viceregal authority not only in Upper Peru but to invade the Plata also and restore viceregal rule there, too. Peruvian armies invaded Upper Peru in 1809, severely punished the La Paz revolutionaries, and reincorporated the area into the Peruvian viceroyalty, pending the restoration of viceregal authority in Buenos Aires. The invasion of the Plata region by Abascal's army, however, ran into stiff opposition from local patriot forces and was turned back.[3]

Armies were subsequently dispatched by the revolutionary government in Buenos Aires to invade Upper Peru, wrest control of the area from the Peruvian viceroyalty, and annex it to the emergent Argentine state. These armies were ultimately successful only in alienating the Upper Peruvians and producing as much, if not more, regional hatred toward Buenos Aires than existed toward Lima. Although the guerrilla forces appearing in Upper Peru were originally allied with the Buenos

Aires armies against the Peruvians, they soon turned against them and struck out on their own against both "foreign" invaders. In the course of the resistance against both the Peruvian and Argentine armies, which continued sporadically in the fifteen years from 1809 to 1824 (the *quincenio*), Upper Peruvian guerrilla forces generated a regional, patriotic sentiment. These guerrilla armies controlled their own enclaves, many of which resembled miniature nations with their own patriotic ethos and quasi-political structures. These *republiquetas*, as they were called, were ephemeral and of questionable political significance. However, they did embody a tradition of patriotic struggle. They added another layer to that tradition of Upper Peruvian separatism that included the early activities of the *encomenderos* (holders of royal grants of Indians) and continued in the thoughts and actions of generations of Audiencia judges.[4]

The guerrilla leadership, or what was left of it from the *republiqueta* period, placed itself immediately under Sucre's command as his army prepared to close on Olañeta.

Liberation or Occupation?

Because of the French invasion of Spain, Holy Alliance politics had come to the forefront of the picture of Spanish-American independence. The chief obstacle to independence was Spain's unwillingness to tolerate it, backed by its military force still present on the continent. Another, more subtle obstacle, now replaced it: The granting of "independence" under Holy Alliance auspices, that is, by means of the alliance actively setting up and backing Bourbon monarchies to rule the new states. This raised the question of whether simply liberating places from Spanish military domination adequately defined the mission of Colombia's army beyond its borders. Might the mission not also be to politically secure liberated areas against cooptation by the Holy Alliance? Wasn't a strategy of political occupation, rather than simple liberation, more appropriate for places where Colombia's military power had broken Spanish control? Whereas Sucre advocated the liberation model, Bolívar favored the political occupation model.

What did a strategy of political occupation mean? Holy Alliance occupations in Europe were designed to protect the legitimist foundations of political systems by using military occupation as a temporary expedient. The occupations were intended to maintain an ethical structure of obedience to dynastic political authority based on the ancient social privilege of aristocracy, as opposed to notions of popular sovereignty. In Spanish South America, however, founding an ethics of obedience on a pre-existing aristocratic right was not possible given the assiduous efforts by the Spanish crown to prevent the development of an American feudal aristocracy. A substitute for the European aristocratic class could conceivably be found, following the Roman praetorian model, in a guardian class drawn from the Colombian military liberators; their heroic achievement could be the functional equivalent of aristocratic prerogative. (This was the idea of the moral censors, made up initially of the Venezuelan liberators, in Bolívar's Angostura Address.) Since the Colombian liberators were foreigners to the areas of liberation, to cast them in a guardian role meant that occupation politics would have to deny the exercise of republican self-determination by native liberated populations. But, theoretically, as the liberators died, their ranks in the state would be filled by new generations of native guardians. These would surpass the original heroic ethic and develop expertise in exercising a moral custodianship of politics based on the accumulating practises and prerogatives of the guardians, higher levels of education of the newer guardians, and their consolidation as an ascriptive class. This model of occupation meant using the heroism of the liberators as a kind of moral capital to be invested in building up solid states that would not fall prey to popular revolutions (as would republican systems) or to the beguiling appeals of legitimist politics as the only way to stabilize the new, unsettled societies.

The liberation model, in contrast to the political occupation model, sought to found a new politics on the celebration of a republican self-determination process featuring the "theater" of elected, native assemblies. This approach was different from the designation of a guardian, ascriptive political class drawn originally from the liberators; it was the difference between the democratic euphoria of liberation and an ethics of obedience to a new order based on the liberators. The liberation model clearly oriented the political objectives of the Colombian army in a direction opposite to the mission of Holy Alliance interventions in Europe where the purpose was to restore existing political systems and to deny popular sovereignty. The political occupation model based on the Colombian liberators was intended by Bolívar to be analogous to Holy Alliance occupation method, even though he insisted on an essential moral difference between Old World occupations and New World occupations.

> Popular revolutions are contagious and they have spread out from Buenos Aires amid acclamations and reached the Juanambú [the river forming the old border between the Peruvian and the New Granadian viceroyalties]. ... Venezuela is a tinder box. Accordingly, we should imitate the Holy Alliance in everything that has to do with political security. The difference ought to be none other than that of principles of justice.

In Europe everything is done for tyranny, here it is for liberty; which certainly makes us enormously superior to those allies. ... The armies of occupation of Europe is (sic) a modern invention and skillful. It conserves the independence of the nations and the extant order established in them, and at the same time avoids the necessity of conquest. ... In order to elevate ourselves to a corresponding level and to be able to sustain a fight [against the Holy Alliance] we can do no less than adopt equal methods.[5]

Bogotá's removal of his command authority over the Colombian army and the repeal of his extra-constitutional powers, meant to Bolívar that he had to act in Upper Peru exclusively in his capacity as dictator of Peru. Although he professed outrage at Bogotá's actions, he actually saw them as conveniently widening his political latitude in Upper Peru. This was the context in which he mentioned, as in the preceding quotation, the need to emulate the Holy Alliance technique. He believed that the Holy Alliance had proved the role that occupation armies could have in securing political systems. The Colombian army might do the same for Upper Peru. The occupation techniques of the Holy Alliance armies should be studied to learn about methods for creating a political status quo based on a foreign military presence.[6] The army being sent under Sucre's command into Upper Peru, he said in this context, was being sent in as an "army of occupation."[7]

Ironically, Sucre's victory at Ayacucho sealed the fate of the Spanish liberal commanders in Peru and, along with them, Sucre's hedge, in the sense of his Yungay letter, against the expansion of Bolívar's Peruvian dictatorship. Ayacucho provided Bolívar with a political *carte blanche* in Peru. His dictatorship reigned supreme. As Sucre looked at the invasion of Upper Peru, his apprehensions about untoward collaboration between Peruvians and the dictatorship escalated. In Upper Peru it was unlikely that another large-scale military encounter like Ayacucho would take shape. The advantage of the big campaign leading to Ayacucho was that it placed the Peruvians under his Colombian command authority. But in Upper Peru, there was reason to believe Olañeta would fold under pressure. Sucre, in fact, saw the invasion, in its military aspect, as a "promenade." He knew that Bolívar wanted to lower the Colombian military profile in Peru for political purposes. Precisely because of the low-level military challenge in Upper Peru, Sucre suspected that Peruvian desires to annex Upper Peru would come to the forefront of the invasion. He, in fact, deeply feared and suspected that the scope of Peruvian influence on Bolívar's thinking would expand as a result of the operations in Upper Peru. He did not see any valid Colombian or American purpose being served by the invasion if it amounted to annexing the area to Peru, and, in effect, extending Bolívar's Peruvian dictatorship. Initially, Sucre did not want to be personally involved. "The greatest tribute you could give me for my role at Ayacucho," he wrote Bolívar, "would be my passport to Guayaquil."[8]

Sucre's fears about the Peruvians compromising Bolívar were sharpened by his awareness of Bolívar's growing feud with Bogotá. His letters to Bolívar in December 1824 and January 1825 are punctuated by warnings against giving the affairs of the Colombian army anything less than his undivided attention. No political action taken in Bogotá could relieve Bolívar of the moral obligation to his compatriots. Nor did it give him the right to expand his own political commitments to the Peruvians at the expense of his oversight of the affairs of the Colombian army. "You brought [the Colombian soldiers] here," Sucre wrote Bolívar, "and you should not have any other considerations than maintaining their strength and glory. Everything else is secondary." There was no doubt about what that "else" was; it was Bolívar's Peruvian dictatorship.[9]

As far as Upper Peru was concerned, Sucre objected to any effort by Bolívar to extend his dictatorship in that direction on the ground that "we are dealing with another country up there." Sucre was aware of the regional patriotism in Upper Peru. Spanish officers captured at Ayacucho undoubtedly told him about that sentiment. Many, including the viceroy, had personal experience fighting the Upper Peruvian guerrillas. Moreover, Sucre did not accept the legitimacy of the distinction that Bolívar was making between his role as president of Colombia and his role as dictator of Peru, much less the implication that the former had been superseded by the latter due to the actions of the Bogotá congress. He left no doubt about his feelings on this score after he had received notice that he should prepare to invade Upper Peru. Bolívar had grown unaccustomed to being addressed with this much candor.

> I have asked you for orders concerning the conduct of our troops (in Upper Peru). Frankly, I will ask that your orders come to me as from the Liberator of Colombia, since you have chosen to make a distinction between your office as such and the one you have as Dictator of Peru. Well, spare me that distinction and give me orders (concerning Upper Peru) as the Liberator of Colombia, since we have to operate in a country (Upper Peru) which does not belong to Peru and does not appear to want to belong to anyone but itself.[10]

Sucre, in effect, began to see Upper Peru as an "escape route" for the Colombian army from Bolívar's Peruvian dictatorship. This tactic would be particularly effective, in Sucre's outlook, if the provinces of Upper Peru could be separated from Peru and turned into, as in his Yungay letter, a "neighboring state" conducting relations with Peru but not compromised in its domestic political system. By emphasizing the separate-ness of Upper Peru, Sucre hoped to pre-empt the application of Bolívar's Peruvian dictatorship there. At the same time, he wanted to indicate to Bolívar that he should define the political purposes of the invasion as Liberator of Colombia. That is, he wanted to make sure that the libera-tion model prevented the political occupation model from materializing in Upper Peru with the inevitable color of Bolívar's Peruvian dictator-ship. Accordingly, Sucre proceeded to design the invasion so as to avoid the occupation of Upper Peru, that is, to make it into a Colombian as opposed to Peruvian operation.

For a brief time, Sucre feared that Bolívar was going to give the inva-sion command to Santa Cruz or authorize him to conduct all of the polit-ical negotiations in Upper Peru. Sucre was displeased by both prospects, but he limited himself to telling Bolívar that "if it is your pleasure to use Santa Cruz" in Upper Peru and "if his opinions ... which you know, coin-cided with your's respecting this country" he had better be sent to join Sucre immediately. Bolívar, however, finally decided to give the com-mand to Sucre and authorized him to undertake surrender negotiations with Olañeta. Santa Cruz went into Upper Peru as an informal agent of Bolívar's, but not in an official capacity.[11]

Sucre was very adamant that the invasion force be composed predomi-nantly of Colombians instead of Peruvians. The trouble was that Bolívar was insisting that Sucre use mainly Peruvian troops. The political impli-cations were unacceptable to Sucre, not to mention his doubts about the military reliability of these troops. It was therefore necessary for him to lay the groundwork for circumventing Bolívar's preferences.

Just prior to Ayacucho, a Spanish fleet had appeared off the coast of Chile. Sucre speculated that its intent might be to rally loyalist forces along the Peruvian coast and to resupply Olañeta. Sucre announced to Bolívar that if it became necessary to interfere with this operation, he would deploy "all" of the Peruvian forces under his command along the southern coasts of Peru and send "all" of the Colombian units to Upper Peru. When the Spanish threat failed to materialize, Sucre sent the First Colombian Division under the Venezuelan lieutenant colonel, Jacinto Lara, to garrison Arequipa, while he brought together the Second Divi-sion at Cuzco in order to have it spearhead the invasion of Upper Peru. In the meantime, he strung out the Peruvian units in between the two Colombian concentrations.[12]

Arequipa was strategically situated between Upper and Lower Peru. Sucre wanted to have control there, military and political. He recommended to Bolívar that one of the candidates for the prefectureship in Arequipa was preferable to the others, who were, by implication, more nationalistic. The preferred one "is our friend and admires the Colombian army." Another candidate was objectionable because "he is a prickly personality and not friendly to Colombia. He could cause me problems."[13]

Having established this configuration, Sucre informed Bolívar that if he wanted him to command the invasion of Upper Peru he would do so only with Colombian troops. He alleged that, given the conflicting claims of Peru and Argentina in Upper Peru, there might be divisions between Peruvians and many of the Argentines still serving as officers in the Peruvian army. Sucre said that his "intelligence" indicated that a military force from the Argentine province of Salta was invading Upper Peru and that this only increased the friction that could be expected if Peruvian troops had to be used. In fact, Sucre had requested the Argentine general, Juan Antonio Alvarez de Arenales, to invade from the south in order to cut off Olañeta's line of retreat. In reality, Sucre wanted to keep the Peruvians out of the invasion by bringing in the Argentines.[14]

In contrast to the Peruvians, Sucre wrote to Bolívar, the Colombian army represented a "neutral party" in Upper Peru and therefore should constitute the majority of the invasion force. Further, with the Colombian army predominating, the purposes of the invasion would be seen as more disinterested politically. He informed the Peruvian ministry of war that the Colombian army was crossing the Desaguadero river into Upper Peru without any orders from its government and with Sucre only guessing what Bolívar's intentions were. "[O]nly in favor of the cause of America does it take the responsibility for doing it." Innocuously, Sucre announced that he would proceed to "organize this country as one liberated by pro-independence forces, and leave to the population its sovereignty in order that they may constitute themselves," pending the making of a "definitive arrangement" between Peru and Argentina. Doing this, he said, was consistent with "what seemed to be the mind of His Excellency, the Liberator President of Colombia." It was obviously less consistent with what seemed to be the mind of the dictator of Peru.[15]

After the invasion was under way, Sucre came under pressure from Bolívar to involve the Peruvians more visibly. He had no choice but to call them up from Peru. But he assigned them to running down Olañeta's disintegrating army in the south of the country, while he concentrated his Colombian forces in La Paz to, as Sucre put it, "rest" them. Under pressure from the pursuing Peruvians, Olañeta's troops mutinied, killed him, and surrendered. But before the Peruvians were brought up in more force, and Sucre's Colombian forces still constituted the overwhelming majority of the extant invasion force, Sucre announced in La Paz that the purpose of the invasion was to inaugurate a self-determination process in order to create an independent state. He put this purpose into the form of a public decree issued in La Paz on February 9, 1825 (but drafted by Sucre on February 1, at Puno in Peru), nowhere in which could be found mention of Bolívar or Peru. Sucre blithely told Bolívar that he did not want to compromise his name in the self-determination process because if it went awry Bolívar would not be implicated. But if it proved viable and was well received, Bolívar could then "give it the spin" he wished. He noted that there could be no implication that the decree, because it did not carry Bolívar's name, was usurping his authority over the Colombian army. "Everyone knows," Sucre pontificated, "that everything we do that turns out well is done under your orders."[16]

Almost simultaneously with the drafting of the decree, Sucre opened negotiations with Casimiro Olañeta. The nephew of Pedro Olañeta and commissar of his army, Casimiro had secretly entered into correspondence with Bolívar and provided intelligence on his uncle's situation. He provided Sucre with political advice regarding Upper Peru, most of it slanted toward creating an independent state— at least toward keeping it free of Argentine control. The *porteños* of Buenos Aires were hated by the Upper Peruvians, Casimiro assured Sucre. As for Peru, the negative feelings were less intense but not cordial. Sucre was impressed with Casimiro. "He is very patriotic," he wrote Bolívar. On the other hand, Sucre added smugly, Santa Cruz was "not esteemed" in Upper Peru, according to Olañeta. That observation seemed to be enough to convince Sucre of Olañeta's integrity; Santa Cruz was, after all, heavily identified with Peru despite his Upper Peruvian nationality. In Sucre's view (encouraged by Olañeta) Santa Cruz's incompetence, had been revealed to Upper Peruvians when he had appeared during the Intermedios campaign in Upper Peru as a "liberator" only to be humiliated by the Spanish, trying to place the blame on Sucre. Whereas Santa Cruz was a "spurious" Upper Peruvian patriot, Olañeta was the real article, in Sucre's estimation. He would change his mind about Olañeta, but not Santa Cruz. Olañeta and Sucre were evidently of one mind concerning the justification for Sucre's decree.[17]

Sucre's decree represented the political seed of the state of Bolivia. He had begun advocating self-determination in Upper Peru during the course of his contacts with Pedro Olañeta. He had hoped to make a deal to avoid an invasion, if Olañeta would agree to self-determination in Upper Peru based on the declaration of its independence from

Spain. After Olañeta refused, Sucre had dangled the same prospect of self-determination in front of Upper Peruvians—civilians, guerrilla leaders and potential defectors in Olañeta's army—to reward them for staging a revolt against Olañeta. For example, in a circular to the municipalities of Upper Peru, he said that "the aim of the Liberating Army will not be used other than to guarantee your liberty; we will leave it up to your own *albedrío* to determine what your wishes are (concerning the political future of Upper Peru) and to organize the country in the manner that is most conducive to your happiness." The unusual Spanish term *albedrío* means an act of free will that has law-creating effect.[18]

The domestic uprising never took place, and the invasion became necessary in order to precipitate Pedro Olañeta's demise. Self-determination could not, therefore, be offered as a reward for the overthrow of Olañeta from within. Yet, there had been fifteen years of protracted struggle in Upper Peru against the viceregal armies of Peru and the revolutionary armies of Buenos Aires. The burden of this long struggle for freedom certainly merited some recognition. So did the fact that the revolt of the *audiencia* in 1808 became the first link in the chain of rebellions that constituted the Spanish-American independence movement. Sucre began to regard this experience as a seminal political legacy in Upper Peru—one which he did not fail to invoke in support of his decree. That decree, Sucre said, was a fitting tribute to the "first sons of the revolution," who deserved more from the victory of Colombian arms than the setting up of an occupation regime. What they deserved was a chance to "decide their own destiny" and that is what his decree was designed to give them.[19]

Sucre's clearly intended his decree to be a pledge of Colombian good faith. It left no doubt that Colombian purposes would be truly served only if the Upper Peruvians were given a definitive—or as the decree said, "sovereign"—role in determining their future. Article 4 announced that by virtue of the internal strife among its provinces, Argentina was not in a position to assert sovereign rights in Upper Peru. It concluded that Peru's claims did not have to be consulted from the fact that Argentina's could not be. The inference drawn from this *non sequitur* was that the political organization of the provinces of Upper Peru should be the result of its own internal deliberation. Article 5 held out the vague possibility of these deliberations being made compatible with some future treaty made between Argentina (when it emerged from its anarchy and formed a national government) and Peru. The other articles gave testimony to the the liberation model.

ARTICLE 1: That on passing the *Desaguadero* the Liberating Army had as its sole object the releasing of the provinces of Upper Peru from Spanish oppression, and to leave them in possession of their rights.

ARTICLE 2: That the Liberating Army had no right to intervene in the domestic affairs of these people.

ARTICLE 3: That since the major part of the Liberating Army is composed of Colombian troops, its incumbent obligation can be no other than to liberate the country and to leave to the people their sovereignty, thereby giving testimony to the justice and generosity and to our principles.[20]

In its operative paragraphs, the decree convoked an assembly of Upper Peruvian delegates to "deliberate the destiny" of their country. Sucre defended his decree to Bolívar by saying that it was an alternative to him arriving in Upper Peru "with the abhorrent aspect of a military occupation."[21]

In January 1825, the Congress of Peru determined to extend Bolívar's dictatorship at least for one more year, when the congress would reassemble and consider whether a further extension was in order. Bolívar "reluctantly" agreed to this continuation. In order to widen the political base of his dictatorship, he expanded it to include an executive cabinet in which the leading figures were La Mar and Carrion.

One argument for the renewal of the dictatorship was that Bolívar's authority was a form of political capital for Peru. The Peruvian Bolivarians believed that under Bolívar's rule, Peru would escape factionalism and have the stability, and the selfconfidence, to begin building a nation. The credibility of the Bolivarian position depended on the identification of Bolívar's goals with the Peruvian national interest. Upper Peru posed an immediate test, for there he was called upon to support Peru's claims that Upper Peru rightfully belonged to it.

Bolívar was cognizant of the need to at least appear to be serving the interests of Peru in Upper Peru. After he ordered the invasion, he had solicited from the Peruvian congress instructions that were to govern his behavior in Upper Peru. Since he was aware that Argentina also had claims in Upper Peru, he wanted some latitude left in the instructions to deal with those claims. The instructions that were finally drafted and published on February 23, 1825, as a resolution of the Peruvian congress, empowered Bolívar to establish a provisional government in Upper Peru until such time as Argentina and Peru fixed their respective borders with Upper Peru and adjudicated the question as to whom the upland provinces belonged. Should the provinces not belong to Peru, the instructions established the right of the Peruvian government to receive indemnification from them for the costs of the invasion.[22]

It was the Brazilian question that caused Bolívar to want to keep his options open, to some extent, in Upper Peru. He believed, as we know, that if the Holy Alliance got the upper hand over Britain in Brazil, it might be necessary for him to attack Brazil in order to support Britain in its struggle against the alliance. By annexing Upper Peru to Peru, he would certainly alienate Buenos Aires, making any alliance negotiations difficult. By the same token, by attending to Argentine claims in Upper Peru and avoiding any arbitrary action there in favor of Peru, Bolívar could facilitate his dealings with Buenos Aires. At a minimum the *porteños* would be robbed of a pretext for not dealing with him. Being politic in Upper Peru might have its advantages.

This Argentine scenario, however, began to lose its attraction for Bolívar as 1825 wore on. With the war against the Spanish over, his political thought was becoming more conservative, moving away from the liberation model toward the political occupation model. But this model was much more problematic in Argentina than in Peru because the Argentine population was less docile. Further, Bolívar became doubtful that Britain would lose control over Pedro, particularly now that Canning was managing British policy in Brazil. As this dawned on him, Bolívar gradually lost his taste for an ideological confrontation with the Holy Alliance and began to think more in terms of accommodation through the medium of British policy in Brazil. Argentina began to appear as an unnecessary and dangerous distraction from where his real opportunities lay—in Peru. It was clear that by March 1825, Bolívar had begun to lose his incentive to join Argentina's war with Brazil. Among other things, he was aware of, and deeply offended by, the racist diatribes against him, which were appearing in the ministerial papers in Buenos Aires. He wrote to Santa Cruz that he wanted his policy in Upper Peru to prove that he had the interests of the Peruvian state at heart, not Colombian aggrandizement. He made the disingenuous statement that "if I were not Colombian, I would have insisted against crossing the Desaguadero; but being Colombian I could not dictate that Peru not augment its territorial scope and power, because that would look like I was trying to keep Peru weak."[23]

Sucre's decree of February 9 was objectionable to Bolívar in three ways. First, it appeared to rule out a role for Buenos Aires in determining the future of the provinces. With Argentine claims pre-empted, the case for Peruvian claims should logically have become strengthened, not weakened. Yet Sucre's decree, as we saw, used the Argentine default in Upper Peru to imply a Peruvian default.

Second, Sucre's decree deprived Bolívar of acting in Upper Peru on the basis of his authority as dictator of Peru, without even getting from Buenos Aires promises of a new authority in Argentina. Bolívar's agent in Buenos Aires, Gregorio Funes, had repeatedly urged him in letters to unify the Argentines under his leadership. Restoring the Upper Peruvian provinces to the Argentine state and laying the groundwork for widening the war against Brazil were the two obvious steps toward Bolívar's assumption of a leadership role in Argentina. From Funes's letters and newspaper reports, Bolívar knew that there was opposition to him playing any political role in Argentina, but that opposition was based in Buenos Aires and identified with Rivadavia's clique. Funes argued that his entry into Argentina would tip the power struggle in favor of the rest of the provinces and against Buenos Aires. We can judge from Bolívar's response to Sucre that, instead of having the chance to make gains for either his Peruvian-based authority *or* for a new Argentine-based authority, he saw himself being offered the role of presiding over a chimerical self-determination process in order to display Colombia's disinterestedness and his own liberality. Bolívar was not impressed. If anything, it was Sucre who was making the gains for his own reputation. He was already the national hero of the Ecuadoreans; now he was the national hero of the Upper Peruvians. For a man who professed to be devoid of political ambition, his action in Upper Peru was a strange testimony.

Third, Sucre's decree seemed to clearly point to the establishment of an independent state in Upper Peru. This was admittedly contemplated as a possibility in the instructions of the Peruvian congress but with the critical difference that the final say in this matter would repose in the congress, acting in consultation with Buenos Aires. Sucre's decree simultaneously denied the Peruvian congress the prerogative to approve the independence of Upper Peru, the right to receive indemnification payments for the cost of the liberation, and even the option of opening up negotiations with Buenos Aires on the subject of Upper Peru's status. This was certainly slight compensation for the money and men Peru had put up for the invasion of Upper Peru.

Bolívar was furious when Sucre's letter and text of his decree arrived at his office in Lima. He had been annoyed with Sucre's innuendos concerning his "compromises" with the Peruvians and the business about sending orders to him only as the Liberator of Colombia and not dictator of Peru. In his letter of February 21, 1825, Bolívar intended to put Sucre in his place. The matter of Upper Peru was not as complicated as Sucre was trying to make it.

> There is no military problem in Upper Peru and regarding the political matter it is very simple. You are under my orders with the army under

your command, and you do not have to do anything except what I tell you to do. The Colombian army has come here at my orders so that, as the head of Peru, I direct it and make war with it against the Spanish. You command the army as a General of Colombia, but not as a general of the nation (of Peru) while I, without commanding the (Colombian) army as a general, do direct it as an auxiliary of the nation over which I preside. I do not give you orders as head of Colombia because I am not; but, yes, as head of the territory (Peru) which is at war against Spain.[24]

Having "straightened out" this matter, the letter observed that the convoking of any assembly of delegates from the provinces of Upper Peru was an act for which Sucre had no authority. Bolívar found it amusing that Sucre had protested so about not wanting to appear as a conqueror in Upper Peru by setting up a military government. "You have a very rare kind of scruple. You do not want to exercise the military authority which corresponds to you, exercising power over the territory occupied by your troops, but you want nevertheless to exercise a legislative authority over that territory." Here Bolívar made an unflattering comparison between Sucre and San Martín who, he said, forgot about the war against the Spanish in Peru while preferring to tinker around with the political system of the country. Bolívar intimated that the only reason Sucre had issued his decree was to ingratiate himself with local opinion and to produce affectionate feelings toward his person. "You are obsessed with being the nice guy," he told him. Bolívar continued in this vein by accusing Sucre of having botched an opportunity to get rid of Riva Aguero at the Callao fort when the congress wanted to depose him. There, he said, you "tried to please everyone and ended up by alienating everyone ... the same thing will be repeated now" in Upper Peru.[25]

Sucre obviously feared that the invasion of Upper Peru would, all things being equal, lead to annexation to Peru. Bolívar knew this but rather than dealing with the question of Peruvian annexation on its merits he shifted the question to Argentina. He knew that he could appear more disinterested by arguing the injury to Argentine rights caused by Sucre's decree rather than the injury to Peru, where Bolívar had vested interests. "You say you want to convoke an assembly of those provinces," Bolívar continued. "That very convocation is obviously an act of sovereignty." It separated, *de facto*, the Upper Peruvian provinces from the Argentine provinces. "Buenos Aires has every right to repudiate your decree." Parenthetically, he alluded to Peru's basis for grievance. "It cannot be very pleasing to it ... that its troops are used to pull off a political operation, without it even being consulted."[26]

Bolívar told Sucre to retract his decree and forget about it. He should confine his commitment to "occupying the country militarily and awaiting orders of the Peruvian Government." Those orders Bolívar said, referring to his instructions from the Peruvian congress, would call for settlement of the status of Upper Peru in a legitimate and legal way, that is to say, through negotiations conducted with the interested parties by the Congress of Peru—on whose behalf Bolívar would be acting when he arrived in Upper Peru.[27]

The fact that Sucre did not have to retract his decree and that he was able to acquire Bolívar's qualified approval of it, was due to a surprising turn in Argentine policy regarding Upper Peru. Far from offending Buenos Aires, Sucre's decree was seen there as a counter to the expansion of Bolívar's Peruvian dictatorship. Coincidentally, a decree that was a mirror image of Sucre's had been on the verge of being promulgated in Upper Peru by General Juan Antonio Alvarez de Arenales, who was acting at this time on behalf of a new national government of Argentina.

Sucre's Search for Argentine Support

On April 10, 1825, Bolívar and his staff rode out of Lima for Upper Peru, to "look for Sucre," as he put it. The entourage headed south on the royal Inca highway. Except for bending inland to cross the cities of Ica and Nasca—centers of ancient, pre-Incaic civilizations that preceded even the spectacular Tiahuanaco civilization centered in the area of Upper Peru—the highway hugged the coast deep into Chile. Bolívar was not in a rush. His trip was more like a triumphal procession, with the local populations swarming out to greet the legendary liberator. The desolation caused by the war was evident along the way. As usual, very little escaped Bolívar's eagle eyes. Where he saw burdensome taxes, damaged government property, poor sanitation, or a place to build a school, he fired off directives to Lima and tried to make arrangements on the spot. His overriding concern was for the people at the bottom of the social structure, mainly the Indians.[28]

At Nasca, he heard from Sucre. The letter was from Potosí, where Sucre had gone on an inspection tour. He had just received Bolívar's fulminating letter of February 21. Sucre's ostensible tone was apologetic and plaintive. He told Bolívar that he was upset with himself because he had given Bolívar "cause to express such feelings concerning Upper Peru, respecting which I have committed an error [convoking the assembly] that was so involuntary ... my sole objective was to comply with your intentions." Sucre emphasized that he was innocent of any self-serving or devious motives, much less of disloyalty to Bolívar. In fact, it was out of loyalty to Bolívar that he had gone to Upper Peru in the first place, against his will. His "duties as a Colombian, as a general, were satisfied at the Desaguadero." He arrived in Upper Peru not knowing how to avoid the "abominable aspect" of being an invader with an army of occupation. He therefore had "taken the most noble and generous road."[29]

After admitting his guilt, Sucre deftly observed that no one knew that Bolívar felt so strongly about Argentine rights. But he would take those feelings at face value. Bolívar should know, Sucre wrote, that anarchy reigned between the Argentine provinces. No national government existed since 1820; the provinces were acting like sovereign units. Sucre said that, in this perspective, his decree did no more than to put Upper Peru on a par with the individual Argentine provinces.

Basking in his triumphal procession, Bolívar's anger toward Sucre had cooled off by the time he reached Nasca. Moreover, he took Sucre's letter as an apology. He had not yet fully appreciated that Sucre's decree positioned Upper Peru to be one of the "neighboring states" mentioned in his Yungay letter that could form alliance relations with Peru but be uncompromised in Peru's internal structure. Bolívar saw the decree, rather, as a result of what he called Sucre's "soft and flexible character"—the quality that had made him too malleable in his prior assignments in Guayaquil and Lima. Bolívar regretted that his letter had offended Sucre, but told him that "he would suffer constantly so long as his feelings are moved by those silk cords of a supreme susceptibility." He invited Sucre to "agree with him, even though it wounds your *amour propre,* that it was his desire to appear "moderate" that caused Sucre to call for the election of an assembly. "You judged it to be a simple matter and you did it without any need (since among other things) the country was not even liberated yet." Bolívar then became conciliatory. He said that he was not a reactionary, and he could even admit that Sucre's decree appealed to his instinct to do the right thing in Upper Peru. Further, he could respect Sucre's argument that in view of the anarchy prevailing among the Argentine provinces, they could not be looked to for guidance in Upper Peru's future. But he then returned to his Peruvian political constraints. The Congress of Peru would not agree with Sucre's logic that because Upper Peru was freed from Argentine guidance by default, Peru should be deprived of its rightful say in deciding Upper Peru's political status. His instructions from the Peruvian congress certainly made no mention of Upper Peruvian sovereignty. He would not allow Peru's rights to be pre-empted by Sucre's decree, whatever justification Argentine anarchy lent it. Peru should not have to be called upon to be a "martyr" by sacrificing its dispositive rights in Upper Peru on the shiny altar of Sucre's decree. Nor did Bolívar intend for his dictatorship to be sacrificed on that same altar.[30]

At the port town of Camaná, Bolívar and his entourage left the old Inca highway and slanted inland, reaching the foothills of the Andean mountains in a week. Bolívar braced himself for his inevitable bout with *soroche*—altitude sickness. He was very vulnerable to it. A week later they had climbed to 7,200 feet and arrived at picturesque Arequipa, the city built from white lava rock, nestling on a plateau in full view of the towering volcano, *El Misty.* Loyalist feeling ran strong here; the city was a stronghold of the Roman Catholic Church. Bolívar's welcome was polite enough. But, whatever may have been lacking in spontaneity among the local elite was more than made up for by the festivities prepared by the Colombian army which was there in strength under Lara's command. It was a time of rejoicing between Bolívar and his officers and troops whom he had not seen since Ayacucho. It was also a time to collect his thoughts and to chart a course of action. Two letters from Upper Peru were waiting for him in Arequipa. One was from Sucre. The other was from General Arenales.

———◆———

Sucre indeed had been very upset by Bolívar's letter. As was his wont, he sulked for a while. He made plans to quit the service and return to Quito. He planned to go to Chuquisaca for a few days, return to La Paz to see Bolívar and then leave. Bolívar had insisted on meeting him in Upper Peru. Sucre had requested to meet him on the Peruvian side of the Desaguadero in the expectation that extricating himself from any further role in Upper Peru would be easier. In this state of mind, Sucre decided to postpone the assembly until Bolívar arrived, when "he could convoke it if he wants." He, however, could not restrain himself from warning Bolívar that although Peru might gain from the cancellation of the assembly, Colombia would regret it, and "we have the epithets of these people instead of their blessings for having gotten rid of the Spanish." Even while he was pouting, however, Sucre was assessing his situation with the strategic eye of the excellent chess player that he was.[31]

In addition to his rhetoric about doing the noble and generous thing, Sucre cited another purpose behind his decree. This was none other than using the unification of the Upper Peruvian provinces as a political magnet to attract the wayward Argentine provinces and pull them free of their anarchic struggle against the centralists of Buenos Aires. Like Bolívar, Sucre was offended by the racial insults toward Colombia that were editorialized in the official Buenos Aires papers. But he knew also that a different, and more Americanist, sentiment existed in the provinces. Sucre was in contact with the political leaderships of the larger Argentine provinces, and he took pains to bring his decree to their attention. He encouraged these *caudillos* to be sympathetic to his initiative. He protested that Colombia's role was completely disinterested. By joining the Argentine provinces to Upper Peru to form a new state, Sucre avowed to Bolívar that he would be able to isolate and punish Buenos Aires for its attacks on Bolívar and Colombia. He confided to Bolívar that it would have been a "nice trick" to play on Buenos Aires. In this way, Sucre began to try to get Bolívar to think of an Upper Peruvian state not as an impediment to his Peruvian dictatorship (which they both knew it was) but rather as a basis for attack on Bolívar's enemies in Buenos Aires. This represented the first phase of a complex three-year effort undertaken by Sucre to link Upper Peruvian statehood to Argentine politics in order to shield the former from annexationist pressure emanating from Peru and to lure Bolívar out of his Peruvian dictatorship. The twists and turns in Sucre's Argentine policy—always correlated with the degree of Peruvian pressure on him—are clearly traceable in Sucre's unpublished letters to Dean Funes in Buenos Aires. Unfortunately, these letters have been neglected to date by historians.[32]

As Sucre began to reassess his situation, he had to ask where his primary plan, of placing Upper Peru beyond the reach of Bolívar's Peruvian dictatorship (and hence beyond Peruvian annexation), stood in light of Bolívar's repudiation of his decree. Could it stand at all? Was it still possible to use linkages to the Argentine provinces to offset pressures for Peruvian control over Upper Peru? As Sucre re-evaluated the situation, he began edging toward an alliance strategy.

In his exploratory talks with Arenales, Sucre began to discern that a common cause existed between his liberation scenario and the political needs of the central government in Buenos Aires. He was determined to capitalize on this fact.

In early 1824, while Rivadavia was still in Europe on his diplomatic mission, Juan Gregorio de las Heras was elected governor of the Buenos Aires province and replaced Martín Rodríguez. Heras named Martín García, a co-minister of Rivadavia in the preceding government, as his minister of state. At this time, another effort was under way to see if the Argentine provinces could come together and form a national government. The provincial government of Buenos Aires hosted the congress of delegations from all of the provinces. Things appeared headed toward success. It was decided to draft a constitution for a national government. Pending its adoption, it was agreed that the government of Buenos Aires province should act as the executive arm of the projected nation, while the provincial delegates would serve as an interim national legislature.

Heras and García expected to wrestle with this congress over the matter of deciding on a policy toward the conflict with Brazil over the Eastern Bank—whether to pursue a military or a diplomatic approach to resolving it. That discussion had to defer to discussion of the new situation created in Upper Peru by reason of Sucre's victory at Ayacucho. It was obvious in the discussions that ensued that Pedro Olañeta's position was seen as untenable. Barring support from Pedro, it was expected that Olañeta's followers would be demoralized by Ayacucho and the loyalist cause permanently disabled. The question raised in Buenos Aires concerned *how* Olañeta should be taken out of the picture. Should it be by indigenous revolt? Should it result from military invasion by Bolívar's forces? Or should Olañeta's elimination be secured by some kind of intervention by Argentina in Upper Peru?

The original plan was to position Arenales with an army in Upper Peru in order to force armistice terms on Olañeta before Bolívar's forces arrived. It was felt that Olañeta would prefer this to surrendering to Bolívar: Bolívar could be expected to annex Upper Peru to Peru, whereas Argentina was prepared not to insist on incorporation but to allow the voice of the Upper Peruvians to be heard. That was all they would ask of Olañeta. Arenales had informed Buenos Aires that since Olañeta had been eliminated before he arrived, the best vehicle for the intent of his instructions (i.e., to block Peruvian annexation of Upper Peru) was to circulate a decree in the name of Argentina, calling for an assembly of Upper Peruvians to decide their political future. Since Sucre's decree accomplished the same result, Arenales advised Buenos Aires that he would withhold his own decree and endorse Sucre's.[33]

García suspected that the Upper Peruvian question was being perceived by the federalists in the Argentine congress as a potential vehicle for foiling *porteño* designs for centralist domination of the Argentine state. Delegations from the Upper Peruvian provinces could be expected to enlist in the federalist coalition in the congress and turn the numbers against the centralists. The Upper Peruvians were known for their aspirations of autonomy and for the ill-will they bore toward Buenos Aires. Upper Peru's incorporation into the Argentine state was almost a guarantee against Buenos Aires's supremacy. García therefore tried to dampen the congressional enthusiasm for taking action in Upper Peru. He quashed a proposal to send in an Argentine army to attack Olañeta and restore the provinces to the Argentina.[34]

The position of the executive, however, stopped short of advocating a policy of complete neutrality toward Upper Peru. There was a strong apprehension, indeed one shared by both the provincial delegations and the executive, that if they did nothing, then Upper Peru might well be annexed by Peru. The creation of a Greater Peruvian state on the Argentine border was viewed skeptically; having to live next to the Brazilian empire was bad enough. To have to face a Peruvian colossus also, would be unacceptable, unless, of course, the military strength being assembled in Peru could somehow be deflected toward Brazil as a common enemy of the Spanish-American republics. But in the eyes of the Argentine executive (less so in the congress where attitudes toward Colombia were more favorable) the prospect of Peruvian annexation was seen to be essentially mixed up with the spreading of Bolívar's power, since he controlled the Peruvian state. If Argentina did nothing, Olañeta might well be defeated by a combined Colombian-Peruvian invasion force that would proceed to extend Bolívar's Peruvian dictatorship into the area or create a client state of Colombia. García was therefore willing to support an Argentine role in Upper Peru that would head off either of these developments. The whole prospect of Bolívar's power getting closer to Argentina was feared by *porteño* politicians. The great anti-Bolivarian phobia of Rivadavia, who was absent on a diplomatic mission to Europe at this time, was present in the apprehensions of Heras and García.[35]

Heras and García finally hammered out an agreement with a congressional commission. The city of Buenos Aires would supply no forces of its own, but it would agree to finance an army to be raised in the province of Salta and sent into Upper Peru. The purpose of the expedition would be essentially political, not military. Arenales, as the governor of Salta, was given responsibility for the undertaking.

The instructions Arenales received from García (dated February 6, 1825) opened with the observation that there was no need for another battle to be fought in Upper Peru.[36] Ayacucho had ended the military phase of the independence struggle. Pedro Olañeta's only option was to accept the best surrender terms he could get. The inference is clearly that he would be more enticed by the surrender terms Argentina would offer him than the ones he could expect from Bolívar. The reason was that Argentina was prepared to insist only that Olañeta dissolve his army. It would not impose any condition that Upper Peru be restored to the Argentine nation. On the other hand, surrender to Bolívar would inevitably entail the Peruvian domination of Upper Peru and probable annexation. Surrender to Argentina would give Olañeta an alternative to surrender to Bolívar. Arenales was therefore authorized to sign a treaty with Olañeta stipulating the dissolution of his army and the placing of the provinces of Upper Peru in absolute "liberty to arrange their interests and government." A decree of Heras promised ratification in advance of any treaties Arenales made with Olañeta, provided only that they were conditioned on Upper Peruvian self-determination.[37]

Arenales was an astute choice. He was one of the few governors of the provinces that had been on good terms with Rivadavia. (Of all the Argentine provinces, Salta had the best relations with Buenos Aires; in fact, it was an outpost of the *porteños* and the place where the liberal initiatives of the port were most closely imitated.) Arenales enjoyed the trust of Heras and García. At the same time, Arenales was respected in provincial circles as a man of integrity who had achieved notoriety for his military exploits under San Martín in Peru. He was known to be an admirer of "the great Bolívar" but, at the same time, deeply suspicious of Peruvian designs on Upper Peru and very partial to the restoration of the Upper Peruvian provinces to the Argentine union. At the time the instructions from Buenos Aires arrived, Arenales had already started raising on his own a military force in Salta to invade Upper Peru. He was doing so on the request he had received from Sucre to attack Olañeta from the south, while Sucre attacked from the north. When the instructions were being drafted in Buenos Aires, the invasion of Upper Peru by Sucre was not yet known.[38]

Thus, a common cause was in the making between Sucre and Argentina in Upper Peru. For the time being, Sucre was prepared to suspend his plan to identify Upper Peru with the struggle of the Argentine provinces to free themselves from domination by Buenos Aires. He determined instead to try to firm up a commitment from the new national government in Argentina to the cause of Upper Peruvian independence. This might impel Bolívar to retract his negative response to the assembly idea. Hadn't he been the one to insist on Buenos Aires's consent in the first place? Hadn't he chastised Sucre for not taking into account the *porteños'* wishes?

Sucre needed to draw out the commitment of the Argentine government to the Upper Peruvian Assembly as a sovereign body. He immediately wrote Heras apologizing for addressing the Argentine provinces individually in order to announce the convocation of the assembly in Upper Peru; he had not known that a national government existed in Buenos Aires and that the internecine strife among the provinces was apparently concluding. "This step (the effort to unify the Argentine provinces) is of immense importance to the cause of America." He said the assembly was being delayed due to logistical difficulties but that this would provide time for the new Argentine government to "establish its relations with this Assembly." This contact could also take advantage of Bolívar's imminent arrival in Upper Peru and "abbreviate" the latter's relations with the Peruvian government. Sucre's unmistakable intent here was to have Bolívar and Argentina negotiate with the assembly, while keeping Peruvian input to a minimum. In this way, he intended to draw Bolívar out of his Peruvian dictatorship and into negotiations with Argentina, looking toward Upper Peruvian statehood.[39]

In the meantime, Sucre was persuading Arenales that the assembly was not a cover for Peruvian annexation and would not be if sufficient Argentine backing could be built into it before Bolívar stepped into the picture. Sucre was at his likeable best in his talks with Arenales. He perceived Arenales to have been genuinely interested, while he served with San Martín in Peru, in providing help to Sucre in the Quito campaign. If the Peruvian nationalists had ruined that opportunity for genuine collaboration by pressing on San Martín their claims to Guayaquil, here was a new American opportunity where the Peruvians should not be allowed to get in the way again. "I will never forget the help that you tried to give us in 1822," was Sucre's way of opening his letter to Arenales.[40]

Arenales's behavior in Upper Peru predisposed him to cooperate with Sucre. Upon learning of the defeat and death of Pedro Olañeta, Arenales had proposed to García that Argentina convoke an assembly of Upper Peruvian delegates as "proof of the legal and disinterested" policy of its eastern neighbor. That assembly would be charged with the task of "pronouncing upon the future destiny of the provinces" in complete freedom and without any outside pressure. He wrote García that convoking such an assembly would stem the outbreak of anarchy in Upper Peru attendant upon the dissolution of Olañeta's army. The convocation of the assembly would help also to refurbish the image of Argentina in Upper Peru, which had suffered due to the abominable activities of the Buenos Aires armies. Simultaneously, it would pre-empt any attempt by Peru to grab the area. Arenales was by this time aware of Sucre's invasion and of the presence of considerable numbers of Peruvians in his ranks. He requested instructions in case "the forces of Peru (with Sucre) should try to mix into these matters."[41]

It was not simply Olañeta's demise that threatened to undermine Arenales's proposed assembly but also the presence of the Colombians and Peruvians. In fact, virtually all of Upper Peru came under the control of Sucre's forces while Arenales was waiting for authority from Buenos Aires to issue a decree convoking the assembly. This development would seem to have pre-empted the self-determination scenario had it not been for Sucre's surprising February 9 decree. Arenales was prepared to ask Buenos Aires to transfer the requested approval of his decree to Sucre's, given the similar objectives in the two decrees: Upper Peru's freedom to choose the political status it preferred. Argentine policy could theoretically operate as well through Sucre's decree as Arenales's decree. The question was, how trustworthy was Sucre's decree? Could Sucre guarantee free deliberations in the assembly if he came under annexationist pressure from Peru, particularly if Bolívar backed that pressure? Arenales went to Potosí to see Sucre and explore this question.

Arenales showed Sucre his instructions from García and a copy of his letter to García requesting authorization to call an Upper Peruvian assembly. He emphasized to Sucre the disinterested basis of Argentine policy in Upper Peru; incorporation of the provinces was not being insisted on, only freedom of choice for the inhabitants. He applauded Sucre's decree. He said that his main concern was that freedom of choice be guaranteed to the assembly. Arenales must have mentioned his fears of Peruvian coercion. Sucre insisted that the assembly's decision would be made spontaneously. "In the matter of politics," Arenales wrote García, "the most animated protests and sentiments expressed with the greatest verve, leave room for doubts." But, he continued, when he saw "the enormous concern [Sucre] takes ... to avoid doing anything that might offend or displease the ... Plata provinces," Arenales felt warranted in concluding that he could be trusted; that Sucre's profession that "his own preference was for the Upper Peruvian provinces to decide to join the Plata provinces" could be taken at face value. The contemplation of a power move in Upper Peru was extremely unlikely "in view of the personal character of His Excellency, his extreme candor, the total interest he shows for the prosperity and *concordancia* (harmony) of all of the states of America."[42]

On the basis of his Potosí interview with Sucre, Arenales proceeded to argue to García that there was no difference between Sucre's decree and the one he intended to issue in Upper Peru, and, as such, Sucre's decree deserved the full endorsement of the Argentine government. He finished his report to García by noting that opinion in Upper Peru was decidedly against rejoining the Argentine provinces. He expected that in time these anti-Argentine feelings would subside and that a more favorable attitude might assert itself. He therefore took the position that the assembly should postpone any final decision concerning the political status of Upper Peru until opinions had time to settle down. In the meantime, he felt that the Upper Peruvians should establish their own provisional government, as per Sucre's decree. He concluded by saying that he was going to Chuquisaca "in consortium with" Sucre to represent Argentine desires to the assembly. Arenales saw his role as one of convincing the delegates that Argentina wanted good relations with Upper Peru "as one country to another."[43]

The trail to Chuquisaca took less than a week. The descent provided relief from the climactic rigors of Potosí. Potosí was even higher than La Paz and aggravated a chest ailment of Sucre's, which by this time was becoming chronic. It was an affliction of many tropical Venezuelans who campaigned in the Andes. In many cases, as in Bolívar's, it turned into terminal tuberculosis. Chuquisaca, the garden spot of the Spanish mining community at Potosí, was just what Sucre physically needed; his condition seemed to markedly improve by bathing in the local mineral water springs. But it was not only the temperate climate that agreed with him; he found the historical atmosphere also invigorating. Hadn't the struggle for sovereignty been nurtured here for 250 years by the viceroy-defying activities of the *audiencia*? He could walk right around the corner from the governmental palace on the town square and be at the *audiencia's* old headquarters. Walking the other way one block off the plaza would bring him to the famous Jesuit-founded University of San Francisco Xavier, where the *creole* professors and their students goaded the *audiencia* into its declaration of territorial sovereignty in Upper Peru in 1809. The city was the living embodiment of Upper Peru's separatist aspirations. If the assembly met in Chuquisaca, it would seem to be a foregone conclusion that it would opt for independence. Of all the people in Upper Peru, Sucre's decree caused the most excitement among the *chuquisaqueños*, especially the lawyers. Casimiro Olañeta, Sucre's political confidant, hailed from here. So did most of Santa Cruz's other enemies.[44]

Sucre's talks with Arenales were fruitful in Potosí and got more so as they conversed during the ride to Chuquisaca. Sucre had every reason to expect that Buenos Aires would send formal approval of the Upper Peruvian Assembly. In his letter from Chuquisaca, Sucre therefore decided to approach Bolívar gingerly. He now stated that the assembly would be postponed until either Bolívar arrived "or" the government in Buenos Aires gave its consent. Sucre said that the pronounced emphasis placed by Bolívar on the need to observe *porteño* wishes made him believe that if they approved of the assembly being held in Upper Peru, Bolívar could not possibly object to it. What Sucre would like to see happen, he now said, was for the Upper Peruvians to have their own government for "12 or 20 months" during which time they could observe the performance of the governments of Peru and Argentina and decide which one they would like to join.[45]

After arriving in Chuquisaca with Sucre, Arenales, at Sucre's prompting, notified Bolívar of his mission to Upper Peru and paraphrased his instructions from García. He assured Bolívar that the Argentine government was an ardent admirer of his accomplishments on behalf of independence and liberty in America. He expressed the hope that Bolívar would not permit the "germs of discord" to develop now that Ayacucho had sealed independence. By the "germs of discord," he meant Peruvian moves toward a take-over in Upper Peru. Only if real self-determination were bestowed on the Upper Peruvians could Argentina feel secure in pursuing a disinterested policy there. The implied message was unmistakable: Argentina would respect Sucre's decree, but it expected Bolívar to do the same. Arenales's letter was mailed from Chuquisaca on the same day (April 27) as Sucre's.[46]

———◆———

Bolívar pondered these twin missives. He resisted being drawn down the road that Sucre was indicating, in effect collaborating with the Argentines to create an Upper Peruvian state. Bolívar preferred to see Argentina's deference to Sucre's decree as a favor to the Peruvians. This would make it easier for Bolívar to exercise his influence in Upper Peru unilaterally in favor of Peru because Argentina had voluntarily taken itself out of the picture. He sensed that he might bolster his Peruvian authority by endorsing Sucre's decree rather than by protesting it.

In accordance with this strategy, Bolívar informed his council of state in Lima that Sucre's decree had been indeed ill-advised. He said that the convocation of a sovereign assembly in Upper Peru violated his orders from the Peruvian Congress that Sucre establish a provisional government in Upper Peru, pending the negotiation of the Peruvian and Argentine claims to the area. The Arenales mission had changed the picture, Bolívar said. To repeal the decree would run counter to the "explicit desires" of the Argentine government that the Upper Peruvians be allowed to voice definitively their political preferences. Even more, there was good reason to expect that the Upper Peruvian Assembly would feel enormous "gratitude toward its liberators and more ready to do more for them than for others." Certainly Peruvian stock was currently much higher in Upper Peru than Argentine stock. Sucre's decree provided the opportunity to ratify that fact. "Now is the time for the assembly," Bolívar told the council.[47]

Bolívar knew that Peruvian opinion would fear that the Upper Peruvians would opt for independence instead of joining with Peru. Could a Peruvian lever be kept on the Upper Peruvians' decision? Was it possible to make the assembly sovereign enough to satisfy Argentina but enough not sovereign to satisfy Peru? Bolívar's gymnastic "Arequipa decree" sought to accomplish this. The interaction between this decree and Sucre's decree provided the political dialectic in Upper Peru over the next three-and-a-half years.

In his Arequipa decree, Bolívar tried to combine Sucre's decree with his February 23 instructions from the Peruvian Congress. In his cover letter to Sucre, Bolívar said that his authority was not retroactive, and he therefore could not repeal Sucre's decree. He had to accept it, reluctantly, as a fact. He said that "unofficially," however, he admired the liberal purpose of the decree and that his and Sucre's thinking actually coincided on the merit of "leaving these provinces in complete liberty." His Peruvian commitments, however, prevented him from proceeding on this basis. Taking an oblique swipe at the Bogotá Congress's actions curtailing his power, he said that he was constrained to "fulfill his duty, not doing anything else except obeying those [Peruvians] who have given me the authority I now exercise—an authority I cannot contravene for anything, even though its decisions may be opposed to what the most liberal policy is."[48]

The fact that Argentina was now apparently pursuing a liberal policy in Upper Peru through Arenales's instructions, enabled him, Bolívar told Sucre, to lean more in the liberal direction. He told Sucre that he had decided to take Arenales's letter at face value. He recognized that the Argentine government could not be held to its policy of nonintervention if it appeared that the assembly deliberations contemplated by Sucre's decree were being rigged. He therefore ordered Sucre to remove himself and the liberating army outside of a radius of ten leagues (thirty miles) from the center wherever the assembly chose to meet. He announced that he would delay his own arrival in Upper Peru until after the assembly had completed its deliberations. Argentina should see that "we," meaning the Colombians, are relinquishing any right, which "we" do not have anyway, "to introduce any matter in this assembly which could produce a fundamental principle for their institutions." In this oblique manner, Bolívar was saying that the assembly should not be allowed to assume a constitutive role. He would let the assembly meet, but he did not want any constitutional issues being raised or discussed; its sessions were to be "purely deliberative." In particular, he wanted no more political surprises from Sucre. Sucre could and should write a speech for the assembly when it opened, stating the above ground rules and explaining his own activities to date in Upper Peru, but in the military vernacular of a "soldier who is speaking to civilians." Bolívar asked that a draft of his speech be sent to him before it was read so that he could "express an opinion as to its merit."[49]

In his Arequipa decree of May 15, Bolívar stated that the provinces of Upper Peru should meet in the assembly, in conformity with Sucre's decree, in order to "express freely in it their will concerning their interests and government." Article Two, however, stated that the deliberations of the assembly would not be "sanctioned" until the new Peruvian Congress was installed in 1826. This created a virtual Peruvian veto power over the Upper Peruvian Assembly's decisions, a fact that Bolívar subsequently used as a lever to encourage the Upper Peruvians to invite him to write a constitution for their new state. Bolívar might have begun to think about writing such a constitution at just this time. By adopting for themselves a Bolivarian constitution, the Upper Peruvians could be ensured that the Liberator would prevail on the Peruvians to recognize their statehood, if such indeed was the decision of their assembly.[50] Bolívar eventually went further and conjured up the idea of building a nexus between the two Perus in the form of their joint adoption of the Bolivian Constitution, as an alternative to outright Peruvian annexation of Upper Peru, which he originally preferred. But whether it was Peruvian annexation or a Bolivarian union, this drift in his thinking toward reuniting the two Perus ran opposite to Sucre's hopes of using Upper Peru to dislodge Bolívar from his Peruvian base. In effect, Sucre wanted to use Upper Peru as a springboard for Bolívar's entry into Argentine politics and into the war against Brazil. From this point onward, the question of Argentine internal politics, the monarchy in Brazil, and the Eastern Bank, began to form part of his calculations.

Argentina's Response to the Invasion

Pedro's military build-up in the Eastern Bank and Juan Antonio Lavalleja's heroic invasion of the bank ignited a patriotic reaction in the Argentine provinces, calling for a declaration of war against the empire and an invasion of the Eastern Bank with regular armed forces. Whether the Argentine armies could handle the imperial forces in the Eastern Bank without Colombian help was, however, questionable. But equally so was the question of whether the politicians in Buenos Aires could handle Bolívar, and the Argentine *caudillos* who would inevitably flock to him, if Colombian forces were brought into the war. Sucre's alliance proposal, however, served to give the situation a new twist from the perspective of Buenos Aires.

The recently elected governor of Buenos Aires province, and acting head of the Argentine union, Juan Gregorio de las Heras did not have cordial relations with Rivadavia. But the latter's partisans exerted a strong influence on his Heras's government and continued to set the tone of official thinking through the ministerial newspapers. Like Rivadavia, Heras was a centralist. But he was also a military officer who had served under San Martín in Peru. He was not an admirer of Bolívar, especially; like many Argentine officers who returned from Peru, he harbored animosity toward Bolívar for undermining San Martín's authority in that country. But Heras had a grudging admiration for Bolívar's military career, including his liberation of Peru. In contrast to Heras, Rivadavia and his partisans saw Bolívar as a practitioner of the kind of military adventurism that their policies protested against.

These differences spelled a different way of looking at the problem in the Eastern Bank. For Rivadavia, it would be an "evil day" (*un día funesto*) when Argentina had to enlist Bolívar's help in order to escalate the fight against Brazil.[51] Heras, however, did not assume that a military escalation would automatically undermine the centralist position. That position would be strengthened, in fact, if a centralist-controlled army could score important victories against the Brazilians and, just as importantly, be able to absorb into its national ranks the insurgent forces of the bank. Heras did not even rule out accepting the cooperation of Colombian military forces in this endeavor. He felt that Sucre's decree in Upper Peru, taken at face value, contradicted the *rivadavianista* thesis that wherever Colombian armies went, militarism and dictatorships soon followed. If Colombian power was not behaving arbitrarily in Upper Peru, perhaps Rivadavia's fears were unfounded. The convocation of the assembly in Upper Peru indicated to Heras, and to some of his advisers, that Bolívar was not intent on flexing his muscle there. That being true, perhaps he did not want to muscle into Argentina either; therefore, it would be safe to sound him out about backing up Argentina in the struggle against Brazil.

In any case, the Heras government, like Pedro's in Rio, could not ignore the military dimension of the Eastern Bank after April 19, 1825, the day that Lavalleja's followers staged the invasions of the bank from Buenos Aires and triggered Pedro's escalatory response. In fact, Lavalleja's purpose was to put pressure on the Heras government to increase its military support for the struggle in the bank. Lavalleja's initial significant successes had forced the imperial army to retreat from the countryside into the fort at Montevideo to await reinforcements. Lavalleja convoked a congress to establish a provisional government in the bank, which immediately appealed to Buenos Aires for assistance and sent a delegation to take its place in the national congress. The options facing Heras and Foreign Minister García were either to ignore that call and press for a diplomatic arrangement with Pedro, or to respond with a powerful, centralist-controlled army that could take charge of the war and prosecute it in the name of the whole nation, not the local insurgents.

The crucial question at this juncture was: How should the appearance of Colombian power on the scene affect the centralists' choice? One thing was clear—the prevalent attitudes in Buenos Aires were deeply divided on the subject of Bolívar.

The pending arrival of Bolívar in Upper Peru immensely complicated the internal political struggle of the Argentine state. Ostensibly, his appearance in Upper Peru, and the immediate prospect of him assuming a role in the war against Brazil, undercut the national leadership pretensions of the centralists; in the event of a Bolivarian take-over in Buenos Aires, Rivadavia and his clique could be expected to go the way of Riva Aguero and his clique in Peru. Two years previously, Manuel Dorrego, a *porteño* federalist, had hoped that San Martín, upon his return from Peru, would establish his own national dictatorship in order to lead the country into war against Brazil. He reasoned that the federalist forces could gain the upper hand over the centralists under the umbrella of San Martín's patriotic dictatorship. This kind of thinking resurfaced with regard to the prospect of a Bolivarian assumption of power in Argentina.[52]

The picture, however, was by no means black and white. If Bolívar consented to supporting Argentina militarily, without imposing a dictatorship in Buenos Aires, the added confidence in victory over Brazil might be just what was needed to push the centralists into full support of the war effort in the Eastern Bank. A victory there achieved by Buenos Aires's armies, backed by forces from the major provinces it was able to command, like Salta's, and "some forces lent by Bolívar," (a phrase used by the centralist, Vicente Gomez in a letter to Alvear), could be portrayed as a victory of the centralist leadership and the old bete noire of the centralists—their collaboration with the monarchy against Artigas in the Eastern Bank. Alternatively, a treaty commitment from Bolívar might be enough to scare Pedro out of the Eastern Bank without an actual war.[53]

Theoretically, the centralists could stand to benefit from the addition of Bolívar's power to the Argentine effort against Brazil. The crucial question was how much political *entrée* Bolívar wanted in Argentina as price for his sharing the war. The approach of Bolívar to Argentina via Upper Peru created a large element of suspense in Argentine public opinion concerning his intentions. As we know, the official press did its best to picture his intentions as threatening to Argentina's political integrity. The opposition tried to picture Bolívar as an American hero, in speeches in the congress and in other forums of opinion. A stream of letters and envoys were directed to Bolívar in Upper Peru in order to discover what his intentions really were toward the monarchy in Brazil and the struggle in the Eastern Bank.

Pedro García, a *porteño* business man with mining interests in Upper Peru, confessed in a letter to Bolívar his enormous anxiety to know "every move you make as you get closer to my country." As a practical man concerned with the future well-being and stability of his country and with his investments in Upper Peru, Pedro García, like many of his *porteño* compatriots, applauded the progress of Buenos Aires under Rivadavia's ministry. But they doubted that the civilian centralists could either control the *caudillos* in the provinces or force Brazil out of the Eastern Bank. Bolívar, however, could do both. In particular, García was convinced that Bolívar should be called upon by Heras to help his government "by intervening directly in the affairs with Brazil." García told Bolívar how "opportune [Bolívar's] intervention would be due to the fortunate position in which you are today situated, your name being famous in Europe and America due to the *de facto* influence which you have over all [American] states, able to dissipate with one breath all of the obstacles which to others seem insuperable."[54]

These sentiments were not viewed favorably by the Heras government, which remonstrated vehemently with García against the idea of giving Bolívar a blank check in Argentine affairs. García insisted to Heras, however, that his view reflected the feelings of the "right-thinking" (*sana*) portion of his countrymen, who recognized that they could "rest easily over the future of their country once [Bolívar] decided to take it under his protection." He predicted that the Heras government lacked the confidence to confront Brazil in the Eastern Bank and would be forced to evade any possibilities of an open war until it knew whether it would have Bolívar on its side. The official negotiators from Buenos Aires, in seeking

Bolívar's help, would be acknowledging his status as "the arbiter of continental destinies." It was a petition worthy of Bolívar, a means for him to finish off the "last enemies who remain on the continent ... and at the same time fulfill the hopes of an American nation, which with the greatest expectations comes to put its request directly in front of you."[55]

Gregorio (Dean) Funes had been acting as a Colombian agent in Buenos Aires since 1820, when he had befriended the Colombian envoy, Joaquín Mosquera, during his frustrated mission to Buenos Aires. Although Argentinean himself (he was a native of Córdoba), Funes admired Colombia and wanted to bring the two countries together. He was a crusty octogenarian, a deacon in the Catholic Church, a dogmatic exponent of the independence cause, and an erudite teacher-historian. He had written and published a long tome expounding his thesis of Brazil's systematic efforts to expand its borders. If the Eastern Bank fell to the Braganzas, he predicted that Paraguay would be the next to go, followed by large portions of Upper Peru and Peru that bordered on Brazil. Casimiro Olañeta, Sucre's alter-ego for a while on the subject of Upper Peruvian statehood, had been a student of Funes' at the University of Córdoba prior to the outbreak of the independence movement in Argentina. Funes became a strong advocate of Upper Peruvian statehood, once it was declared, and he collaborated actively with Sucre, as we will see, in trying to form the relations between Bolivia and Argentina into an alliance against Brazil. Funes was a shrewd man with pronounced biases against the *porteños*. Suspicious of their intrigues and their Eurocentric mentality, and dubious of their ability to command the patriotic energies of the Argentine people, Funes looked to Bolívar for the leadership of his countrymen.[56]

Funes was resident in Buenos Aires during the tenure of Rivadavia in the ministry. He found that government particularly distasteful because of its failure to see that Bolívar's struggle in Peru was vital to the cause of all of America's independence and to stopping Brazilian expansionism. Acting as Colombia's agent, Funes had solicited from the government its cooperation in the war in Peru. He ran into a stone wall. The war in Peru was seen by the *porteños* as Bolívar's war. The prevailing view of the ministry, including Rivadavia, was that American independence, and Argentina's in particular, would be consummated in Europe, not on any American battlefield. Britain could be relied upon to produce both a Spanish and a general European acceptance of independence. Ironically, Rivadavia and Bolívar ultimately shared the same Eurocentric outlook. The difference was that Bolívar wanted to force Europe's hand by creating a stable order of independence guaranteed by Colombia's "occupation armies," while Rivadavia sought to appeal to European liberalism against American militarism. For Rivadavia, the fighting in Peru was mainly a distraction that simply raised the level of militarism in America and made it that much harder for Europe to see that Spanish America could sustain liberal societies. Rivadavia believed that unless Europe could see that independence did not mean turning America over to the *caudillos*, it would never be comfortable with the idea, nor would America deserve independence. The real victory for independence was to be won by political and moral suasion, backed by examples of liberal and civilian governments in America, without the cost of more blood and treasure being expended on American battlefields.[57]

Funes found Rivadavia's mindset complacent and misguided. Like Sucre, he felt that the British would not go out on a limb to protect American independence. Military intervention by the Holy Alliance was certainly not out of the question. More accurately, it appeared that, in the wake of the key French role in the Holy Alliance's intervention in Spain in August 1823, France and Spain were looking to carve up America between them. For their part, the British were mainly interested in trade. "It is clearly verifiable," Funes wrote Bolívar on April 16, 1824, "that if we are to be free, we will be so only by our own efforts. Peru and the Plata provinces have nowhere to look except to you." Bolívar was his "only consolation" in the face of the self-serving, Eurocentric calculations of the government. Funes defined his own mission as that of "trying to convince these people of the transcendent effects that your [Bolívar's] triumphs in Peru will have and that they are seeking in vain for those effects in Europe."[58]

As a known Bolivarian, Funes's political clout increased enormously in Buenos Aires after the victories of Junín and Ayacucho. The circumstance that most pleased Funes about Ayacucho was that Peru "owed its liberty to [Bolívar's] hand alone." He had "wanted no other consorting in that glory and his wishes had been fulfilled." Funes was pleased that it was precisely on an American battlefield where Peruvian liberation was achieved.[59]

In expectation of the victories that Bolívar would achieve in Peru, Funes requested that he be Bolívar's personal agent in Buenos Aires, in addition to his role as agent of Colombia. He felt that Bolívar's Peruvian power would decide Argentina's political behavior not only toward Peru but toward itself. "Assuming that Peru will owe its liberation solely to you, I am foreseeing that the mention of your name alone will serve to decide the most important questions that will arise concerning the form of [Argentina's own] government and the question of the location of the border between the two states [Peru and Argentina]."[60]

It was largely along the lines laid down by Funes that Bolívar had planned to extend his Peruvian dictatorship into Upper Peru and exercise direct leverage over Argentina's behavior. Funes's relationship with

Sucre was thus ironic: Sucre wanted Bolívar's role in Argentina to take the place of his role in Peru, while Funes wanted that role to be a direct extension of Bolívar's Peruvian power base. They were both Americanists, however.

Dean Funes's steady stream of letters to Bolívar informed him of the state of "panic" that reigned in the ministerial party over Bolívar's arrival in Upper Peru. The progress of Lavalleja in the Eastern Bank placed this party in severe straits. Lavalleja had declared a provisional government in the bank, declared its reincorporation to Argentina, sent a delegation to the congress in Buenos Aires, and urgently requested military aid. The Heras government and its supporters in the congress, however, were reluctant to respond positively despite the arguments from Funes and others in the congress that failure to admit the bank delegation and to recognize the Lavalleja government would lead to the defeat of the bank "insurrection" and the loss of a "sister province." García, however, was "disgusted" with Lavalleja's rabble-rousing tactics, which were reminiscent of Artigas. Although not ruling out the military option, he preferred to hope that the bank could be recouped without a war. Britain did not want one, a position Canning had made very clear to Rivadavia. Britain could be counted on to mediate the dispute; its enormous influence in Rio should be exploited by Argentina. The value of British mediation was that it would serve as a screen for keeping Bolívar's power out of Argentina. Rivadavia took the position with García that war should only be waged against Brazil if the British absolutely refused to mediate. According to Rivadavia, Canning still had a way to go in assuming active mediation because of his fears of setting a precedent for the Holy Alliance's intervention in American disputes.[61]

Funes objected to the whole drift of García's approach to the Eastern Bank war. The need to recognize Lavalleja's government was urgent. That recognition should take the form of a declaration of war against Brazil and immediate preparation for a massive military build-up in the bank. Long-term plans would only allow the Lavalleja forces to succumb or expire. A "rapid war" was needed. The failure of the congress to admit the bank delegation was a patriotic disgrace, for Funes. "In my soul," he wrote Bolívar, "I pass in silence the ignominy of a Government which in front of all eyes allows a sister province to sacrifice itself." García was losing credibility. The plight of Lavalleja became more acute while the government was becoming more irresolute. "Many here want you to close in with a big army," Funes told the Liberator.[62]

Porteño politicians, even those identified with centralist politics, began jockeying for Bolívar's favor. Thus, the congressional leader, Manuel Sarratea, wanted Bolívar to know that he and Rivadavia did not like each other and "did not even say hello in the street." Sarratea was worried that Bolívar believed that he was a friend of Rivadavia's. One of Sarratea's greatest honors, he wrote Bolívar, would have been to be a member of the delegation that the government was preparing to send to Upper Peru. "I can assure you," he wrote obsequiously, "that I would not yield to anybody in sincere cordiality (toward Bolívar) in the course of effectuating that mission."[63]

A somewhat more ambivalent position was adopted by Valentine Gómez, who was an ardent supporter of Rivadavia. He was kind of a mentor to Carlos Alvear, who along with the secretary of the congress, José Miguel Díaz-Vélez, were the two individuals designated to head the mission to Upper Peru. Alvear was the choice of the executive and Díaz-Vélez, the choice of the congress. Gómez tried to brief Alvear before the mission left and afterward by letters. He wanted Alvear to assure Bolívar that in his (Gómez's) role in the congress he was independent of the ministerial party. He had confronted García in session and attacked the government for lethargy in prosecuting the war in the Eastern Bank. He had accused it of delays in getting the mission to Upper Peru instructed and sent off.[64]

Gómez had become alarmed that Bolívar had a list of *porteño* politicians identified with Rivadavia whom he saw as his enemies. He thought that he was on the list, which he was. His comments to Alvear, in this connection, are revealing and display an ambivalent combination of respect for and fear of Bolívar's power. That there were apprehensions concerning Bolívar's methods among the *porteños* should not be attributed by Bolívar, Gómez wrote Alvear, to gossip and rumors "but to the nature of things." It was because of the "nature of things" that Colombia's offer of a treaty alliance in 1820 had been rejected. Argentina did not want to accept interference in its domestic affairs. Bolívar should know that Gómez, for his part, was independent-minded. His record of debates with García in the congress would testify to this. But, he wrote Alvear, and this was the revealing part, "it is essential that you make Bolívar aware that the *porteño* population is completely different from those he now has under his direction—at least speaking of Peru—and that in this regard, the majority is generally apt and informed (*dispuesta y ilustrada*) and to this degree vigilant and protective of everything it has undertaken and this is what constitutes its best political welfare (*su mejor bienestar político*)." *Porteños* were ready to "pay homage to [Bolívar's] services, to his name and his glory [but] "opinion cools off and becomes alarmed in the face of any thing perceived as a threat to their liberty." The message was clear: Bolívar could bring his power and his reputation with him and enlist them in the cause of the war against Brazil and be welcome among the *porteños*. But he would have to leave his dictatorial methods behind in Peru.[65]

Notes

1. The first "Atlanticist" judge was Juan de Matienzo (d. 1587) who drafted a plan for a "second founding of Buenos Aires" under the *audiencia's* sponsorship. The Atlantic strategy is elaborated by Matienzo in his *Gobierno del Peru.* Buenos Aires, 1910, II: chaps. 15–17, esp. pp. 278–85 for his alternative proposals for establishing communication lines between Upper Peru and Spain via Buenos Aires, as opposed to the Pacific lines through Arica and Lima. See Ruiz-Guinazu, *Audiencia de Charcas.* Buenos Aires, 1962, I: 331ff; José Barnardas, *Charcas: Orígenes de una Sociedad Colonial.* La Paz, 1973, 459–61. Blocking of the intendant initiative: John Lynch, *Spanish Colonial Administration, 1782–1810: The Intendant System in the Viceroyalty of Río de la Plata.* New York: Greenwood Press, 1958.

2. Impact of Carlota's plan on the *audiencia*: Gabriel Rene-Moreno, *Los Últimos Días Coloniales.* La Paz, 1970, 332–75. Complicity of Pueyrredón and other Buenos Aires political figures in Carlota's plan and John's "Empire of America" scheme: Alan K. Manchester, *British Pre-eminence in Brazil: Its Rise and Decline.* Chapel Hill: University of North Carolina Press, 1933, 122, 139. Revolt of the *audiencia* and creole politics: Valentine Abecia Baldivieso, *Criollismo.* La Paz, 1964. Rene-Moreno gives more revolutionary weight to the internal dynamics of the *audiencia.*

3. Fernando Diaz Venteo, *Las Campañas Militares de Virey Abascal.* Seville, Spain, 1948; Ferdando Abascal, *Memoria de Gobierno,* edited by Vicent Rodríguez de Casado and José Antonio Calderon Quijano. Seville, Spain, 1944.

4. Charles Arnade, *The Emergence of the Republic of Bolivia.* Gainesville: University of Florida Press, 1957. Arnade minimizes the political significance of the *republiquetas* movement in Upper Peru. For treatments that stress their military and patriotic significance: Sabino Pinilla, *La Creación de Bolivia.* La Paz, 1975, escpecially pp. 167–68; Bartolomé Mitre, *Historia de Belgrano y la Independencia de Río de La Plata.* Buenos Aires, 1927, II: 423–77; Juan R. Munoz Cabrera, *La Guerra de los Quince Anos.* Santiago, 1867. See also José Santo Vargas, *Diario de un Comandante de la Independencia,* with an introduction by Gunnar Mendoza. Mexico, 1982. Arnade's thesis is based largely on this text about life and fighting in the *republiquetas.*

5. Bolívar to Santander, February 23, 1825, in Lecuna and Barret de Nazaris, *Simón Bolívar: Obras Completas.* Havana, Cuba, 1950, I: 1048.

6. Bolívar to Santander, September 13, 1822, and September 14, in ibid., 680–82, 682–83.

7. Bolívar to Santander, February 23, 1824, in Vicente Lecuna, ed., *Cartas del Libertador.* Caracas, 1929, IV: 266–73.

8. Sucre to Bolívar, January 8, 1825, Pedro Brases and Esther Barret de Nazaris, eds., *Archivo de Sucre.* Caracas, 1973–1985, V: 27.

9. Ibid.

10. Sucre to Bolívar, December 20, 1824, Daniel F. O'Leary, *Cartas de Sucre al Libertador.* Madrid, 1919, I: 271–72.

11. Ibid.

12. Spanish fleet: Sucre to Bolívar, January 23, 1825, in O'Leary, *Cartas,* I: 288–91. Sucre's troop deployments: Sucre to Bolívar, January 26, 1825 in ibid.,

292–93. For the reasons Sucre gave to Peru for switching the Lara Division toward Upper Peru instead of to Arequipa as originally planned, Sucre to Peruvian minister of war, December 23, 1824, in *Archivo de Sucre*, IV: 565–66.

13. Sucre to Bolívar, February 1, 1825, in O'Leary, *Cartas*, I: 299.

14. Sucre's conditions for accepting the invasion command: Ibid., 296–97. Sucre's intelligence on the Argentine invasion and prediction of conflict between Argentine and Peruvians under his command: Sucre to Bolívar, January 8, 1823, in ibid., 279–81. For Sucre's request for an Argentine invasion simultaneous with his own, Arenales to Bolívar, April 27, 1825, *Documentos Referentes a la Creación de Bolivia*. Edited by Vicente Lecuna. Caracas, 1975, I: 194–95.

15. Sucre to Bolívar, February 1, 1825, in O'Leary, *Cartas*, I: 296; Sucre to Peruvian Ministry of War, February 1, 1825, in *Archivo de Sucre*, V: 141.

16. Decree text, *Documentos Referentes a la Creación de Bolivia*. Edited by Vicente Lecuna. Caracas, 1975, I: 94–96. "Every one knows": Sucre to Bolívar, February 3, 1825, in O'Leary, *Cartas*, I: 301–03.

17. Sucre to Bolívar, February 3 and 5, 1825, in O'Leary, *Cartas*, I: 301–03 and 303–05. Sucre used the term "spurious" in regard to Santa Cruz's Upper Peruvian patriotism in a later letter to Bolívar, July 3, 1827, in ibid., II: 168.

18. Sucre circular to the municipalities of La Paz, Cochabamba, Chuquisaca, and Potosí. January 1, 1825, in *Documentos Referentes a la Creación de Bolivia*, I: 43–44. For the connotations of the term *albedrío*, see *Appleton's Revised Cuyas Spanish Dictionary*. New York: Appleton Century-Crofts, 1961, 22.

19. Sucre address to the Upper Peruvian Assembly, August 6, 1825, in *Documentos Referentes a la Creación de Bolivia*, I: 285.

20. Text, *Documentos Referentes a la Creación de Bolivia*, I: 94–96.

21. Sucre to Bolívar, January 1, 1825, in *Documentos Referentes a la Creación de Bolivia*, I: 11; Sucre to Santander, April 23, 1825, in *Archivo de Sucre*, V: 489. Bolívar and Sucre were in late June–early July, in the vicinity of Yunahuanca, Peru, the town where Sucre said he and Bolívar conversed about the idea of holding an assembly in Upper Peru. They had made plans to concentrate their forces at Yunahuanca in order to force a battle with the Spanish, which occurred at Junin on August 7. Bolívar to Sucre, July 7, 1824, in Lecuna and Barret de Nazaris, *Obras Completas*, II: 20–21.

22. Text, *Documentos Referentes a la Creación de Bolivia*, I: 108; Gabriel René-Moreno, *Ayacucho en Buenos Aires*. Madrid, n.d., 198.

23. Bolívar to Santa Cruz, March 11, 1825, in Blanco-Fombono, 293–96.

24. Bolívar to Sucre, February 21, 1825, *Documentos Referentes a la Creación de Bolivia*, I: 105–06.

25. Ibid., 107.

26. Ibid., 106.

27. Ibid., 107.

28. Daniel F. O'Leary, *Bolívar and the War of Independence*. Trans. and ed. by Robert F. McNerney, Jr. Austin, Tex.: University of Austin Press, 1970, 277.

29. Sucre to Bolívar, April 4, 1825, in *Documentos Referentes a la Creación de Bolivia*, I: 147–51.

30. Bolívar to Sucre, April 26, 1825, in Blando-Fombona, 316–18. This letter includes Bolívar's "martyr" reference to Peru. *Documentos Referentes a la*

Creación de Bolivia, I: 190–93, copies an incomplete draft version of the letter that lacks the "martyr" reference.

31. Sucre to Bolívar, April 23, 1825, in *Documentos Referentes a la Creación de Bolivia*, I: 487. Sucre's secretary José María del Castro comments on Sucre's chess-playing skills in his book on Sucre.

32. Sucre to Bolívar, July 11, 1825, in *Documentos Referentes a la Creación de Bolivia*, II: 269; June 2, 1825 in *Archivo de Sucre*, VI: 224–25. Sucre's (unpublished) letters to Funes exist in the Biblioteca Nacional de Argentina (Buenos Aires), A. J. de Sucre to Dean Funes, 542/37–117, June 18, 1825 –November 14, 1826.

33. See Chapter 4 section, Sucre's Search for Argentine Support.

34. Rene-Moreno, Àyacucho, 94 ff.

35. Ibid., 95, 102, 136.

36. Instructions Text, *Documentos Referentes a la Creación de Bolivia*, I: 92–93.

37. Decree, (Heras and Garcia) February 8, 1825, Ibid., 94.

38. "Great Bolívar": Arenales to Rudicindo Alvarado (Argentine officer in Bolívar's service), March 23, 1825, in *Documentos Referentes a la Creación de Bolivia*, I: 139; Moreno, Ayacucho, 82, 102 ff. Sucre's request for Arenales' invasion of Upper Peru: See Chapter 4 section, Sucre's Search for Argentine Support.

39. Sucre to Heras, April 6, 1825 in *Archivo de Sucre*, 377–78.

40. Sucre to Arenales, April 6, 1825, *Historia de Tarija*, ed. by Cristina Minutolo de Ortiz, Tarija, 1986, II: 319.

41. Arenales to Garcia, April 4, 1825, in *Documentos Referentes a la Creación de Bolivia*, I: 147.

42. Arenales to Garcia, April 21, 1825, ibid., 176–78.

43. Ibid., 178.

44. Gerhard Masur, *Simón Bolívar*. Albuquerque: University of New Mexico Press, 1948, 688 and n. 21. The author argues that it was advanced tuberculosis that caused Bolívar's death. Sucre's first mention of his chest pains is his letter to Bolívar of January 8, 1825, in O'Leary, *Cartas*, I: 279–80. He postponed at least one trip to Potosí from Chuquisaca because of his fear of pulmonary attack; Sucre to Leon Galindo, prefect of Potosí, May 15, 1826 in *Cartas de Sucre al Galindo*, ed. by Carlos Blanco Galindo. La Paz, 1964, 27–29. The climate and patriotic sentiment made Chuquisaca the "best of Upper Peru" for Sucre personally. Sucre to Bolívar, April 27, 1825, in *Archivo de Sucre*, 493–95. The political atmosphere of Chuquisaca is vividly portrayed in Gabriel Rene-Moreno, *Últimos Días Coloniales en el Alto Peru*. La Paz, 1970. Also Valentíne Abecia, *Historia de Chuquisaca*. Sucre, 1939; Guillermo Francovich, *El Pensamiento Universitario de Charcas*. Sucre, 1948.

45. Sucre to Bolívar, April 27, 1825, in *Archivo de Sucre*, V: 494–95.

46. Arenales to Bolívar, April 27, 1825, in *Documentos Referentes a la Creación de Bolivia*, I: 193–95

47. Gabriel Paz (Bolívar's secretary) to the Peruvian council of state, May 19, 1921 (sic 1825), in *Documentos Referentes a la Creación de Bolivia*, I: 221–23.

48. Bolívar to Sucre, May 15, 1825, in *Documentos Referentes a la Creación de Bolivia*, I: 214–15.

49. Ibid., 215–16.

50. Text, *Documentos Referentes a la Creación de Bolivia*, I: 220–21.

51. Rivadavia to Alvear, September 23, 1826, in Gregorio Rodriguez, *Contribución Historica y Documental*. Buenos Aires, 1931, II: 328–29. See also Rivadavia to Alvear, September 15, 1824, in ibid.,II: 328–29.

52. Forbes to Adams, September 12 and 14, 1823, in Manning, I: 625–26.

53. The phrase "with some forces from Bolívar" belongs to Vicente Gomez: Gomez to Alvear, September 19, 1824, in Rodriguez, II: 262.

54. The letters from "various Argentines" to Bolívar are in O'Leary, *Memorias*, XI, as indicated in the contents; "How opportune Bolívar's intervention would be": Pedro Garcia to Bolívar, November 3, 1825, in ibid., XI: 316–17.

55. Pedro García to Bolívar, December 4, 1825, in ibid., XI: 318–19.

56. Silva, presents valuable biographic data on Funes in addition to a portion of his letters to Bolívar, which are extracted from O'Leary, *Memorias*, XI.

57. Funes to O'Leary, April 16, 1824, in O'Leary, *Memorias*, XI: 180; Funes to O'Leary, September 1, 1824, in ibid., 183–84; Funes to Joaquin Mosquera, Colombian envoy, April 16, 1824, in ibid., 179–81.

58. "Have nowhere to look except to you": Funes to Bolívar, April 16, 1824, in ibid., *Memorias*, XI: 113–14; "seeking in vain for those effects from Europe": Funes to Bolívar, July 19, 1824, in ibid., 120–21.

59. Funes to Bolívar, January 25, 1825, in ibid., 123–32.

60. Funes to Bolívar, June 2, 1824, in ibid., 118.

61. Funes to Bolívar, June 16, 1825, in Silva, 283–85; August 26, 1825, in ibid., 283–93; October 18, 1825, in ibid., 296–98; October 26, 1825, in ibid., 300–304.

62. Funes to Bolívar, August 26, 1825, in ibid., 290–301; October 18, 1825, in ibid., 297–98.

63. Sarratea to Bolívar, May 17, 1825, in O'Leary, *Memorias*, XI: 110–10.

64. Gomez to Alvear, July 27, 1825, in Rodriguez, II: 260–70.

65. Gomez to Alvear, September 10, 1825, in ibid., 278–81.

5

Sucre Poses the Challenge to the Monarchy

THE COLOMBIAN INTERVENTIONS IN PERU and Upper Peru makes it clear that the efforts to create unity within Spanish-American societies were likely to find more fertile soil for growth in playing upon nationalistic fears and resentments toward other Spanish-American states than in the development of a republican *esprit d'corps*. One reason for this was that these states had to rely on outside help to liberate themselves, help that was largely made up of armies recruited in the other Spanish-American states. This produced jealousies and resentments instead of solidarity: The Chileans resented the Argentines; the Peruvians resented the Colombians; the New Granadians resented the Venezuelans; the Venezuelans resented the New Granadians; the Upper Peruvians resented the Peruvians (and tried to make use of the Colombians as a lever against Peruvian interference). Only the Argentines and the Paraguayans were exempted from this syndrome. But the Argentines would have to face the question of accepting help from the Colombians in their war to liberate the Eastern Bank from Brazilian occupation. Given the "price" that the Peruvians were perceived to have paid for Colombian liberation of Peru, the Argentines could understandably question the compatibility of Colombian power with the republican cause. All of this meant that efforts to organize the independence movements in terms of shared republican principles were undermined by efforts to organize a politics of nationalism that fed off the interventions by Spanish-American states in each other's domestic affairs.

Yet, it fell to Sucre to insulate Colombian power from the growing, nationalist politics of the Peruvian state so that it could be aligned with the cause of advancing republican government on the South America continent. At the heart of this effort was his attempt to align Bolivia with Argentina in the war against the Brazilian monarchy, in the hope that Bolívar could be enlisted in this republican challenge to the monarchy and thereby dislodged from his authoritarian dictatorship in Peru. This was an almost impossible challenge, given the enormous distrust that had developed between Bolívar and the Argentines. Yet Sucre was very resourceful.

Sucre's Brush with the Imperial Brazilian Army

After the downfall of Olañeta, many royalist functionaries in Upper Peru, including Sebastian Ramos, the governor of the western Upper Peruvian province of Chiquitos, had to consider making their peace with the new order. Ramos initially offered to submit to Sucre's authority but changed his mind upon learning that he was a target of locally motivated reprisals. Ramos, then, asked the provincial government of Mato Grasso, across the border in Brazil, to occupy the province of Chiquitos and place it under the protection of the empire. The municipal authorities of Mato Grasso acceded to Ramos's request, apparently in an effort to augment the authority of the city in the provincial political structure and to win the approval of the emperor for their actions, which would push Brazilian boundary further westward and create a buffer against possible attacks by Sucre. Chiquitos was duly invaded in early April 1824 by Brazilian soldiers. Sucre was informed by a letter from their commander that Chiquitos was now part of the Brazilian empire.[1]

Sucre's immediate reaction to the invasion was to teach the Brazilians a lesson and to instill in them the "fear of Ayacucho." "A short while ago," he responded to the Brazilian commander's note, "18,000 of [Colombia's] proudest enemies were humiliated and its [Colombia's] armies are ready to make themselves respected and to punish wrongdoers." Chiquitos was under the protection of the liberating army along with the rest of the Upper Peruvian provinces. If the Brazilians did not immediately evacuate, Sucre promised to "march against them and not to only liberate our border but to invade the land that had declared itself our enemy, carrying to it desolation, death and terror in order to avenge our country." Sucre wanted the retaliation also to generate Upper Peruvian patriotism. The population of Santa Cruz should be "persuaded that the cause is national and even more just than was the war just concluded against the Spanish."[2]

Sucre had a larger twofold purpose in ordering the retaliation against Brazil. He contemplated the idea of triggering an overthrow of the monarchy by fomenting the republican principle inside Brazilian borders as his army invaded. He believed that republican sentiment inside the empire could be galvanized by the invasion; that the distance from the border of Upper Peru to Rio de Janeiro, although geographically vast, was not that great politically. At the same time, Sucre wanted to use the invasion to pave the way to an alliance between Upper Peru and Argentina. These purposes were clearly intimated in his various letters to the commander of the "expeditionary" force being assembled in the Santa Cruz province and in his letters to various local officials explaining the situation to them.[3]

The orders Sucre gave to the commander of the military reinforcements he was sending to Chiquitos were couched in the same language as his response to the Brazilians. The mission was not just to eject the Brazilians but to "take them on inside Mato Grasso and carry terror to this enemy population." Sucre assured the president of the Santa Cruz department, José Videla, that troops were available in Upper Peru for the Brazilian invasion: The Colombian Second Division stationed in La Paz "was ready for the campaign and prepared to carry the standards of liberty or revenge to Rio de Janeiro itself." Sucre pointed out that it was because Argentina did not show firmness that the Brazilians were able to wrest the Eastern Bank from them. That same mistake would not be made in this case. He said the liberty of Chiquitos must be defended against the Portuguese. Agitators must be sent into Mato Grasso to "proclaim liberty, democratic principles and to foment disorder and confusion."[4]

Sucre soon backed off from the plan of using either Colombian or Peruvian troops in the Chiquitos operation. The advantage of using them was that it would widen the coalitional basis of the war against Brazil. But getting the approval of the two governments might be difficult or at least cost time. He, therefore, decided to employ mainly Upper Peruvian troops commanded by surrendered Spanish officers and some Colombian officers.[5]

There was also a political advantage in using the Upper Peruvian troops. Sucre wanted to draw Argentina into an alliance against Brazil without raising its immediate fears about bringing Peruvian and Colombian troops closer to its borders as a result. Further, Sucre wanted Argentina to see that Upper Peru as a separate state could be useful to it in its endeavor to reconquer the Eastern Bank. By opening another front against Brazil in Mato Grasso, Upper Peru could distract Pedro from the Eastern Bank and make him vulnerable there. If Argentina were placed under an obligation to Peru for the use of its troops to invade Mato Grasso, especially in the early phase, it would be constrained to recognize Peruvian claims in Upper Peru and to back away from its own May 9th endorsement of Sucre's decree. But if mainly Upper Peruvian troops were used for the Brazilian invasion in the beginning, Argentina would have to treat Upper Peru as an allied state. In fact, the whole of Sucre's management of the Chiquitos affair—from the upping of the ante to his subsequent emphasis on using only Upper Peruvian troops in the invasion of Brazil—was intended to set the stage for a military alliance between Upper Peru and Argentina. This would be a prelude to Bolívar joining the alliance later with Colombian and Peruvian forces.

Sucre's Proposal of Alliance with Argentina

Sucre's purpose in the Colombian interventions in Ecuador and Peru was to blunt the growth of Bolívar's dictatorial authority, to moderate its scope, and also to moderate the scope of the occupation-style politics that it generated. In pursuit of this objective, Sucre tried to pave the way for Bolívar to exit from his dictatorship in Peru by having him get involved in Argentina's war against the monarchy and thereby link Colombian forces with the republican opposition inside of Brazil. This strategy was predicated on the creation of Bolivia as an independent, republican state. Sucre hoped that Bolívar would abandon his Peruvian dictatorship with its authoritarian links and place himself at the head of an alliance of republican states (Bolivia and Argentina at the minimum) intending to attack the monarchy in Brazil. Toward this end, Sucre had to struggle against Bolívar's attempt to use Colombia's military power as a basis for creating an authoritarian, monarchic-oriented politics that was based in Bolivia and Peru, aimed at replacing the republican system of Colombia, and linked to European interests. Sucre's proposed alliance of Bolivia with Argentina was the key to his policy of creating an alternative, republican orientation for Colombian power.

Just prior to the opening of the Upper Peruvian Deliberative Assembly in August 1825, Sucre had advised Bolívar that he was awaiting the response from Buenos Aires to his invitation to send observers to the assembly and open relations with it. In the meantime, he deliberately delayed the publication of the Arequipa decree. He wanted a favorable response from Buenos Aires to arrive first in order to reassure the delegates, given the demoralizing effect that he predicted the Arequipa decree would have on them.[6] Sucre intended to dampen the effects of the Arequipa decree on the assembly by playing up the effects of Argentina's endorsement of the assembly, if that endorsement was forthcoming.

The signs in Buenos Aires were immediately good. In the official ministerial newspaper, *Argos,* Sucre's February 9 decree and cover letter, as well as his earlier circular of January 20, were published along with the text of the instructions that had been given to Arenales for his mission in Upper Peru. The clear inference was that Sucre's policy in Upper Peru was in complete accordance with the desires of the Argentine government as expressed in the Arenales instructions. The arrival of Sucre's letter of April 9 produced, in the words of the American ambassador in Buenos Aires, "a tranquilizing and satisfactory effect." Sucre's letter caused this relief because it seemed to promise that Bolívar's Peruvian dictatorship would not be extended to Upper Peru, and it appeared that self-determination would be adhered to. In the creation of sovereignty in Upper Peru, the Heras government saw a barrier against Peruvian annexation and against the extension Bolívar's Peruvian dictatorship.[7]

Sucre predicted that the Argentine government would recognize the sovereign right of Upper Peru to either declare independence or rejoin the Argentine provinces but would "protest any act of incorporation into Lower Peru, because it [the Argentine government] cannot consent or have placed on its border a state so powerful as that of Upper and Lower Peru reunited, etc., etc." He told Bolívar that it was gratifying to see, in the developing position of the Argentine government, that "his conduct (in issuing the February 9 decree) was not only approved but applauded— conduct which you believed so much would be rejected by the Government of the Argentine Provinces." At this time, Sucre was beginning to receive considerable intelligence about Buenos Aires politics from various sources, including newspapers relayed by Arenales, reports from the military courier he had dispatched with his April 9 letter, and from Dean Funes, Bolívar's agent in the port city. Sucre's letters to Funes are unpublished. Historians' ignorance of these letters has prevented a proper appreciation of the degree to which Sucre involved himself in Argentina's internal politics.[8]

The Heras government had responded with alacrity to Sucre's offer to open up formal relations with the deliberative assembly. A letter from the minister of foreign affairs, Manuel José García, accepted Sucre's congratulations on the installation of a national government and said that "they produced even more pleasure in Buenos Aires because they were accompanied by [news of] the complete liberty of the four provinces of Upper Peru resulting from the destruction of General Olañeta and by the notice of the measures which he [Sucre] had taken to organize them and save them from anarchy." The García letter enclosed the copy of a law passed by the congress on May 9, 1825, in response to the executive's advisement of the arrival of Sucre's letter of April 9. That law further conveyed the feeling of relief that Bolívar was not planing to annex Upper Peru to Peru but would proceed there in the spirit of Sucre's measures. This meant that the Liberator could be approached more gingerly by Argentina on the subject of getting help from him against Brazil. Thus, Article 1 announced that in response to Sucre's offer, a delegation was being prepared to travel to Upper Peru to convey to Sucre "the most sincere gratitude and recognition which animate the provinces of the [Argentine] union over the heroic and generous efforts of the Liberating Army which, after having given freedom to the provinces of Upper Peru, has taken upon itself the noble endeavor of sustaining in them order, liberating them from the horrors of anarchy, and expediting for them the means of organizing themselves by themselves (*de organizarse por sí mismos*)." The assumption here is that this freedom of choice would not result in a decision to join Upper Peru to Peru, or even to Argentina for that matter. Article 2 thus stated that the delegation would "reconcile with Bolívar, as the supreme Head of Peru, whatever difficulty might arise between that state and this one [Argentina] as a consequence of the state of liberty in which today are found the four provinces of Upper Peru, which have always belonged to Argentina." Argentina would forego any claims in Upper Peru, provided Peru did also. That would be the basis of the position of the Argentine envoys in their dealings with Bolívar and with the assembly. These instructions clearly fell into step with Sucre's intimation that by dealing directly with Bolívar and the assembly, the Argentine government could obviate the need to pay attention to possible Peruvian claims in Upper Peru.[9]

By explicitly linking of his decree convoking the deliberative assembly to the May 9 Argentine law, Sucre had paved the way politically toward an alliance between Upper Peru and Argentina. But there remained the problem of Bolívar's Peruvian commitments as an obstacle to separating Upper Peru from Peru. Sucre, therefore, had to try to involve Bolívar in Argentina in order to distance him from his Peruvian commitments. Further, the commitment of Bolívar's power in Argentina would necessarily aim it at the monarchy in the name of the republics; his power in Peru was aimed at Colombia's republican system. If Bolívar could be brought into the war against Brazil—if Colombian forces could be linked with the republican opposition inside Brazil—then Bolívar's antagonism toward Colombia's constitution and his flirtation with Páez, which greatly worried Sucre, would be moderated.[10]

The May 9 law signaled that Argentina was less defensive about the spread of Bolívar's dictatorship into Upper Peru. Sucre concluded that the *porteños* might be more prone to approaching Bolívar for military help in the Eastern Bank against Brazil; they would not have to feel that such an approach would whet Bolívar's appetite to expand his dictatorial system. On May 20, 1825, Sucre made his approach to the Argentines.

Sucre's letter of this date to Heras announced the Brazilian invasion of Chuquitos. He said the Brazilians would be ejected but that, in addition, Sucre had under consideration the project of insurrecting all of the adjacent Brazilian provinces and forming a "punitive expedition" to invade and occupy them. He proceeded to invite the Argentine government to "take advantage of this occasion." He told Heras that Upper Peruvian troops would constitute the bulk of the invasion force. They would "invade Mato Grosso, Cubaya etc. etc., take a large part of Brazilian territory, carry the standard of revolution into the Empire in its weakest part and ... force the Emperor to cede territory or make such transactions as would restore the Eastern Bank to the United Provinces." He said that the project "merited detailed meditation and a formal commitment" by Argentina in order to undertake it. The imminent arrival of Bolívar in Upper Peru meant that he could be brought into the picture *after* Upper

Peru and Argentina had defined their own *casus belli* against Pedro, and the prospect of wider republican collaboration in the war could be studied. Thus, Sucre's letter and his actions in readying a strike force in Chuquitos should be seen by Argentina, he said, as laying the groundwork for the alliance and for a possible joint invasion of the empire by Upper Peruvian and Argentine forces. Colombian and Peruvian forces could come into the picture pending the authorizations of their respective governments. The Argentine-Upper Peruvian alliance should be seen as the spearhead of the larger republican alliance against Brazil.[11]

Four days later, Sucre included a copy of his letter to Heras along with his own letter to the ministry of war at Bogotá. Characteristically, he concealed his political plan behind a feigned simplicity of motive. "In the uncertainty over whether Upper Peru belongs to Río de La Plata, Lower Peru or to itself, I have believed that in any case the public cause and the aggression of the Brazilians against this country (Upper Peru) requires [sic] me to take this step [of formulating the invasion plan in conjunction with the alliance proposal]." Sucre felt obliged to later send a copy of his alliance letter to Lima, with a curt cover note saying only that the full logic of his policy on Chiquitos would be taken up with Bolívar when he arrived in Upper Peru. Obviously, the council of state in Lima would find it difficult (if the Colombian government did not) to see that Sucre's policy stemmed from his "uncertainty" over the question of to whom Upper Peru belonged: His alliance proposal was a palpable move toward ensuring that it did not belong to Peru. In addition, Sucre's proposal of alliance was intended to stimulate the pro-Bolivarian party in Argentina.[12]

Sucre's Argentine policy was thus entering a new phase. Initially, as we saw, he had considered annexing the Argentine provinces to an Upper Peruvian state, leaving Buenos Aires isolated. He was now proceeding in a more subtle manner. His new purpose was not to isolate Buenos Aires but to subordinate it politically within the Argentine state to the pro-Colombian sectors. In that way, Bolívar would be able to think positively about involving himself in Argentina through the war against Brazil. Because of his intelligence from Buenos Aires, Sucre could inform Bolívar that there were essentially two parties in the capital: "that of Colombia and you which is based in the opposition party to the Heras government and that of the ministerial party running the government which is your enemy. Our party is gaining every day although the other is strong."[13]

Sucre wanted Bolívar to appreciate that the decision of the Argentine government to send a delegation to Upper Peru to treat with him was a "political triumph." With the fears of a Peruvian annexation of Upper Peru taken out of the picture by Sucre's decree, the anti-Bolivarians (including Heras) had been disarmed, and the issue of a military victory, with Bolívar's help, in the war in the Eastern Bank became paramount.

Bolívar had gained almost free access. "Without you even having to say a word to them, you already have complete latitude to go even to Montevideo with the consent of the very people who have maligned your glory." Sucre predicted an even larger momentum for the Bolivarian mandate in Argentina. "I hope that my last letter offering to help them recover the Eastern Bank (by invading Mato Grasso) will have a marvelous effect."[14]

Argentina's Response to Sucre's Alliance Proposal

Whether an actual alliance against Brazil would be developed out of Sucre's proposal to the Argentine government depended on the establishment of trust between Bolívar and the *porteños*. The latter had to decide whether Sucre was a camouflaged scout for Bolívar's Peruvian dictatorship or, whether Sucre's efforts on behalf of Upper Peru's self-determination could be relied on to prevent a Peruvian annexation of Upper Peru. If the latter was the case then a buffer would be available against the danger of a reproduction of the Peruvian dictatorship in Argentina if Bolívar were brought into the war against the monarchy. For his part, Bolívar had to know that Buenos Aires was not looking for a "free ride"—that is expecting to reap the benefits in the Eastern Bank of a successful challenge to the monarchy without paying the cost of accepting the role of junior partners in the alliance with him. At Potosí, Bolívar and envoys from Buenos Aires dueled over the question of waging a joint war against the Brazilian monarchy. The Argentine envoys came with elaborate instructions, which were the result of the political analysis that was triggered by Sucre's alliance proposal.

---◆---

By June 10, 1825, García had drafted the original instructions for the envoys Alvear and José Miguel Díaz Vélez. These instructions contained two objectives. The first was to open relations with the Chuquisaca assembly, hopefully before it had made any definitive decision on the sovereignty question, but if not, the choice made should be reported to Buenos Aries immediately. If that choice were for independence, or for joining Upper Peru to the Argentine state, the *porteño* emissaries were to open official relations with the assembly. If the decision was for reincorporation to Peru, relations were to be broken off and the mission would "await the decision" of Buenos Aires. The second objective of the mission was to deal with Bolívar.[15]

García expected that Bolívar would make an issue of the Panama assembly and the fact that Argentina, in consequence of the general disunity of the provinces since 1820 and the specific rejection by Rivadavia of Colombian invitations to participate in an American league, had to date not agreed to send delegates. The instructions, in this connection, reflected the persistent *porteño* fear that the American league was a tool for Colombian political hegemony on the continent. García felt, along with many *porteños*, that a wide European political role on the continent would blunt Colombia's sense of its American hegemony.[16]

The mission was instructed, in this light, to find out what the "real objects" of the Panama Congress were; to explore Bolívar's own ideas about the domestic structures of American states, and "where he thought that they should be going." This part of the instructions reflected the apprehension, clearly expressed in an article in *Argos*, which accused Funes of complicity, that Bolívar planned to establish a personal protectorate over South America and make himself an emperor.[17]

The *porteño* concern was how much of an issue Bolívar would make out of Argentine nonattendance in Panama. Alvear requested more guidance on this matter, particularly about how far he could go in committing Argentina to send a delegation if Bolívar used it as a condition to receive his backing against the monarchy. Alvear was told to avoid rejection of the league idea and to even indicate a conditional approval with "assertiveness," if this appeared necessary to get Bolívar to provide military support against the imperial army in the Eastern Bank.[18]

The envoys were to find a way to take advantage of Bolívar's military power against Pedro without risking the establishment of a Bolivarian dictatorship in Argentina. The method decided upon was that of the republican alliance. The Brazilian empire was to be presented not just as a problem for Argentina, but as a problem for all of the other republics on the continent. Bolívar should be convinced of the deep "aversion with which Pedro looks at the new Republics and his decided opposition to anything that tends to consolidate" their foundations. His invasion of the Eastern Bank was an attack on the republican idea as much as anything else. This being true, what was urgently needed was for the republics (Colombia, Peru, Chile, Argentina) to "act in accord" to stop Pedro's designs and to force him to withdraw from the bank inside the boundaries of the empire. As the first step toward building a united front, an ultimatum should be delivered to Pedro, in the name of the four allies, demanding the evacuation of Montevideo and self-determination for the bank under a treaty that could possibly be guaranteed by Britain. Britain had "obvious reasons" for wanting to avoid a war among American states and could be expected to support the ultimatum. The chances that a war over the bank could be avoided in this manner were good. An expanded war against the empire would only distract the Spanish Americans from the urgent tasks of laying the domestic foundations for their new states. However, should the ultimatum fail and Pedro remain intent on maintaining Brazil's annexation of the bank, the four allies would have to seek to liberate Montevideo "by all means necessary."[19]

By relying on the device of an ultimatum, the Argentine government sought to avoid a war and to maximize a role for the British in the arrangement of the bank. The value of this approach was that it would bring Bolívar's power to bear on Pedro without bringing it directly into Argentina. But the essential safeguard for Argentina against Bolívar's auxiliary power was to place that power in the alliance context. Should it come to war against Brazil, Argentina could have the security of relating to Bolívar within the coalitional framework rather than having to relate to him, like the Peruvians, as the "invited" leader of an auxiliary army on national soil.

The basic weakness of the alliance device was that it was not obvious that Chile, Peru, or Colombia were involved in the Eastern Bank question. The envoys could speak speculatively of the Eastern Bank invasion being an "illustration" of the enmity that Pedro bore to all of the republics on the continent and as an indicator of his future intentions. But it was by no means clear that this was true. Moreover, the instructions to the envoys avoided recommending that a war against Pedro be the primary object of the alliance. Furthermore, once the war broke out, it was not clear that the alliance framework would be able to protect Argentina from Bolívar's auxiliary power. The reality, therefore, was that the alliance device was a ploy in order to prevent Bolívar from making proposals about assuming a direct role in Argentina.

The situation, however, had changed dramatically as a result of the Chiquitos invasion and Sucre's independent proposal of an alliance against the empire. What was originally a lame ploy in the original instructions to Alvear and Díaz Vélez now became an earnest policy for moving toward a coalitional war against Brazil. García proceeded to redraft the instructions in light of Sucre's initiative; now the alliance could be advocated with vigor.

The strike into Chiquitos made it clear that Brazil was not just Argentina's problem. In García's view, the invasion revealed that the security of all of the republics was manifestly threatened by "the voracious power arising in the heart of the continent." Peru and Colombia could consider themselves attacked as a result of Chiquitos; both of their troops were on Upper Peruvian soil.[20]

García observed that Sucre's belligerent response to the Brazilian invasion, and his attempt to link that response to the Argentine struggle with Brazil in the Eastern Bank, opened a new horizon of joint action against Brazil—a "more effective plan of operation" that was "more in accord with the present (i.e., post-Chiquitos) situations of Peru and Colombia." For García, as long as the problem of Brazil remained confined to the Eastern Bank, and to that extent the problem was Argentina's alone, Bolívar's help against Brazil could be purchased only at the price of the direct interposition of his power in Argentina. It was dubious that alliance relations could be built up to offset that fact, as long as Colombia, Peru, and Chile did not see themselves as directly threatened by Brazil. But now Chiquitos made it possible to strengthen the alliance framework of Bolívar's intervention and to widen the basis for waging a war against Brazil. What García advocated were simultaneous assaults on Brazil: Bolívar and his forces (Colombian, Peruvian, and Upper Peruvian) attacking the "weakest part" (Sucre's phrase) via Mato Grasso; Colombia attacking by sea with its naval power, aided by Chilean naval forces; and Argentina attacking through the Eastern Bank. Not only would the alliance framework of the war be strengthened, but Bolívar's power would be deflected from Argentina directly into the empire. For this reason, García was now enthusiastic about escalation of the war, in notable contrast to the earlier instructions.

In the new instructions, the role of Britain was de-emphasized. Nowhere was it mentioned that Britain would be opposed to a "war of principles" breaking out among American states. Now Bolívar could be encouraged to "carry insurrection into the center of the empire. ... The spirit of ambition and conquest could be eliminated from the American continent." Bolívar could be assured that the "plans of the Emperor that have started and will continue to develop are nothing but the consequence of his policy and of the efforts which the Party of Legitimacy is making against the liberty and security of the new Republics of the continent."[21]

Notes

1. Ron Seckinger, *The Brazilian Monarchy and the South American Republics.* Baton Rouge: Lousiana University Press, 1984, 73–79; Ron Seckinger, "The Chiquitos Affair: An Aborted Crisis in Brazilian-Bolivian Relations," *Luso-Brazilian Review,* 1974, XI: 19–40. For an excellent and well documented Bolivian monograph that analyses Sucre's strategy of escalation in the Chiquitos crisis, see Jorge Alejandro Ovando-Sanz, *La Invasión Brasileña a Bolivia en 1825; Una de las Causas de la Asamblea de Panamá.* La Paz, 1977.

2. "Terror to the enemy population": Sucre to Francisco Lopez, May 11, 1825, in Pedro Grases and Esther Barret de Nazaris, *Archivo de Sucre.* Caracas, 1973–1985, VI: 83.

3. Ibid., VI: 84–105.

4. "To Rio de Janeiro itself": Sucre to José Videla, May 11, 1825, in ibid., VI: 80–82, and May 14, 1825, 103–05.

5. Use of surrendered Spanish officers: Sucre to Videla, May 30, 1825, in ibid., VI: 206–07; Sucre to Santa Cruz, May 30, 1825, same, 213; Sucre to Las Heras, May 20, 1825, in Vincente Lecuna, ed., *Documentos Referentes a la*

Creación de Bolivia. Caracas, 1975, II: 224–25. Seckinger mistakingly reports Sucre's letter to Las Heras as saying that "using only troops from Peru, the banners of the revolution could be brought into Brazil." *Brazilian Monarchy*, 111. He actually said "using only troops from Alto Peru."

6. Sucre to Bolívar, June 3, 1825, in *Archivo de Sucre*, VI: 226. Also, on Sucre's delay in publishing the Arequipa decree: Sucre to Bolívar, August 3, 1825, in ibid., VI: 473–74; Arenales to Bolívar, June 28, 1825, in Daniel F. O'Leary, *Memorias de General O'Leary.* Caracas, 1880, XI: 313–14.

7. Sucre to Bolívar, June 25, 1825, in *Archivo de Sucre*, VI: 354; "Tranquilizing effect": John M. Forbes, U.S. chargé d'affaires to Henry Clay, May 2, 1825, in William R. Manning, *Diplomatic Correspondence of the United States Concerning the Indpendence of the Latin American Nations.* New York: Oxford University Press, 1925. I: 647–50. This includes translations of Sucre's circular of February 20, his letter of April 9, and the instructions drafted for Arenales on February 6, as they appeared in the official newspaper *Argos.* Heras's view of Upper Peru as a buffer: Ibid., 647; Sabino Pinilla, *La Creación de Bolivia.* La Paz, 1975, 131.

8. "Gratifying for him to see": Sucre to Bolívar, June 25, in *Archivo de Sucre*, VI: 354. The Funes letters to Sucre are in O'Leary, *Memorias*, XI: 179–242. See also J. Francisco V. Silva, *El Libertador Bolívar y El Dean Funes.* Madrid, 1916, which carries (339–95) a portion of the letters to Sucre in the O'Leary volume. Sucre's (unpublished) letters to Funes exist in the *Biblioteca Nacional de Argentina.* Buenos Aires, A. J. de Sucre to Dean Funes, 542/37-117, June 18, 1825–November 14, 1826.

9. García to Sucre, May 14, 1825, in *Documentos Referentes a la Creación de Bolivia*, I: 213–14.

10. Sucre's caution to Bolívar about Páez's motives: Sucre to Bolívar, August 12, 1826, in Daniel F. O'Leary, *Cartas de Sucre al Libertador.* Madrid, 1919, VI: 470–472. Sucre to Bolívar June 6, 1826, in ibid., 34–37. His caution to Bolívar about "frightening the people with the word king": Sucre to Bolívar, August 24, 1826, ibid., 93–94.

11. "Carry the standard of revolution into the Empire": Sucre to Juan Gregorio de las Heras, May 20, 1825, in *Archivo de Sucre*, VI: 148–51.

12. "The aggression of the Brazilians requires me to take this step": Sucre to Colombian secretary of war, May 24, 1825, in *Archivo de Sucre*, VI: 157–58. Logic of his Chiquitos policy would be taken up with Bolívar: Sucre to the Peruvian Ministry of War, May 27, 1825, in ibid., VI: 188.

13. Two parties in Buenos Aires: Sucre to Bolívar, July 11, 1825, in ibid., VI: 405.

14. Sucre to Bolívar, July 11, 1825, in ibid., VI: 404.

15. Text of instructions, in Ernesto Restelli, ed., *La Gestión Diplomatica del General de Alvear en el Alto Peru.* Buenos Aires, 1927, 6–10.

16. García to Alvear and Díaz-Vélez, August 10, 1825, in ibid., 55–61.

17. García to Alvear and Díaz-Vélez, June 10, 1825, in ibid., 11–12.

18. Alvear and Díaz-Vélez to García, June 14, 1825, in ibid., 13–15; García to Alvear and Díaz-Vélez, June 16, 1825, in ibid., 15–18.

19. García to Alvear and Díaz-Vélez, June 10, 1825, in ibid., 7–8.

20. García to Alvear and Díaz-Vélez, June 26, 1825, in ibid., 21–23.

21. Ibid., 22.

6

Failure of the Challenge

THERE WERE TWO SCENARIOS of Bolivia's statehood. One was Sucre's and the other Bolívar's. Sucre's contained the idea of involving Bolivia in an alliance with Argentina against Brazil. Bolivar's contained the idea of writing a quasi-monarchical constitution for Bolivia that would serve as a model for Peru and Colombia, with the three states eventually coming together into the Empire of the Andes. The debate in the assembly on declaring Bolivia an independent state evinced a strong republican spirit but it was overshadowed by the growing realization that it would be Bolívar, and not the delegates, who would write the constitution of the new state. This made it difficult for Bolivia, as a quasi-monarchical state linked to the Andean empire, to play a key role in forming a republican alliance against the Brazilian monarchy. There was another, even more basic obstacle to Bolivia playing the role of challenger: The delegates to the assembly distrusted the motives of Peru and Argentina as much as the motives of the Brazilian monarchy. Bolivia as an independent state would be wedged between three more powerful and potentially hostile states. Bolivia's security seemed to lie not in republican unity vis à vis the monarchy but in the maintenance of a balance of power.

At the crucial Potosí negotiations, Bolívar, in effect, vetoed a role for Bolivia in the alliance with Argentina against Brazil thereby dashing Sucre's alliance plan but also unleashing raw Argentine geopolitical pressure on Bolivia, the first move toward converting Bolivia into a buffer state. By failing to lead the republican alliance against Brazil (with Bolivia being the equal of Argentina), Bolivia became an object of not only Argentine depredations but those of all of the rest of its neighbors. No distinctions were to made between the encroachments of the Brazilians and the encroachments of fellow Spanish-American states; this was about territorial aggrandizement and balances of power, not ideology and republican solidarity.

Divided Purpose of Bolivian Statehood

The imposition of Bolívar's constitutional fiat in Upper Peru conflicted fundamentally with the politics of liberation that Sucre was trying to develop. The seed of the project was planted by the activities of Santa Cruz in Upper Peru. He saw a Bolivarian constitution for Upper Peru as a way of fending off annexation to Argentina or an outright declaration of independence. He harbored a militant antipathy toward Argentine efforts to draw Upper Peru into that state's orbit. The Bolivarian constitution, since it would be written by Bolívar as dictator of Peru, would in effect amalgamate the two Perus under Bolívar, exactly what Santa Cruz wanted. The idea that Upper Peru should become an independent state struck him as chimerical. Based on a specious argument, advanced by the creole academics and lawyers based in Chuquisaca, the *audiencia* was alleged to be the historic progenitor of an Upper Peruvian sovereignty. As a *paceño* (inhabitant of La Paz), Santa Cruz was naturally suspicious of the "doctors" of Chuquisaca. But it was likewise difficult for him to identify with the nationalism of the people of La Paz. He had been a loyalist officer during the first stages of the rebellion at La Paz in 1809 and participated in the repression. His father was killed by the rebellious citizenry in 1814 during the course of its resistance to the Peruvian viceroyalty's efforts to control the city.[1]

Andrés Santa Cruz was born in La Paz in 1788. His father was a Spanish loyalist and military officer. His mother was a full-blooded Aymara Indian. He had high cheekbones and wiry black hair parted on the side. In his youth, Santa Cruz's face was very gaunt, an aspect that was offset by a pleasant, quizzical countenance and a mouth on which there was the permanent trace of a smile. He was very reserved in manner and elliptical in utterance. He was reticent, suspicious and elusive—acquired traits, perhaps, that are typical of any conquered population like the Aymara. The fact that during the formative period of his career he was an Upper Peruvian among Peruvians, Argentines, Colombians, and Chileans caused Santa Cruz to have to walk a razor's edge; the need to change his ground and hedge his bets came with the territory.

After a brief period of study in a seminary in Cuzco, Santa Cruz opted for a military career in the king's service and joined the army that Viceroy Abascal had sent to crush the rebellion in La Paz. He saw extensive action with this army, fighting against both the Argentines and the Upper Peruvian guerrillas. The Argentines took him prisoner in 1817 and transported him to detention centers in Tucumán from where he escaped and fled to Rio de Janeiro by sea. For him at this time, the Brazil of the Braganzas was friendly territory, and Argentina was enemy territory. He made his way to Lima and enlisted in the service of the viceroy only to be captured again by the Argentines—this time by San Martín's forces in southern Peru. He saw the light during this second captivity. In some sense his mother's nativism may have won out over his father's Hispanicism. In any case, he abandoned the royalist cause and offered his services to San Martín, who accepted them. From that base, he started to work toward his goal of uniting the two Perus.[2]

Ironically, his first assignment led him away from Upper Peru. He was ordered to northern Peru to quell a royalist revolt in the provinces. San Martín then ordered Santa Cruz to lead a battalion of Peruvian troops to Ecuador in order to assist Sucre in the liberation of Quito. He did this, as we saw, despite the embarrassing counterorders from San Martín, instructing him to avoid collaboration with Sucre and concentrate on liberating Guayaquil so that it remained free of possible Colombian annexation. In fact, Santa Cruz questioned these orders and argued with Lima that the success of the campaign against Quito should take precedence over fighting over Guayaquil's status. After the victory at Pichincha, and despite Sucre's contemptuous attitude toward him, Santa Cruz was openly solicited by Bolívar while both men were at Quito. They surely discussed Bolívar's coming to Peru to take over the war. Judging from his later correspondence with Bolívar, Santa Cruz encouraged him in their Quito talks to do so and apparently agreed to retire his battalion from Ecuador without occupying Guayaquil as he had been ordered to do by Lima. He ignored these orders and gave Bolívar a free hand in Guayaquil, while he returned with his men to Lima. He had already written San Martín off, and he was beginning to structure his behavior on the assumption that the Colombians would replace the Argentines in Peru, a change he by no means disfavored.[3]

During 1825, Santa Cruz acted in concert with Bolívar on the matter of joining Upper Peru to Peru. He was more optimistic than Sucre concerning Bolívar's political future in Peru. Santa Cruz felt that the continuation of Bolívar's dictatorship in Peru was necessary in order to consolidate that nation and to set the stage for the joining together of the two Perus. He was very disappointed that Bolívar had bothered to convoke the Peruvian congress in 1825, much less allow it to discuss the longevity of the dictatorship.[4]

In Santa Cruz's view, Bolívar's authority provided a bridge between Peru and Upper Peru. Divided, both would be weak and vulnerable states, especially Upper Peru because of its isolated and virtually landlocked position. United, they could be a formidable power on the South American continent. He thought that the two countries should draw themselves together under Bolívar's authority and begin to consolidate themselves as a single Bolivarian nation. The reunification of the two

Perus provided the essential objective of Santa Cruz's extraordinary political and military career, which lasted until January 20, 1839.[5]

Santa Cruz had arrived in Upper Peru after the invasion and began to observe with growing skepticism the political process started there by Sucre's decree. He felt the decree was ill advised. He hesitated about participating in the assembly even though he was elected as a delegate from La Paz. Sucre argued that he should honor the La Paz election and serve. He was, after all, a native of Upper Peru. Santa Cruz, however, invoked his Peruvian citizenship as the reason for demurring and appealed to Bolívar's wishes in the matter. Bolívar instructed Santa Cruz not to become compromised in the assembly because, as he explained to Sucre, "he [Santa Cruz] was in a position to perfectly serve the cause of Upper and Lower Peru."[6]

Santa Cruz arrived in Chuquisaca after a brief stay in La Paz. As a Peruvian citizen, he announced to Sucre that he would exile himself from Upper Peru if the provinces were joined to Argentina. From this declaration, Sucre wrote Bolívar, "You can deduce his ideas." Sucre portrayed Santa Cruz's outlook as dogmatically Peruvianist.[7]

Santa Cruz did not serve in the assembly, but he monitored the debates and conveyed reports to Bolívar. He saw that a decision in favor of creating an independent state was a foregone conclusion. The "better minds" in the assembly would favor incorporation to Peru, he said, but a "mania for liberty" was likely to prevail and create a rush to independence. "They don't want to be even under the sky," he commented. Only Bolívar's authority could hold in check the political recklessness of a recently liberated people. "I will chart my course on this premise," he wrote to a Peruvian friend, "and I will stick to it until the Liberator arrives."[8]

While Santa Cruz scrutinized, the delegates debated the question of whether Upper Peru could exist safely and viably as an independent state. What if Brazil, backed by the Holy Alliance should attempt another invasion? There were other tiers of problems. Upper Peru lacked a port on its seacoast to take the place of the Peruvian port of Arica. It lacked a navy and an army. The frontier with Peru was almost impossible to garrison. Were the necessary state-building resources present? This question involved not just material resources for security and prosperity, but also the moral resources. Were there enough patriotism and public spirit available in this Indian-dominated, hinterland society to make statehood meaningful? Were there great men available to undertake the challenges of public administration and staff the offices of state? Would the climate of independence elicit virtue and foment leadership qualities, or would it simply cement anarchy?[9]

Some delegates, who saw Upper Peru as deficient in state-building resources, argued that separate statehood for Upper Peru would deny it "that degree of respect which is required in order for other states to recognize it and leave it to the peaceful enjoyment of its rights." But the majority tended to emphasize the patriotic grit displayed by Upper Peru during the *quincenio* years of warfare against the occupation forces of Spain, Peru, and Argentina. As for the problems of security and dearth of political and administrative talent, all states at their founding, including many which were currently in full bloom, faced these same problems.[10]

It was expected that Upper Peruvian statehood would raise problems with Argentina. To be sure, Argentina seemed to sanction the idea. Its May 9 law certainly went much further in that direction than Peru had gone publicly. At the same time, even the May 9 law contained some subtle reminders that Upper Peru had been a part of the Plata Viceroyalty. It was no secret that the *porteños* felt they had proprietary rights in the Upper Peruvian provinces. A rumor even circulated in the assembly that Rivadavia was in London selling the mines of Upper Peru and letting out contracts. It was also quite apparent to the delegates that Argentina needed the Upper Peruvian markets. An independent Upper Peru that managed its European trade through its own port on the Pacific would deal a crucial blow to the Buenos Aires port. In Olañeta's view, which he conveyed to Bolívar, the separation of Upper Peru from Argentina would lead to the economic ruin of Buenos Aires, and the *porteños* could be expected to evade it by all means fair and foul. He warned Bolívar to be on guard against the bad faith of the *porteño* delegates sent to treat with him.[11]

Despite Sucre's efforts to capitalize on Argentina's May 9 law, fears persisted that it was a ploy; that "the generous expressions of the Argentine Republic might have been made with the object of letting us become dependent only on ourselves in order to attack us on the slightest pretext."[12]

On the other hand, Peru was seen as a potential military threat to Upper Peru if the latter became a separate state. The national army of Peru had been swelled by the incorporation of the defeated Spanish regiments, many of which had combat experience in Upper Peru. Its army was more feared than Argentina's. Whereas the threat from Argentina was expected to be subtle and indirect, the threat from Peru, like that from Brazil, was perceived as military in nature. "Bolivia is surrounded," Olañeta wrote Bolívar, "by two powerful states and one bent upon intrigue."[13]

Yet the assembly attitudes toward Peru were by no means completely negative. Some delegates argued that it was precisely by pooling its resources with those of Peru that Upper Peru "could achieve all that it did not have." The capital of the enlarged Peruvian state could be located at Arequipa or Cuzco to eliminate the problem of Upper Peru's distance from Lima.[14]

Many delegates perceived a dilemma from which the only escape was statehood. Joining Argentina would offend Bolívar. Joining Peru would offend Argentina. The only way out was separation from both, in which case neither had to be feared: "[Peru] because the power of our Liberators will contain its ambition and [Argentina] because it has solemnly protested that it will recognize and respect our deliberations." This theme of protection by the liberators was repeatedly invoked as the discussion moved toward declaring independence from both Argentina and Peru. The reputations and power of Sucre and Bolívar inspired crucial confidence in the idea of Upper Peruvian statehood. The two men were both praised, but Sucre was eulogized as the "noble instrument of the political existence of Upper Peru." Moreover, Sucre's opening address to the assembly was perceived as an invitation to declare statehood by identifying Upper Peruvian interests with the creation of an "equilibrium of power among the states which form" South America. This idea was was an echo of Sucre's Yungay letter.[15]

On August 6, the delegates signed a declaration of emancipation from Spain. It was also declared that Upper Peru would "not ... associate itself with any of the neighboring states but (would) instead erect itself as a sovereign state independent of all other nations, whether of the Old World or the New." The fifteen-year struggle of the *republiquetas* proved Upper Peru's desire for freedom and that tradition was profusely invoked in the declaration.[16]

Sucre's decree provided the obvious source of authority for making the statehood decision, but it could not be cited as such. This would give it an ascendancy over the Arequipa decree of Bolívar, which the assembly feared would affront the Liberator and complicate Sucre's relations with him. It was to be hoped that Bolívar would retract his Arequipa decree, at which time Sucre's decree could be elevated to its proper position. In the meantime, the May 9 law of Argentina would have to act as a surrogate for Sucre's decree, by providing the legal spark of the Upper Peruvian state. Neither Sucre's or Bolívar's decrees were mentioned in the declaration.

The sentiment in the assembly was overwhelmingly republican. It was also constitutive. Thus, the declaration of independence prominently said in the operative paragraph that "its irrevocable vow (*voto*) is to govern themselves by themselves, and be under a Constitution, laws and authorities which they themselves give to themselves and believe to be most conducive to their future felicity as a nation."[17]

The problem here again was the Arequipa decree. The assembly wanted to begin legislating and drawing up a republican constitution, without having to await Peruvian approval of statehood. Accordingly, a decision was made to send a delegation to Bolívar to press him to abrogate the Arequipa decree. In the meantime, the assembly on the constitutive question limited itself to a resolution stating that the country would adopt a republican form of government, unitarian and possessing a tripartite separation of powers. Efforts to placate Bolívar by including language and clauses that explicitly acknowledged the Arequipa decree were expunged in the expectation of success in getting Bolívar to suspend the decree. Bolívar would therefore have to be placated in other ways. On August 11, the assembly decreed these further actions: The new state was to be known as the Republic of Bolívar; supreme executive power was vested in Bolívar during the time of his stay in Bolivia; Chuquisaca was renamed Sucre; portraits were to be painted, medals struck, and equestrian statues cast in honor of Sucre and Bolívar. In addition, one million pesos were to be "opportunely" distributed to the liberating army as prize money.[18]

The redeeming feature, which Santa Cruz identified in the delegates' declaration of independence was the expressed willingness to place their statehood in Bolívar's hands. The eulogies of Bolívar that emanated from the assembly—intended to cajole him, to be sure, into revoking his Arequipa decree—were nevertheless reassuring to Santa Cruz. He cultivated this sentiment among the delegates and took it upon himself, unquestionably in response to a suggestion from Bolívar, to suggest that the delegates really show their confidence in Bolívar by inviting him to write a constitution. He thought that his suggestion would be accepted. However, it was discussed and rejected as an undue restriction on the sovereignty of the assembly.[19]

The decision to send a delegation to Bolívar was made in a secret session the day before the signing of the declaration of independence. The purpose of the mission was publicly to praise Bolívar and to extract from him the cancellation of the Arequipa decree. Failing that, the mission should consult whether the assembly could proceed to draft legislation and flesh out a system of public administration for the country.

On August 15, José María Mendízabal and Casimiro Olañeta were appointed to the mission and fully instructed. Sucre was to be publicly eulogized at length as the "great father of the country" and Bolívar (more laconically) for his "heroic services." According to the articles governing the private talks, Bolívar was to be assured that he also had a "great part" in the decision for statehood, despite the May 16 decree, which was to be attributed to Bolívar's political compromises in Peru. But because of changed circumstances, namely the declaration of statehood on August 6, the original reasons for the Arequipa decree "ceased to exist (Article 1)." If Bolívar agreed to suspend the Arequipa decree, he should declare the assembly constitutive (Article 2). Should he not consent, then the person left in charge of Bolivia after Bolívar left should operate within a provisional constitutional framework which the assembly "or" Bolívar could draft (Article 3). Bolívar should immediately appoint a representative to Argentina to ensure that government did not change its mind on the May 9 law (Article 4). Arica should be ceded by Peru to Bolivia and Bolívar should press the Peruvian congress on this question (Article 5). Sucre should stay on in Bolivia "some years" with the status and powers that the assembly determined to give him (Article 6).[20]

Santa Cruz became alarmed that these instructions did not include the invitation to write a constitution. He called the omission to the attention of the assembly and succeeded in having the invitation added to the instructions of the delegation. Santa Cruz brought this addition to Sucre's attention. He conceded that some delegates opposed giving Bolívar the right of constitutional fiat over Bolivia. But he argued that the invitation was "so useful and convenient for Upper Peru" and the opposition of "a few bad delegates" should not be credited. That the delegates were made aware by Santa Cruz that Bolívar was expecting to be asked to write the constitution also apparently helped them change their minds on the subject.[21]

Two members of the La Paz delegation to the assembly, Fermín Eyzaguirre and Eusébio Gutiérrez, acted as Santa Cruz's allies in the assembly, although only Gutiérrez actually voted against statehood. They reintroduced the motion to discuss the constitution-writing question and Bolívar. Unquestionably Gutiérrez, like Santa Cruz, saw that Bolívar writing Bolivia's constitution was, in fact, a method for tying Bolivia to Peru. Despite objections that the matter had already been discussed, it was again discussed. This time it ended in a vote to add to the mission's instructions the article asking Bolívar to write a constitution for Bolivia. Santa Cruz's intervention evidently made the difference, along with some new arguments that the assembly would not be really abrogating its sovereignty if it reserved the right to make changes in the constitution (or even reject it). The gains for the Bolivian state in terms of the luster and prestige of having the Bolivarian imprimatur stamped on it were considered, in the final analysis, to outweigh the cost of alienating the constitutional prerogative. An equally important gain would be the deepening of Bolívar's commitment to Bolivia, so important to securing Colombia's protection and the continuation of Sucre in the country. By the same token, Peru's readiness to accept Bolivian independence would appear to be enhanced; it was unlikely that the Peruvian congress would insult the Liberator by refusing to recognize a nation that bore the emblem of his own constitutional handiwork.[22]

Santa Cruz was pleased with the final state of opinion in the assembly. He wrote Bolívar that naming the new state the Republic of Bolívar and extending the invitation to write a constitution bore "testimony that the majority of the delegates saw that they cannot better assure Bolivia's political existence than by invoking your authority and they have done so, not only for advice and protection but also for drafting the laws of the state."[23]

For Sucre, however, the method to "assure Bolivia's political existence" was that of alliance with Argentina based on framing a challenge to the Brazilian monarchy. He therefore anxiously awaited Buenos Aires' response to his alliance proposal.

Bolívar's Move Against Sucre's Policy

Brazil's invasion of Chiquitos and the opportunity that "arose" for him to draft a constitution for Upper Peru related to two different images of Brazil in Bolívar's thinking. The Chiquitos invasion should rightly lead, if Sucre were correct, toward forging an alliance with the Argentines against the monarchy in Brazil in the name of republican solidarity. In this first image, the Colombian *liberation* of Upper Peru would take the form of its conversion into a self-proclaimed independent republic and its role as such in the war against Brazil at Argentina's side. In the second image, a Colombian political occupation of Upper Peru, taking the form of Bolívar's quasi-monarchic constitution, would signal the accommodation of the Brazilian monarchy. This accommodation would be later buttressed by joining Peru and Bolivia together each under its Bolivian constitution, thereby creating the Empire of the Andes (which Colombian might then be added to). This structure would duplicate the Brazilian empire thus constituting the twin pillars of the South American system.

Bolívar's thinking gravitated toward the second image. Rather than challenging the monarchy in Brazil, he became more interested in emulating it in the constitution he wanted to write for Upper Peru, thereby setting an example for the other states of South America. The imposition of Bolívar's constitutional fiat in Upper Peru conflicted fundamentally with the politics of the liberation that Sucre was trying to develop.

For Bolívar, the basic problem presented by the Chiquitos invasion was whether the it was part of Brazilian expansionism directed by the Holy Alliance against the Spanish-American republics. If so, it warranted the creation of a countersystem of Spanish-American republics united in an alliance against Brazil and the principle of legitimacy. Sucre was clearly trying to build the response to the invasion as if this were the case. By making the plan to invade the empire, fomenting republican principles within it, and postulating a connection between the expansionism of Brazil in the Eastern Bank and the Chiquitos invasion, Sucre was ruling out the Chiquitos invasion as a local matter. Bolívar, however, wanted to treat the invasion as a local matter and avoid making what might be a gratuitous challenge to the Holy Alliance. But he could not be certain that Sucre's view of the invasion was not the correct one; that the invasion was a legitimate occasion to begin shaping a republican alliance against the monarchy. The pattern of Bolívar's thinking concerning the Chiquitos invasion was revealed in four letters he wrote in Arequipa in May and June 1825.

In one letter from Arequipa to Santander, Bolívar included a copy of the "barbarous and insolent demands of the Portuguese commander." He said that General Sucre replied in similar terms, "impelled, no doubt, by the indignation that such an abominable atrocity must have aroused in him. Nevertheless I do not approve of such rejoinders. The outbreak of a new war would benefit no one." Elaborating, he said that

> the Holy Alliance ... could not have advised his [Pedro's] hostile act, which can only destroy their commerce and injure their cause. By his actions, therefore, he actually risks losing his throne. Hence, I conclude that the invasion of Chiquitos is an absurd and rash act that was committed by the commander Araujo. If it originated with the Emperor, without counsel from the Holy Alliance, the matter is a piece of folly and of no consequence. But if it was prompted by the Holy Alliance, then it is of the utmost gravity and importance. If the latter is true, we must prepare ourselves for a long conflict with the greater part of Europe. I believe the first thing we must do, if the Holy Alliance mixes in our affairs, is to have Peru and Buenos Aires occupy Brazil immediately.[24]

At the same time, Bolívar wrote Sucre that according to his reading of the European and South American newspapers, and his own correspondence, he found it hard to believe that "Brazil's aggression was a project of [Pedro's] Court or an effect of the principles of the Holy Alliance initiated in America by the Emperor of Brazil." He therefore "prohibited" Sucre from launching an invasion of Brazil and limited him to securing Upper Peruvian territory. "Bear in mind," he wrote Sucre, "that the Holy Alliance will exploit the least move made by the governments of the American states in order to attribute to us ambitious and extensive designs to destroy the only throne that exists in America." Bolívar's main concern here was that Sucre was getting out of control in Upper Peru. In this letter, he essentially sought to reposition Sucre's policy in Upper Peru within the framework of his Arequipa decree, on which the ink was barely dry.[25]

But, Bolívar pursued the thought that Sucre's view of the invasion might in fact be the right one and that he might indeed have to get involved in a coalitional war against Brazil. The fact that Iturbide by this time had been overthrown in Mexico and killed and that a republican system had been adopted there, may have moved Bolívar more toward accepting the formation of a republican alliance against "the only throne in America" as the only basis for unifying Spanish America: The Chiquitos invasion might have to serve as the *casus belli* for the republics. This train of thought is reflected in his letter on the Chiquitos invasion that he wrote from Arequipa to the Mexican foreign minister. He observed in it that the Chiquitos invasion made it necessary to accelerate the creation of the confederation of American states in Panama on the grounds of opposing the monarchy in Brazil and the threat to the republican principles of Spanish America. He represented the Chiquitos invasion as "an almost certain indication of the opposition of the [Brazilian] Empire to the existence of our republics. If, as might be conjectured, the policy of the Holy Alliance is operating through Brazil, the interest and the existence itself of [the Spanish-American republics] invites us to close ranks, to form a common pact and put up a united front against our enemies."[26]

The criterion of analysis that Bolívar was using concerning the Chiquitos invasion was clearly revealed in his fourth letter from Arequipa to the Peruvian council of state which he told, in effect, that the scenario of his Arequipa decree might have to be forgotten because of the events in Chiquitos. If Upper Peru was on the cutting edge of the republican alliance against Brazil and the Holy Alliance, then to manage its statehood question in the framework of the Arequipa decree would be inordinately parochial and even irrelevant. But before any definite judgement on this question could be made, it was necessary to explore the politics of the republican alliance against Brazil. That meant finding out: (1) how Britain would view a war of the republics against Brazil, if it took place; (2) whether the Holy Alliance was implicated in the Chiquitos invasion; (3) whether the invasion was done on orders from Pedro; (4) and if so, whether, he was counting on the support of the Holy Alliance to back-up the invasion. British envoys in all of the American capitals should be sounded out assiduously on these questions.[27]

Even as he entertained these thoughts, Bolívar's "image" of the Brazilian monarchy underwent a definite change. Early in 1825, he was willing to see the monarchy linked with the Holy Alliance in a deadly conspiracy to wipe the republican idea off the face of the South American continent. He was apocalyptic in his prediction of a struggle in South America that would end up as a global contest for supremacy between the forces of constitutionalism and the forces of legitimacy. Much of this was rhetoric intended, partly, to jolt Santander. But when he said in a calmer vein that "the Holy Alliance and Brazil are one, and if we the free people of South America do not form another we are lost," he seemed to mean it.[28]

Upon further analysis, however, Bolívar concluded that what was going to happen in Brazil depended on the outcome of a duel arranged between Great Britain and the Holy Alliance for control over Pedro's monarchy. The issue of that contest was in doubt for Bolívar through the middle of 1825. All that was clear was that a schizoid element was being instilled in Pedro; he was inclined in both directions at the same time, "which creates a monster."

> He [Pedro] professes mortal hatred of our republics in the name of the Holy Alliance, and he is proud of English protection. ... [The British] want to patronize him for reasons of their convenience. Britain wants to dominate Portugal through Brazil and Brazil through Portugal and for that purpose is a friend of the one and the other. The Holy Alliance wants Pedro for ideological reasons, England for convenience."[29]

By July 1825, Bolívar strongly favored the view that it was British "convenience" and not Holy Alliance "ideology" that was going to win over Pedro. He was in no doubt of this if the British could deliver Portugal's acceptance of Brazilian independence. In Bolívar's view the turning point came when the British mission to Lisbon led by Charles Stuart succeeded in extracting from John, in early 1825, a commitment to sign a treaty acknowledging Brazil's independence. This represented an enormous step forward in Canning's policy of positioning a national, constitutional monarchy securely on the South American continent. Having engineered Portugal's concession of Brazilian independence, Britain had established itself as Pedro's chief benefactor instead of the Holy Alliance. Canning was convinced that this was true and felt that the Spanish Americans should be grateful. Bolívar, for one, was.[30]

That the Stuart mission was successful was apparent to Bolívar by June 1825. Thus, Bolívar informed Santander that thanks to Stuart "the Emperor has good reason to be proud, and to expect much from the British." Stuart, in fact, was en route to Rio with a draft treaty signed by John which effectively conferred independence on Brazil. That treaty was signed, under the conspicuous auspices of Stuart, on August 9, 1825. The success of Stuart's mission to Lisbon was known to Bolívar before he encountered the Argentine delegation at Potosí. A letter from Funes, dated August 26, reported to Bolívar the treaty signed in Rio on the ninth, which Funes characterized as being "designed to minimize Pedro's political relations with the Holy Alliance." Bolívar used this letter in the actual talks at Potosí with the Argentine delegation. It can therefore be established that he was aware of the independence treaty while he was in Potosí. In fact, Funes's letter arrived on October 20.[31]

For Bolívar, the prospect of a conspiracy between the Holy Alliance and Brazil against the republics was radically diminished because of the momentum of British diplomacy and the treaty coup scored in Rio on August 9. Bolívar, however, used another barometer of the depth of Pedro's involvement with the Holy Alliance: the sequel to the Chiquitos invasion.

As we saw, Bolívar's initial reaction to the invasion was guarded; he saw Sucre's plan for an invasion as reckless. However, we know also that Bolívar saw the Chiquitos invasion as a test case of the Holy Alliance's influence in Brazil. If Pedro stood behind the invasion and, in fact, had ordered it, there could be little doubt that he felt that he had the Holy Alliance backing. If such were the case, Bolívar was fully prepared to capitalize on Sucre's initiative and to lead the Spanish-American states against Brazil as part of a global coalition of republican forces against legitimist forces.[32]

When news of the Chiquitos invasion appeared in the newspapers in Rio, Condy Raguet, the U. S. Consul, commented that "[s]hould Bolívar have the inclination to make common cause with the United Provinces of La Plata in a war against Brazil, he will probably find abundant justification for such a course, in the occurrence of" the imperial army's incursion into Chiquitos. But, according to Raguet, Pedro was stage managing this event. He commented on the tardiness with which the imperial government officially acknowledged the Chiquitos invasion—not until August 6, four days after newspaper reports of it arrived in Rio from Buenos Aires. On that day, an official disavowal was issued. But the government was in possession of reports from Matto Grasso dated April 15, although he was not certain how long it had them before its disavowal. But Raguet's contacts voiced suspicions that "the municipal Government of Matto Grasso would never have ventured upon so hazardous an exploit as the invasion of Peru, without orders from Superior authority, furnished before the month of February at a time when the last advices from the country [Peru] represented the republican cause to be tottering and the Royal arms [in Peru] in a situation to be benefitted by the aid and cooperation of the imperial army." In his previous dispatch, Raguet reported the arrival of Canning's envoy, Stuart, in Rio on July 17 and the intense effort he was making to mediate Brazilian independence as part of Canning's effort to avoid a conflict between Brazil and the Spanish-American republics. It is plausible to speculate that Stuart's activities had something to do with the official disavowal of Chiquitos invasion which was published in the Rio press on August 6. It stated that the invasion was "opposed to the generous and liberal principles upon which His Majesty has established the policy of his cabinet, and to the intention not to interfere in the actual contest of the inhabitants of Spanish America, among themselves or with the Metropolis." Clearly, Pedro wanted to downplay the Chiquitos affair. He publicly reprimanded the responsible officers. Additionally, he sent a personal apology to Bolívar and included with it a copy of the official disavowal. By doing this, Pedro was clearly attempting to discourage Bolívar from any thought of retaliating against him.[33]

Although there had been some reports of imperial troop movements in Mato Grasso in response to Sucre's escalation, the Brazilians had promptly withdrawn their forces across the border. Sucre had to admit, as early as June, that the invasion was probably a caprice of the local Brazilian commander. By the time of the Potosí talks, both he and Bolívar had agreed that their policy in Chiquitos should be to remain in a state of observation pending determination of whether Pedro had actually ordered the invasion. But it was clear to them that the Chiquitos invasion was losing credibility as a reason for war and Sucre so told Funes, much to the latter's disappointment. Sucre's attempt to link incursion into Chiquitos with Pedro's reoccupation of the Eastern Bank, lost its plausibility from Bolívar's point of view. He increasingly felt that the Chiquitos invasion should be adjudicated in Panama instead of being treated as a republican *casus belli*.[34]

In the meantime, he began to assemble materials for his Bolivian constitution.

⚬

Bolívar was determined to contribute to the political reconciliation of South America with the Old World now that the independence of the whole continent was achieved. What this meant, for Bolívar, was that the political systems of the republics should be voluntarily slanted in a direction acceptable to the Old World—that is, away from democracy and toward aristocratic and hereditary principles—now that they were no longer under the gun of the Holy Alliance. Bolívar was impressed with a comment made by the French ambassador to Canning to the effect that the British and the Holy Alliance should join together in encouraging the South American republics to adopt at least aristocratic systems of government. He had instructed the Colombian agent in London to encourage the Holy Alliance to think that "mixed governments of aristocracy and democracy" were indeed possible all over South America, and that he, Bolívar, was not above leading the cause to "reform our constitutions."[35] It was in Bolivia that his leadership in "reforming our constitutions" would commence. Writing to Santander about his thoughts on the Bolivian constitution, he announced that "it would be liberal but it would be strong—it will have something of lifetime (*vitalicia*) rule in it."[36]

Bolívar used various models for his Bolivian constitution—Plato's Republic, the papal and conciliar structures of the Roman Catholic Church, the British parliamentary monarchy, the Haitian life-time presidency, the Napoleonic code, and the Spanish constitution of 1812.[37] But the most crucial political tie was to the Brazilian constitution of 1824. By building quasi-monarchical features in to the Bolivian constitution, Bolívar was making, in effect, a bridge between Spanish-American states and the Brazilian monarchy. The Bolivian constitution said, in effect, that the Brazilian monarchy was not part of the problem; it was part of the solution that Spanish-American states must strive toward themselves.

A strong circumstantial case can be made that Bolívar had studied the Brazilian constitution prior to drafting the Bolivian constitution. It is probable that Bolívar had a copy of the Brazilian constitution shown to him at Cuzco by Facundo Infante, a Spanish liberal military officer who had traveled overland in 1824 from Rio de Janeiro to Upper Peru. He had fled to avoid being arrested by Sucre and surfaced at Cuzco, where he held extensive talks with Bolívar who was at the time en route to La Paz from Lima. Possibly, Bolívar interrogated Infante about his impressions of Pedro's government in Rio and the outlook for the new Brazilian constitution. Infante somehow completely won Bolívar's confidence, and Bolívar determined to make use of him in shaping the new political order in Upper Peru. Infante returned with Bolívar to La Paz, where Bolívar presented him to Sucre as a person of indispensable talents for shaping the political future of Upper Peru. In fact, Infante became the second most powerful person, after Sucre, in the government Sucre organized after Bolívar departed the country in early 1826. Infante played a key role in gaining Bolivian acceptance of Bolívar's constitution, especially the controversial lifetime presidency feature. In the meantime, Infante was placed on Bolívar's general staff, and he played a key role in discouraging Bolívar from waging a war against Brazil if that meant an invasion of the empire by way of Matto Grasso.[38]

There are, to be sure, differences between the Brazilian constitution and the Bolivian constitution. The Brazilian document created an overt monarchy with all of the court trappings, ceremonial protocols, noble orders, and ecclesiastic support. It also tacitly sanctioned slavery by not mentioning it. The Bolivian constitution eschewed all of these arrangements. It clearly intended, however, to form a political aristocracy by virtue of the hereditary and ascriptive features with which it endowed public offices. It adumbrated the features of the political occupation model.[39] The chief feature of the Brazilian constitution—the "moderating power" of the emperor—is reproduced in the powers of the lifetime Bolivian president. He is described by Bolívar as the "sun" around which the whole system revolves and from which it draws sustenance and stability.[40]

Sucre was supremely embarrassed by the lifetime feature of the presidency. It was a supreme irony, given his own republican predilections, that when Bolívar's constitution was adopted by the Bolivians in July 1826, Sucre became the "President for life of the new country"—a fact that the Rivadavia press in Argentina made use of to "prove" that Sucre was Bolívar's stooge and that a Bolivarian dynasty was in the making in Bolivia. Sucre had no choice in the matter. Bolívar insisted that he occupy the lifetime presidency as a means of coordinating the country with Peru, where Bolívar intended to have the same constitution adopted in place of his dictatorship. These two Bolivarian nations would then invite Colombia to join them as a third—once it had adopted the Bolivian constitution also. The Bolivians, although supremely unhappy about the lifetime feature of their new constitution, were anxious to lock Bolívar's enormous prestige and protection into their new country and to gain Peru's acceptance of their statehood. Bolívar assured Sucre of Peruvian recognition of Bolivia, on the condition that his constitution was adopted. The Bolivians would hear of nobody but Sucre as their first president. He was their liberator and founding father. And who would have to worry about the lifetime presidency turning into a despotism with Sucre, the great, self-effacing republican, as its first occupant?[41]

Before Bolívar could effect the political occupation of Upper Peru by means of his constitution, the vestiges of Sucre's strategy of liberation needed to be eliminated. That strategy pointed Upper Peru away from union with Peru and toward an alliance with Argentina against the Brazilian monarchy; away from the accommodation of the monarchy that the projected Bolivarian order was predicated upon, and toward a direct challenge to it. Bolívar effected the demolition of Sucre's strategy in the Potosí talks.

Failure of the Challenge at Potosí

After Bolívar concluded his negotiations with the delegation from the assembly in La Paz, he and Sucre, accompanied by staff and Bolívar's honor guard, left La Paz on September 20 for Potosí and the rendezvous with the delegation from Buenos Aires. The ride took about a week. They followed the old colonial road south across the moonscaped plateau (*altiplano*). Most of the towns and hamlets along the way contained small Indian communities. Oruro and Paria were larger, mining towns with considerable mestizo and Spanish residents.

At Paria, the trail began the ascent to Potosí. At nearby Porco, the Incas had worked mines to supply silver to the royal court at Cuzco. Biscayan adventurers from Spain worked them briefly until abandoning them for the richer veins of Potosí. They were worked sporadically afterward but were, like the rest of the mines in the three districts of La Paz, Oruro, and Potosí, idle and in most cases flooded. The cumulative effects of high duties imposed by the Spanish government, the Indian revolts of the early 1770s, the ravages of the fifteen years of war, and a general dearth of technology and capital had virtually paralyzed the industry by 1825. An enormous capital investment and overhaul were in order if the industry were to be revived and the spectacular mineral wealth of the country exploited.[42]

Bolívar spent some time at Oruro. In addition to listening to tales of woe from representatives of the local mining community, he took time to decide upon the negotiating line he would take with the Argentine delegation, which was expected to arrive at Potosí in mid-October. His attitude toward the *porteño* press was already colored by the racial slurs (the term "mulatto" was used to refer to Colombians, especially Venezuelans, including Bolívar) that cropped up regularly in editorials just as they had cropped up in the official press in Lima during San Martín's period. Bolívar's army was portrayed in the *porteño* press as a dusky version of the *montoneros* (from the Spanish word *montones* meaning large amorphous quantities), which had poured out of the provinces to engulf Buenos Aires in 1820. Bolívar was outraged that his victories in Peru over the Spanish received the execration of the *porteño* press instead of the patriotic praise they deserved. Particular issues of *Argos* and *El Nacional*, sent to him by Funes, raised the Bolívar's anger and caused him to order counterpolemics in the Lima newspapers. He wanted "these gentlemen" of Buenos Aires set straight about their accusations that he was scheming to find a way to take over Argentina by using as a pretext the war with Brazil. The article in the Peruvian press was to say that Bolívar was needed at home by Colombia and that "the Argentines can compose themselves without him since they are so ungrateful for Ayacucho." While he was at Oruro, Bolívar received a particular issue of *Argos* that made what he called a "bold-faced attack" on his Arequipa decree, saying in effect that it was a cover for controlling Bolivia through his Peruvian dictatorship. He also instructed Santa Cruz to start counterpolemics in the local newspapers of Upper Peru.[43]

Bolívar's party arrived at Potosí, stark and spectacular under its dome of blue sky, in the afternoon of October 5. Pedro García and Manuel Dorrego, were on hand to greet Bolívar. Dorrego gave letters from Funes to both Sucre and Bolívar. Díaz-Vélez and Alvear finally arrived in Potosí on the night of October 7. Their trip from Buenos Aires by mule and horseback, accompanied only by their secretary, had been a long and excruciating one.

Potosí came alive with the display of South American virility. "I found here," wrote an English traveller, "the illustrious Bolívar, the brave Sucre, the politic Alvear, the gallant Miller [prefect of Potosí], Generals Santa Cruz and Urdininea [an Upper Peruvian military figure active in the *quincenio*] ... a galaxy of military splendor and dazzling uniforms, which seemed to excite the highest admiration among, and to awaken the attractions of, the ladies of Potosí." This Englishman, one Captain Andrew, interviewed Bolívar, who greeted him "with a cordial, downright English shake of the hand." Bolívar was a man of enormous energy and a very rapid, incisive thought process. In interviews, he stabbed the air with his hand to emphasize points and spoke in clipped tones that increasingly resembled orders being given. His trait of avoiding eye contact bothered Captain Andrew "as the habit of any one not looking you fairly in the face in society is apt to do." He was further discomfited by the Bolívar's staccato speech and its monotonic quality. Bolívar seems to have lost his "urbanity," in Andrew's estimation; his personality had become "tinctured with the stormy, warlike, and singular character of the checkered scenes he had encountered." General Alvear, by contrast, was the quintessential *porteño*, "of athletic make, lofty carriage and handsome person. He is remarkably wellbred, and polished in manners. The united provinces of Río de la Plata could not have selected a better representative for (the) mission" of trying to win over Bolívar to their cause against the Brazilian monarchy.[44]

Andrew was more taken with Sucre than with Bolívar and he made inevitable comparisons. Bolívar "has been accused of ambitions toward absolute power. Time alone can settle this point. [However, Sucre] stands without blemish on his reputation." Sucre was not a handsome man physically; "unprepossessing" was the term Miller gently applied to Sucre's physiognomy. But Andrew found himself charmed by Sucre, even by his ineffable, plain face.

> General Sucre is about thirty-two (sic, thirty) years of age, of slender build, five feet eight in stature, of a dark and weather-beaten countenance; his visage is oval, eyes dark and his face lightly marked with small pox. The expression most prominent in his countenance to the observer, is benevolence, without anything to mark the qualities for which he is so distinguished. Yet his face is one which excites great interest in the observer at first glance, without his being able to tell why or to designate any particular character of it as the cause."[45]

Bolívar's opening contact with the delegation was not encouraging. A letter on the official stationery of the Republic of Peru from Bolívar's secretary informed them that Bolívar could not treat with them officially, since the foreign affairs authority of Peru was in the hands of the council of state in Lima and in Bogotá in the case of Colombia. The Liberator, however, would be glad to conduct private, informal talks with the delegates. These took place during the upcoming week.[46]

From the early talks, the two Argentines formed slightly different impressions of Bolívar's state of mind. Both found him almost obsessed by the attacks on him in the *porteño* press and suffering from wounded vanity. Díaz-Vélez felt that Funes had poisoned his mind against the *porteños*. Díaz-Vélez thought that Funes was "an old man, weak of character whom I believe sees his mission as one of flattering him [Bolívar] with stories which have a great effect when the will is prepared." Díaz-Vélez, however, steadfastly believed that Bolívar would rise above his dislike for Buenos Aires and join the fight against Brazil. Moreover he did not feel that Bolívar would do so in order to "intervene in our domestic affairs and to give them direction ... although perhaps he would not resist this temptation if we were overtaken by disaster." Alvear was less sure. Writing to García about Bolívar, he said that "he has been warned against all of you. You know that he has his eyes fixed on those [Argentine] provinces and tries to know by all means what is happening." Once Bolívar was in the fight against Brazil, restraining or deflecting his power from playing a role in Argentine domestic politics would not be easy. "You should keep in mind that the Liberator is of a very decisive character, determined, and enterprising beyond what is calculable. ... He is adored and obeyed by the Army and respected by the people. His voice is like an oracle which finds no resistance."[47]

The delegates opened the talks by urging the formation of an alliance of the republics against Brazil. Bolívar evaded that by alleging that he lacked authority to commit either Colombia or Peru; that furthermore, Colombia and Peru would not sign treaties with any American states until the Panama Assembly had perfected the American league rules. Alvear gamely noted that the United States was going to attend the conference, and it was not suspending its treaty-making rights. Bolívar retorted that he was adamantly opposed to the invitation of United States by the Colombian government and that he had made his displeasure known in Bogotá. Moreover, Bolívar maintained that instead of forming a coalition by treaties, any arrangements for united action against Brazil should be made under the auspices of the assembly in Panama. It was there that Argentina should make its case for continental support against Pedro. As anticipated in the instructions of the mission, Bolívar expressed considerable pique at the noncommittal attitude adopted by Buenos Aires toward the Panama Assembly.[48]

The two Argentines emphasized the gravity of the Chiquitos invasion and explored the possibility of Bolívar invading Brazil as an act of retaliation and without any formal coalitional arrangements among the republics. When Bolívar interposed possible British objections to a widening of the war against Brazil and cited evidence (including the public apology of Pedro that Bolívar showed to them) that the Chiquitos issue was petering out, the Argentine delegates suggested that Bolívar send an aide to Rio to press the Argentine cause, and demand formal satisfaction for the Chiquitos invasion and insist on the evacuation of the Eastern Bank by imperial forces. The delegates again returned to the desirability of forming a republican alliance to give force to the ultimatum to be delivered in Rio. It was imperative, they said, that the republics speak and act with one voice against Brazil.[49]

Alvear and Díaz-Vélez insisted to García that they stuck closely to the principle of their instructions. According to Bolívar, however, the line taken by the delegates was not so carefully construed to keep his power out or Argentina. They emphasized how weak Argentina was against Brazil and conceded the indispensability of Bolívar's help, without Argentine conditions. They apparently exceeded their instructions which, as we saw, emphasized the need to bring Bolívar into a formal, alliance framework. Bolívar gathered from these talks that "Buenos Aires is in the same state as Lima when they called me from Guayaquil and for this reason they are making me a thousand offers of leadership (*mando*) etc." The delegates told him that he should establish a "protectorate" of his own over all of South America as the only means of saving it from its evils, especially from the threat posed by the emperor of Brazil."[50]

Bolívar questioned whether the pleas for his entry into the war were shared by the Heras government. He was unenthusiastic about an attack on Brazil via Mato Grasso because of the deficiency of Chuiquitos as a *casus belli*. However, he despised Paraguayan dictator José Gaspar Francia for holding prisoner Aime Bonpland, the companion of Alexander von Humboldt, the German scientist-traveller. Bolívar said that he would be willing to invade Paraguay with his forces and position them for an attack on Brazil, in the event that Pedro's response to his ultimatum was not satisfactory. By this move, his army would draw nearer Brazil, but also nearer Argentina. Bolívar had learned from Funes that his effort to gain Heras's acceptance of this proposal had failed entirely. Heras had complained that the use of force to restore a province to the Argentine union would be embarrassing to the centralist's new strategy for uniting with the other Argentine provinces. Funes also stressed the enormous preoccupation that García exhibited over British disapproval of a war with Brazil, an observation that reinforced Bolívar's own analysis of British policy. In view of Heras's response to Funes, Bolívar had trouble accepting the sincerity of the delegation's professions that the closeness of Bolívar's power to Argentina would be no problem so long as it was moving nearer to Brazil. He said that keeping his military away from Argentina seemed to be more important to the *porteños*. Either that, or there were "two governments" in Buenos Aires: one the delegation was purporting to speak for and the official one.[51]

Alvear and Díaz-Vélez were thrown off guard by the Paraguay ploy of Bolívar. Trying to buy some time, they insisted that Funes had misunderstood the official position. But new instructions arrived from García reiterating that an invasion of Paraguay by Bolívar would be indeed politically unacceptable to Buenos Aires and that he should confine his miliary movements to the Brazilian border with Bolivia. Bolívar agreed to send an aide (O'Leary) to Rio with a demand for satisfaction over Chiquitos and with expression of support for Argentina in the Eastern Bank matter. He insisted that this mission, coupled with the appearance of his forces in Paraguay, would cause Pedro to back down. Alvear's response was polite; he could not tell Bolívar that new instructions arriving from García confirmed what Funes had already told Bolívar.[52]

Bolívar excluded Sucre from the bulk of his talks with Alvear and Díaz-Vélez. This was symptomatic of the tenuousness of the coalitional subject in the talks. Bolívar basically wanted to proceed under his Peruvian authority in the talks and stay within the framework of the Arequipa decree. Sucre's identification with his own decree, the whole matter of Bolivian independence, and his proposal for an Argentine alliance, would have been at cross purposes with Bolívar's approach in the talks. At one point Bolívar confided to the Argentines that Sucre "had been tricked (*engañado*) by the lawyers of Chuquisaca into issuing his decree" in the first place.[53]

Bolívar brought Sucre into the talks in their latter stage in order to respond to Alvear's claim that the agricultural province of Tarija rightfully belonged to Argentina whatever Bolivia's claims might be. That Alvear raised this as an issue signified that the talks had already rejected, as a serious possibility, Bolívar's entry into a war against Brazil; talk of forming a republican alliance against the monarchy became perfunctory. Tarija was the wedge for introducing a territorial basis for managing Argentine-Bolivian relations. This happened at the same time that challenging the monarchy in the name of a republican unity, backed by Bolívar's power, ceased to be the goal of the Bolivian-Argentine relationship.

The city of Tarija, and the neighboring district, was situated in the southern center of the *audiencia* of Upper Peru. Located in a fertile basin on a tributary of the Berméjo River, Tarija, like Chuquisaca and Cochabamba, came into existence as a "garden city" serving the recreational needs of the mining community at lofty Potosí. Francisco Pizarro's followers had originally settled in the Tarija basin, but the city was founded in 1574 by decree of the Peruvian viceroy. During all of the colonial period it was administered from Potosí. The attitudes and economic activities of the *tarijeños* were oriented toward Upper Peru, of which they felt themselves a part. These feelings sparked a protest when in February 14, 1807, by virtue of an edict of the Spanish crown, the administration of Tarija was transferred from the intendancy of Potosí to the Argentine provincial capital of Salta.[54]

The wishes of the local population were, in July 1825, strongly in favor of sending a delegation to the Chuquisaca Assembly and against sending one to participate in the national congress meeting at Buenos Aires. Sucre was so advised, as were the authorities at Salta. Notwithstanding the wishes of the local population, however, Tarija lay outside of the limits Bolivia could legally claim under the principle of the *uti possidetis* of 1810: The viceroyalty of the Plata, through Salta, had exercised the last colonial authority over Tarija.

Sucre had discussed with Arenales the question of Tarija since the time they had first met at Potosí. They agreed there to postpone any decisions until Bolívar arrived. In the meantime, Sucre, in response to a note from the *tarijeños* requesting him to remove by force an objectionable governor, ordered Colonel Burdett O'Connor, an intemperate Irishman in Colombia's service, to "look into this request and if you find merit in it, remove the governor of this province and put in another in his place." O'Connor arrived with only an aide, threw out the incumbent governor and named a new one "in the name of the [Bolivian] Republic."[55]

In the meantime, Arenales, much to Sucre's chagrin, agitated in Tarija to have a delegation sent to the national congress in Buenos Aires. In September 1824, Bolívar decided to occupy Tarija militarily pending the disposition of the matter in the Potosí talks. Sucre ordered O'Connor to occupy Tarija with a Peruvian unit under his command but to avoid the appearance of any political objective. "But since," he wrote him, "in the nature of things Tarija belongs to [Bolivia] you should foment opinions in favor of it being a dependency of Potosí, offering them improvements in their administration and stability, in order to keep them united to this country."[56]

From the outset of the talks at Potosí, the Argentines had indicated their government's willingness to recognize the political existence of Bolivia. But as it began to appear doubtful that Bolívar would join the war against Brazil, the Argentine delegates began to equivocate on this matter. They insisted that the province of Tarija be ceded to Argentina as a condition for recognition of Bolivia. Alvear indicated that in claiming only Tarija as the part of Bolivia that belonged to Argentina, Argentina was foregoing claims to any other part and this amounted to tacit recognition of the Bolivian state; laying claim only to Tarija thus reinforced what was already promised by Argentina in the May 9 law. Bolívar took this dubious argument at face value. Acting somewhat precipitously, he agreed, in the name of Bolivia, to recognize Argentine rights to Tarija. The Tarija cession was seen by Bolívar as a *quid pro quo* for Argentine recognition of Bolivian independence.[57]

When he was on the verge of making this deal with Alvear, Bolívar decided to call Sucre into the talks. Sucre already knew that Bolívar had dampened the Argentines' expectations concerning the war against the monarchy. In a sharp exchange with Alvear, Sucre argued that Tarija was the breadbasket of Bolivia; that opinion there favored joining Bolivia; that "foreign" control of Tarija would create potentially an enormous military disadvantage for Bolivia. Alvear responded, saying that Argentina was already weakened vis à vis Brazil by the separation of Upper Peru. It was the state in the most direct and dangerous position and the policy "of America" should be to strengthen it, not weaken it, "so it can serve as a formidable barrier to Brazil."[58]

The grappling of Sucre and Alvear over Tarija was indicative of a fundamental change that occurred at Potosí in the relations between Argentina and Bolivia. It became evident to Sucre and to Alvear that there would be no extension of Bolívar's power through Bolivia and into Argentina as a basis for widening the war against the monarchy. Their joint purpose in forming a Bolivian-Argentine alliance as a conduit for extending Bolívar's power in the direction of the monarchy therefore disappeared. As a result, the relations between Bolivia and Argentina began to intensify on a bilateral basis of competing geopolitical interests. Sucre adopted this new language. The Argentines betrayed a desire to exercise control over Bolivia through Tarija in order to prevent it from being absorbed into a Peruvian-based Bolivarian system. Alvear confessed to García that the talk about weakening Argentina as a bulwark against Brazil had been a smokescreen. Argentina needed to conserve Tarija in the "event that military operations" became necessary against Bolivia. He thought it was important that the government be made aware of Sucre's "mode of thinking" about Tarija. In his letter to García commenting on an Argentine mission currently in Santiago, Alvear stressed the need for a Chilean alliance in the war against Rio de Janeiro "or wherever else necessary." This phrase "wherever else" was a quintessential expression of a new order of things in which enmity began to be dispersed among the Spanish-American states according to their geopolitical rivalries. The political and ideological problem posed by the monarchy for the Spanish Americans was dissolved into this larger, more diffuse structure of power relations on the continent. It was clear that the "honeymoon" period in Argentine-Bolivian relations was over.[59]

A toast delivered by Bolívar at a public reception for Alvear and Díaz-Vélez made it clear that the monarchy of Pedro was not to be a *casus belli* for the Spanish-American republics. At noon on October 21, the two Argentines were escorted from their quarters to the Government House by Bolívar's honor guard. At the foot of the large stairway, Bolívar's personal secretary, Santiago Esteños, was waiting. He showed them up the stairs and into the banquet hall where Bolívar and Sucre stood side by side, with a group of Colombian and Peruvian officers at their back, and behind them the heads of the various civic and ecclesiastic corporations of Potosí and assorted notables.

Alvear opened with some brave remarks about the obnoxiousness of Pedro's regime, his aggressive policy, and the need for Bolívar to vindicate "American honor" by leading the coalitional attack against Pedro. Bolívar's answering toast was an elegant demurral. Pedro may have committed offenses against neighboring republics and even broken the "law of nations" but these events properly should evoke only "surprise" from Spanish Americans rather than morally uniting them against the monarchy. After all, Pedro was "an American prince, recently independent of Europe and a part of our noble insurrection for independence." Furthermore, and to his great credit, "he has erected his throne not on weak foundations (of European legitimacy) but rather on the indestructible basis of the sovereignty of the people and the sovereignty of the laws." Pedro's actions, while they were objectionable, especially his continued occupation of the East Bank, were not proof of the incompatibility between his regime and the other governments on the continent. Rather, those actions merely interrupted Pedro's "true destiny," which was to be a "friend of the neighboring republics."[60]

Bolívar intended his toast to demolish the moral basis for forming a republican cause against the empire. Bolívar told Santander that the reason for this "terrible answer" to Alvear's toast, was that in regard to the overall problem of Brazil, Canning was now in control. "Brazil will be protected by Britain in order to keep Portugal in a state of dependence … everything will be arranged peacefully in Brazil by Stuart." Santander therefore did not have to worry that Colombia would find itself in a war with Brazil.[61]

Sucre was obviously disappointed. The tone of his own toast was discordant with Bolívar's. It was more militaristic and predicated on the idea that the war between Brazil and Argentina was one in which all of the republics had a stake. In fact, his toast can be read as a warning to Bolívar about implicating the Colombian army in his Peruvian dictatorship—a more dangerous possibility now that the army was apparently going to be denied a role in fighting against Pedro. Sucre started by pointedly praising the liberal progress made by Buenos Aires under Rivadavia initiatives. And then he observed that the Colombian army

> fighting for liberty, for the justice of America in its struggle, for the cause of humanity, has marched over a glorious career and today enjoys as the reward for its sacrifices the most sublime compensation: the admiration of all men and the blessings of the people. The army will conserve the brilliance of its arms, carrying on its bayonets the observance of the laws, the defense of principles, and of rights. [B]ut if at any time it abandons the good cause, the cause of the people, of the homeland—if any time it degrades itself by siding with tyranny, eternal damnation and the execration of men will be its punishment. ... [That army could if ordered] descend from Potosí upon the enemies [Pedro's army] of Río de la Plata like a torrential rainfall and wash into the sea everything that opposes it.[62]

This was not Colombian chauvinism; it was Sucre's way of saying that the Colombian army had more legitimate American business in the Eastern Bank than it did in Peru. As to the matter of actually using Colombian troops to attack the empire, Sucre, it is true, had echoed Bolívar's concerns by writing to Santander that such a step "would alarm the Holy Alliance and do great damage to our cause." And yet he said, more along the lines in his own thought since the Chuquitos invasion, that

> a war against the Emperor of Brazil would not be difficult in regard to seizing from him the positions he has usurped from the Republic of Argentina and even going further than that because our physical forces and the elements of revolution would provide many openings. ... I believe that before resorting to a war we should touch with dignity all of the means of conciliation so that the Emperor returns that which he has seized violently from the Argentines; that in the meantime we can deploy our forces in order to guarantee a certain result [in the event of war], opening every type of relation with Brazil and with the republican patriots in the territory, examining the military forces and means of defense of the Emperor etc. etc. etc. in order to attack [the Empire] upon certain information."[63]

Since Bolívar was apparently looking at Bolivia in connection with his Peruvian power base, rather than in terms of an Atlantic base, the

Arequipa decree began to appear to the Argentines as particularly ominous—as a kind of Peruvian servitude placed on the Bolivian state. García reminded the delegates that this was so and that the assembly's declaration of independence therefore meant little. He suggested that treaty relations be developed between Argentina and Bolivia to offset the threat to Bolivian independence on the Peruvian side. Up to this point, García had not focused on treaty relations with Bolivia. He passed over this matter in Sucre's letter that proposed a Bolivian-Argentine alliance because he was still thinking of managing the extension of Bolívar's power into the Brazilian war through the fashioning of a coalition. Now he began to believe that converting Bolivia into an Argentine client state, or a buffer state, would make it possible to contain Bolívar's Peruvian power structure.[64]

Alvear and Díaz-Vélez had already begun to focus on bilateral alliance relations with Bolivia. They, therefore, urged Bolívar to have Bolivia sign a treaty of military alliance with Argentina against Brazil. They argued that Bolivia and Argentina had shared interests in opposing Brazilian expansionism. They were the bordering states that were the most exposed and had jointly suffered Brazilian aggression. Presenting a bilateral front would deter Brazil from attacking one or the other. Should Argentina fare poorly in the war, Bolivia would be next in line. Together they could "counterbalance" the forces of the empire (the emphasis was no longer on eliminating the monarchy) and contain it within its legal borders. Bolivia, moreover, was under a special obligation to help Argentina because of the efforts made by Argentina to liberate it during the fifteen years war, as well as the disinterestedness that Argentina had displayed in issuing its May 9 law. Signing the military treaty with Argentina was a just payment of the "indemnity" Bolivia owed to its beleaguered neighbor. The Argentine envoys prefaced their treaty proposal to Bolívar by saying that they were "proceeding on the principle of the independence of Upper Peru being recognized [*sea reconocida*]" if it met Argentine conditions.[65]

Infante prepared a Bolivian mission headed by José Mariano Serrano to negotiate recognition in Buenos Aires. It was made aware of these conditions. Alvear advised García of the Serrano mission and argued that Bolivian agreement to the alliance should be the *sine qua non* of Argentine recognition. They suggested further that Serrano be sent to Rio de Janeiro to warn Pedro that if Brazilian forces did not evacuate the bank, Bolivia would sign a military treaty with Argentina and enter the war. Bolívar had agreed with an informal mission to Rio "if it would facilitate and speed up" Argentine recognition of Bolivia. The formalizing of any treaty, however, would have to wait until Bolivia had adopted his constitution.[66]

Sucre's strategy for challenging the monarchy involved moving Bolívar's power toward Argentina through the filter of a "liberated" Bolivian republic instead of it arriving directly in Argentina in the garb of his Peruvian dictatorship. The idea was to use Bolivia to de-Peruvianize Bolívar's power and to make it possible for the Argentines to ally with Bolívar's power without having to fear falling under his dictatorship; to make possible the formation of a real alliance of equals against the monarchy. Bolívar's virtual exclusion of Sucre from the Potosí talks nullified this strategy. Therefore, the subject of the coalitional war against Pedro was alluded to capriciously by Alvear and Díaz-Vélez as a means for the extension of Bolívar's personal protectorate over all of South America—a far cry from the coalition of the republics as equals engaged against the monarchy in Brazil.

The relations between Bolivia and Argentina were a barometer of the Potosí negotiations. At Potosí, those relations shifted subtly out of the Spanish-American framework for challenging the monarchy into a framework of power politics in which everybody confronted everybody else. Alvear, Díaz-Vélez, and Sucre understood this even if Bolívar did not. The Liberator expected that the Potosí talks, by avoiding the challenge to the Brazilian monarchy, would constitute a crucial step toward the objective of incorporating the principles of monarchic rule into Spanish-American constitutions. The next step was his writing of the Bolivian constitution.

Once he had returned to Peru from Bolivia, Bolívar sent Sucre an emphatic set of instructions. He was ordered to do the following: (1) have Bolivia adopt Bolívar's constitution and be prepared himself to accept the lifetime presidency in Bolivia; (2) negotiate the reuniting (*reunión*) of Bolivia and Peru; (3) keep close harmony with the Peruvian Bolivarians, especially Santa Cruz; and (4) not challenge Pedro—"The British are collaborating with us in this matter and they will preserve harmony."[67]

The dispatch of a new British mission headed by Lord John Ponsonby took place after the death of John in Lisbon, opening new diplomatic vistas for Canning in the management of the Brazilian-Portuguese relationship. The Ponsonby mission held out the prospect of a definitive British mediation of the Eastern Bank conflict and the elimination of all of the concomitant tensions between Spanish-American republics and the monarchy. Bolívar informed Canning that the new British diplomatic interposition in the Plata would ensure that the war did not spill over into Bolivia and Peru, thus allowing the Bolivarian order to be securely fastened down in both countries. Concurrently, Britain would be widening its own political role on the continent, which is what Bolívar zealously wanted. "By adopting its mediatory role in the war between Buenos Aires and Brazil, Britain has extended its benign influence among all of the people of America because an internal war in the New World could cause dislocations difficult to avoid." That the monarchy should be simultaneously strengthened in Brazil by a British-inspired settlement to the Eastern Bank war created no problem for Bolívar. He did not "fear the species of political order which the Imperial Government of Brazil will necessarily establish in its country because the tendency of republics [in Spanish America] is toward anarchy."[68]

In February of 1826, back from Bolivia, Bolívar resumed his negotiations with the British consulate C. M. Rickets, whose fascinating reports to Canning date from that point and continued until January 1827. Bolívar told Rickets that he had decided to steer clear of a war against Brazil and to let British diplomacy mediate the Brazilian-Argentine war. He was going to concede the political organization of eastern South America to the Argentine accommodations made to the Brazilian empire under the supervision of British diplomacy. He said that his major concern was that Argentine anarchy did not spill over into Bolivia or Peru. On the subject of monarchy, Bolívar said the American states should individually arrive at their own political forms, which might be more or less monarchic. Colombia could have one form, Peru another, and Bolivia a third. Bolívar intimated, however, that his Bolivian Constitution could be used to define the political systems of both "Upper and Lower Peru." Bolívar's intent was to give only as much power to the people as they could handle, limiting government with built-in checks but fortifying it with lifetime features and with administrative systems modelled on the Napoleonic Code. If Britain would agree to establish its protectorate over the American states, both individually and in their multilateral relationships through an American league, Bolívar was willing to concede considerable latitude to the American states in regard to their domestic political forms, as he had done in his Jamaica Letter. Facts varied. The emperor was good for Brazil, the federal form for Argentina. "He had his own ideas on Colombia and other ones for Upper and Lower Peru." But South America needed Britain to supply a common, tutelary framework within which their political development could take place, secure from the threats of European and North American domination.

As Bolívar cooled off toward Panama, and as he contemplated the situation presented in Colombia by Páez's growing rebellion, he began to have the same ideas for Colombia and for "Upper and Lower Peru."[69] As a result, he decided to return to Colombia and put into motion what had been latent in his mind ever since the Cúcuta Congress rejected his Angostura Address and drafted an "irrelevant" constitution in its place: linking his southern power structure to that of Páez and forcing Santander and the Cúcuta constitution out of the picture. The elements of this plan were founding the Colombian state anew on the basis of the

Bolivian constitution and accomplishing the union of Colombia with Peru and Bolivia in an Andean empire.

As he prepared to leave Peru for Colombia, Bolívar became more imperative in the language concerning his need for rapid Bolivian adoption of the constitution, in order to "show the way" to both Peru and Colombia. The Bolivian constitution was, he told Sucre, "a bridge between Europe and America, between the army and the people, between democracy and aristocracy, between monarchy and republic." Sucre's cooperation was essential to Bolívar's imperial design. Yet Bolívar appreciated Sucre's commitment to Bolivia's independence. He tried to persuade Sucre of the merits of the Andean empire by pointing out that Britain was still the key to America's peace with Europe and its political stability. The alliance of Spanish America to Great Britain was "greater in politics than Ayacucho." Nothing should be done to embarrass Britain's efforts to gain the reconciliation of the Holy Alliance with America. The Empire of Brazil, under British protection and the tacit acceptance of the Holy Alliance, should take its rightful place in the international system of America. Sucre should exercise extreme caution with Brazil, so as not to upset Canning's policy.[70]

He then broached the subject of the reunification of Peru and Bolivia. He urged Sucre to federate Bolivia to Peru through the Bolivian constitution, once Peru had also adopted it. The Peruvian council of state would recognize Bolivia and prepare the federation of the two states. Each could implement the Bolivian constitution with some variations, but they would be one nation, one army, one flag. Given the successful joining of Peru and Bolivia, Colombia would follow suit, possibly federating first into the three states of Venezuela, Cundinamarca and Quito, in which case three more Bolivian constitutions would appear. "Colombia needs a political variation, either federal or imperial. The *status quo* cannot last." The Bolivian constitution "should be implemented first in the south in order that it can go to Colombia with all of the prestige that will accrue to it by virtue of its adoption" by Bolivia and Peru. Bolivia saw for Sucre "a very great and beautiful role" in achieving the unity of Peru and Bolivia under the Bolivian constitution.[71]

Bolívar thought that Colombia could define the politics arising out of the accommodation of the Brazilian monarchy. The purpose of his Andean empire was not to challenge Brazil but to duplicate its imperial system and monarchic constitution on the rest of the continent. Ironically, Colombia could probably have defined the politics of challenging the monarchy and could have strengthened its own republican system in the process. But it was less clear that it could define the politics of the accommodation of the monarchy. For one thing, Colombia would be required to lead a process of creating quasi-monarchies out of the republics in what would amount to a tacit collaboration with the Brazilian monarchy. Such politics were out of tune with Colombia's own constitutional order and that of the other Spanish-American states. The illusoriness of this idea was revealed by the considerable opposition that developed in Bolivia to Bolívar's constitution. The lifetime presidency feature served to introduce the monarchic principle into a society that had struggled for fifteen years against the monarchic principle. For what? "To replace the Spanish Lion with an American Lion?"[72]

Bolívar's fatal miscalculation was that the cost of staging a constitutional *coup d'etat* against Santander would be compensated by the cooptation of Páez into the new order of the Andean empire. He underestimated Páez and the forces of Venezuelan secessionism. His plans were also undone by what he could not have foreseen: the mutiny of the Colombian army he had left behind in Lima. But the underlying reality was that as a result of the abandonment of the effort to define their American unity on the basis of the exclusion of the Brazilian monarchy, the Spanish Americans were moving by default into a system of power politics that pitted them randomly against each other (cf. Alvear's phrase, "wherever else") and made it seem not to matter that Brazil was the only monarchy on a continent of republics—exactly what the Brazilians wanted.

Notes

1. Santa Cruz's skepticism of Chuquisaca lawyers: Santa Cruz to Antonio de la Fuente, July 27, 1825, *Archivo Histórico del Mariscal Andrés Santa Cruz*, I: 171. His father's murder: Nícolas Fernandez Naranja, "Psicológia de Mariscal Andrés Santa Cruz," in Carlos U. Sossa, *La Vida y Obra del Mariscal Andrés Santa Cruz*. La Paz, 1976, I: 52. Santa Cruz's early life and military career in the Spanish service and capture by the Argentines: Julio Diaz Arguedas, "Trayectoría Militar de Santa Cruz," in Sossa, I: 52. Mother's nativist influence: Fernandez, "Psicológia," 52.

2. Carlos U. Sossa, "Andrés Santa Cruz en el Período de la Independencia," in Sossa, I: 74.

3. Arenales's counterorders to Santa Cruz and his evaluation: letters from Santa Cruz to Arenales from February 26 to April 11, 1822, in *Archivo Histórico*, I: 33–45.

4. Santa Cruz to Bolívar, in *Archivo Histórico*, 163–64.

5. Alfonso Crespo, Santa Cruz, *El Condor Indio*. Mexico City, 1944; Sossa.

6. Santa Cruz to Bolívar, June 4, 1825, *Archivo Histórico*, 166–167; Bolívar to Santa Cruz, June 17, 1825, in Blanco-Fombana, 331; Bolívar to Sucre, May 15, 1825, in ibid., 318.

7. Sucre to Bolívar, June 3, 1825, in *Archivo de Sucre*, VI: 225.

8. Santa Cruz to Antonio de la Fuente, July 27, 1825, in *Archivo Histórico*, I: 171.

9. *Redactor de la Asamblea de Representantes; Legislatura del Año de 1825*. La Paz, 1825, 10–41, passim.

10. "Leave it to the peaceful enjoyments of its rights": J. M. Mendiziabal (Chuquisaca), *Redactor,* 1825, 16. Patriotic grit displayed in the fifteen years' war: Juan Manuel de Montoya (Potosí), *Redactor,* 1825, 193–94.

11. Olañeta to Bolívar, October 19, 1825, in O'Leary, *Memorias,* IX: 23–24.

12. Mariano Manuel de Centeno (Cochabamba), *Redactor,* 1825, 17.

13. "Two powerful states," cited in debates: Olañeta to Bolívar, October 19, 1825, in O'Leary, *Memorias,* IX: 21.

14. Eusebio Gutierrez (La Paz) *Redactor,* 1825, 14; Mendizabal, 16.

15. "Will recognize and respect our deliberations": José Antonio Pallares (Potosí), *Redactor,* 1825, 20–21. Protection of liberators and "noble instrument": José Mariano Enriquez (Potosí), *Redactor,* 1825, 17. "Equilibrium of power": Sucre's address to the assembly, *Documentos Referentes a la Creación de Bolivia.* I: 288.

16. Text of Declaration of Emancipation, *Documentos Referentes a la Creación de Bolivia,* I: 292–95. Prize money sequel: Thomas Millington, *Debt Politics After Independence: The Funding Crisis in Bolivia.* Gainsville: University Press of Florida, 1992.

17. Ibid., 294–95.

18. Placating Bolívar: Pinilla, 209–11. Naming Upper Peru Republic of Bolívar and other symoblic actions: Assembly Resolution, *Documentos Referentes a la Creación de Bolivia,* I: 304–06.

19. Santa Cruz to Bolívar, August 20, 1825, in *Archivo Histórico,* I: 174.

20. Instructions to Mendizibal and Olañeta: Text, *Documentos Referentes a la Creación de Bolivia,* I: 307–12.

21. Santa Cruz to Sucre, August 20, 1825, in *Archivo Histórico,* I: 174–75.

22. *Libro Menor de Sesiones Secretas.* La Paz, 1917, 14. Mention is made of an antecedent discussion of the proposal to invite Bolívar to draft a constitution. No record of that discussion exists.

23. Ibid., 15.

24. Bolívar to Santander, May 30 and June 7, 1825, in *Selected Writings of Bolívar.* Ed. and trans. by Vicente Lecuna and Harold Bierck. New York: Colonial Press, 1951, II: 502–03.

25. Bolívar to Sucre, May 30, 1825, in Vicente Lecuna, ed., *Cartas del Libertador.* Caracas, 1928, IV: 333–35.

26. José Gabriel Páez (Bolívar's secretary) to Mexican foreign minister, May 28, 1825, in O'Leary, *Memorias,* XXIII: 167–68.

27. José Gabriel Páez to Peruvian foreign ministry, June 4, 1825, in ibid., 178.

28. Nestor dos Santos Lima, *La Imagen de Brazil en las Cartas de Bolívar.* Caracas, 1978. "Holy Alliance and Brazil are one": Bolívar to Santander, February 9, 1825, in *Cartas del Libertador.* Ed. by Vicente Lecuna. Caracas, 1929, IV: 1040.

29. Bolívar to Santander, September 26, 1825, in Lecuna, *Cartas,* V: 105–113.

30. Britain due Spanish-American gratitude for Stuart's mission's success: Canning to Parish, November 3, 1826, in Webster, *Britain and the Independence of Latin America.* London, 1938. II: 133.

31. "Good reason to be proud": Bolívar to Santander, October 11, 1825, in Vicente Lecuna and Esther Barret de Nazaris, eds., *Simón Bolívar: Obras Completas,* II: 227; "Minimize Pedro's political relations": Funes to Bolívar, August 26, in

Silva, 288–93. For Bolívar's use of the letter at Potosí, see the following section in the text.

32. Bolívar to Hipólito Unanue, May 30, 1825, in Lecuna, *Obras Completas,* II: 146.

33. Background of Pedro's apology in the context of Stuart's mission: Condy Raguet to Clay, August 27, 1825, Manning, II: 828–31.

34. Sucre to Funes, October 13, 1825, Biblioteca Nacional, Buenos Aires, 542/40.

35. "Mixed governments": Bolívar to Hurtado, March 12, 1825, in *Cartas de Bolívar, 1823–1825,* ed. by R. Blanco-Flombona. Caracas, 1921, 303–10.

36. "Something of lifetime rule": Bolívar to Santander, September 12, 1825, in Lecuna, *Cartas,* V: 94–96.

37. Victor Andres Belaunde, *Bolívar and the Political Thought of the South American Revolutions.* Baltimore: Johns Hopkins University Press, 1938, 234–58.

38. Infante allegedly talked Bolívar out of going to war with Brazil: Seckinger, *The Brazilian Monarchy,* 123. See also Ron Seckinger, "Projetada Alianza Gran-Colombiana Rioplatense Contra o Brazil: Um Documento Inédito," Mensario do Arquivo Nacional, 1974, V: no. 1, 33–40. Infante's biography and role in the Sucre government: Thomas Millington, *Debt Politics After Independence,* 50–51. Infante's advocacy in congressional debate of the lifetime presidency as the "fixed point" of Bolivia's political future: *Redactor de la Asamblea Constituyente de 1826.* La Paz, Bolivia, 1917, 503–04.

39. See Chapter 6 section, Bolívar's Move Against Sucre's Policy.

40. "Constitution of the Empire of Brazil" in *Foreign Constitutions.* Ed. by John Palmer. Albany, 1894, 65–138.

41. September debates on the lifetime presidency (approved): *Redactor de 1826,* 542–47. Sucre embarrassed by lifetime presidency and dynastic danger in it: Losa argued this indirectly, September 6, 1826, in ibid., 544. See also Domingo de Alcalá, *Para la Historia de America del Sur.* Lima, 1850, 65, which exposes Losa's view more explicitly. The lifetime presidency "repudiates seventeen years of patriotic struggle in Upper Peru": Martin, September 6, 1826, *Redactor de 1826,* 545.

42. John Barclay Pentland, *Report on Bolivia.* London, 1974, 188, 194–95, 200.

43. Bolívar to Heres, July 9, 1825, in Blanco-Flombona, 335–38. Bolívar to Santa Cruz, September 25, 1825, in Lecuna and Barret de Nazaris, *Obras Completas,* II: 215.

44. Impressions of Potosí and Bolívar: Captain Andrew, *Journey from Buenos Aires to Potosí,* London, 1827, II: 94–95, 100–101.

45. Quotation from Andrew describing Sucre's appearance, in ibid., 96. Miller's description of Sucre: William Miller, *Memoirs of General William Miller.* London, 1829, II: 68.

46. Felipe Santiago Esteños to Alvear and Díaz Vélez, October 9, 1825, in *Documentos Referentes a la Creación de Bolivia,* I: 372.

47. "An old man, weak of character": Díaz-Vélez to García, May 9, 1826, in Rodríguez, II: 161–62; "Would not resist this temptation": ibid., 162–63; "has his eyes fixed": Alvear to García, December 21, 1825, in ibid., II: 145; "Enterprizing beyond what is calculable": Alvear to García, October 22, 1825, in ibid., II: 226–27.

48. Alvear and Díaz Vélez to García, October 22, 1825, in Restelli, *La Gestión Diplomatica de General de Alvear en el Alto Peru.* Buenos Aires, 1927, 691–92.

49. Bolívar's use of Pedro's apology: Ibid., 124–25. Need for republics to act as one against Brazil: November 5, 1825, and Annex on the October 21st conference, in ibid., 160–63; same, December 6, 1825, 194–96.

50. Bolívar to Santander, October 11, 1825, in *Documentos Referentes a la Creación de Bolivia,* I: 374–75, 379.

51. Funes to Bolívar, August 26, 1825, in Silva, 288–93; "Two governments": Alvear and Díaz-Vélez to García, October 21, 1825, in Restelli, 116–18; Alvear and Díaz-Vélez to García, December 6, in ibid., Annex No. 2, 202–05.

52. Bolívar's Paraguayan invasion scenario and O'Leary mission: Alvear and Díaz-Vélez to García, October 21, 1825, in Restelli, 116–18. Paraguayan invasion by Bolívar unacceptable: García to Alvear and Díaz, November 19, 1825, and January 12, 1826, in ibid., 173–74 and 233–34 respectively.

53. Alvear and Díaz-Vélez to García, October 22, 1825, in ibid., 129.

54. J. Valerie Fifer, *Bolivia: Land, Location and Politics Since 1825.* London: Cambridge University Press, 1972, 29, 168–70.

55. F. Burdett O'Connor, *Independencia Americana.* Madrid, n.d., 173–76.

56. Sucre to O'Connor, September 19, 1825, in *Archivo de Sucre,* VII: 88–89.

57. Alvear and Díaz-Vélez to Bolívar, in Restelli, November 10, 1825, Annex No. 1, 206–8; Bolívar to Alvear, March 6, 1827, in Rodríguez, 167–68.

58. Alvear and Díaz-Vélez to García, December 7, 1825, in Restelli, Annex No. 3, 199–205.

59. "Military operations" against Bolivia: Alvear and Díaz-Vélez to García, December 7, 1825, Annex No. 1, 201; "Wherever else necessary": Alvear to García, October 23, 1825, 142.

60. Texts of the toasts, *Documentos Referentes a la Creación de Bolivia,* I: 386–89. Reception details: Rodríguez, 95–98.

61. Bolívar to Santander, October 21, 1825 in Lecuna, *Cartas,* V: 135–44.

62. Text of Sucre's toast: Rodríguez, 98–99.

63. Sucre to Santander, October 11, 1825, in Lecuna, I: 379–80. Seckinger treats this letter simply as a kind of carbon copy of Bolívar's thinking: Seckinger, 111.

64. García to Alvear and Díaz-Vélez, November 19, 1825, in Restelli, 145–46.

65. Alvear and Díaz-Vélez to García, November 10, 1825, in ibid., Annex No. 2, 167–68.

66. "*Sine qua non*": Alvear and Díaz-Vélez to García, in ibid., December 3, 1825, in Restelli, 184–85; "Would facilitate and speed up": Alvear and Díaz-Vélez to García, December 6, 1825, in ibid., 194–95.

67. Bolívar to Sucre, May 12, 1826, in Lecuna, *Obras,* 363–64.

68. Bolívar to Canning, December 22, 1826, in ibid., 500.

69. Rickets to Canning, February 18, 1826, in Charles Webster, *Britain and the Independence of Latin America.* London, 1938, II: 526–37.

70. Bolívar to Sucre, June 21, 1826, in Lecuna, *Cartas,* V: 203–07; April 28, 1826, in ibid., 279–80.

71. Bolívar to Sucre, May 12, 1826, in ibid., 289–95.

72. "American Lion": Bozo, *Redactor de 1826,* 543. See note 41 above.

7

The Monarchy Secure:
The Dawning of
South American Power Politics

THE IDEA THAT THE MONARCHY in Brazil was surrounded by Spanish-American republics that were poised to join forces against it lost its military and political plausibility in 1826. A virulent anti-Colombian atmosphere began to develop in Peru after Bolívar's departure for Colombia on September 1, 1826. It became increasing clear in 1827 that the anti-Bolivarian Peruvian nationalists were intent on expunging Bolívar's influence from Peru and Bolivia and even attacking Colombia in order to recapture Guayaquil, and possibly Ecuador, from Bolívar's clutches. In the face of this movement, Sucre thought less about challenging the monarchy in an alliance with Argentina and more about positioning Bolivia in a system that would increase its chances of withstanding probable Peruvian efforts to overthrow him. The challenge to the monarchy was intended to dislodge Bolívar from his Peruvian dictatorship. After 1826, however, Bolívar was no longer in charge of Peru; his enemies were. The Peruvian threat to Bolivia became direct and even military in nature.

Illusion of an American Equilibrium

In early 1827, Sucre's thinking shifted toward what he called an "American equilibrium." In 1826, he developed some of the regional elements of this concept during his effort in 1826 to ward off pressure from the Bolivarians in Lima to federate Bolivia and Peru. Sucre's idea represented an apolitical version of the monarchy accommodation scenario. He thought that by including Brazil (regardless of its monarchic structure) into an American equilibrium of states, European influence could be excluded, and the system would be American-operated even if not politically unified. Instead of trying to challenge Brazil in the name of republicanism Spanish-American states could make the balancing of Brazil's power part of a wider balancing process that would restrain Spanish-American states from attacking each other. In the context of an American equilibrium, the looming threat posed by Peru to Bolivia could be addressed more directly than by trying to assert Bolivia's independence by challenging the Brazilian monarchy.

------◆◆◆------

On December 10, 1825, Pedro gambled in the Eastern Bank. He made a formal declaration of war against Argentina, began the rapid build-up of the imperial forces in the bank and, more critically, ordered a naval blockade around the port of Buenos Aires. If his Eastern Bank policy were any indication, the Portuguese decision to grant Brazilian independence seemed to embolden Pedro in his behavior toward the Argentines rather than moderate it, as Canning had hoped. The British envoy, Charles Stuart was evidently unsuccessful in stopping Pedro from escalating the conflict in the Eastern Bank.

In the aftermath of the Potosí talks, Sucre became concerned about Bolívar's apparent willingness to allow the British to mediate the Eastern Bank war. He attempted to stay involved in Argentine politics in order to deny the British the opportunity to successfully mediate the war. In Chuquisaca, after Bolívar had left Bolivia, Sucre entered into a certain understanding with Alvear and Dorrego. The "plan," as Funes referred to it, was apparently talked about in Potosí, although apparently without Bolívar's knowledge. Alvear and Dorrego returned to Argentina, intending to create support in the national congress for a federalist president who would be able to lead the nation into the war against Brazil, to picture it as an American struggle against the monarchy, and to accept help from Sucre. Most likely, such a president would be Dorrego.[1]

In view of Bolívar's reluctance to enter the war, Sucre discussed with Alvear and Dorrego (he seems to have trusted Dorrego more) the possibility of him (Sucre) taking command of a alliance army in the Eastern Bank consisting of Argentines, Upper Peruvians, and "some Colombians." Sucre, in effect, was contemplating taking Bolívar's place in the alliance. This was an very independent decision for Sucre to make. It attests to his willingness to part ways with Bolívar on the question of challenging the monarchy. But Sucre was convinced that a higher purpose was being served—that of keeping the solution of the war in American hands as opposed to British hands. He was also at this time tired of war and politics. He was physically ailing with tuberculosis and homesick for Quito. Yet, he brought himself to a secret understanding with

Dorrego and Alvear. He intimated this understanding to Funes in a letter that has remained unknown to historians. Funes received it in February, 1826. It was written on January 21, 1826, soon after Bolívar's return from Bolivia to Peru. The occasion for Sucre's offer to take command in the Eastern Bank was Pedro's decision to declare war on Buenos Aires. The bulk of the letter deals with technical help from Buenos Aires that Sucre was seeking in connection with his reforms in Bolivia. He alluded in the last paragraph to his pact with Alvear and Dorrego. Dorrego had already returned to Argentina, and Alvear was on the verge of leaving for Argentina from Chuquisaca.

> According to the newspapers you all are anxious because the Emperor has decided to go to war. I wish you victory and with all of my heart that I may accompany you with some of our soldiers (*de todo corazón les acompañara con algunos de nuestros soldados*). General Alvear who leaves here for there on the 19th will inform you of our intent (*disposicíon*).[2]

It was not clear whether "by some of our troops" Sucre included Colombians. Lacking authorization for this from Bogotá or from Bolívar, he probably meant Bolivian forces into which he planned to smuggle some Colombian officers and captured Spanish officers still in Bolivia. This was the configuration of the strike force that he had prepared to invade Brazil with in retaliation for the Chiquitos incident.

The "plan" fell apart for a variety of reasons, chiefly the ascendancy of the centralist party in Buenos Aires following the return of Rivadavia from Europe, his election to the Argentine presidency, and the implementation of his policy of overt, uncompromising hostility to anything that smacked of cooperation with Sucre, Bolívar's "pawn." A diplomatic blitz over the Eastern Bank conflict, backed by new British mediation in the shape of the Ponsonby mission, unfolded. This increased the likelihood that the Eastern Bank war would be pre-empted as a focus for a joint challenging of the monarchy.

Even before the Ponsonby mission appeared on the horizon, Sucre had been monitoring the possibilities of British diplomatic inroads into the Eastern Bank war. He found out that Stuart had brought nothing with him relative to the bank question on his mission to Rio. Pedro's declaration of war reassured Sucre that the British were not controlling Rio's policy altogether. He intimated to Funes that Stuart, to the extent he tried to head off an escalation of the war by Buenos Aires, would get nowhere because the British were not prepared to force Pedro to cede the bank to Argentina "and that is the crux of the question." But the Ponsonby mission was more threatening from Sucre's point of view and excited his concerns. In June 1826, he wrote Bolívar that he would find out howsoever he could "what the relations are between Buenos Aires and the British Government concerning the matter of the Eastern Bank." Stuart had not been instructed or prepared to undertake mediation, so there was not much to fear from his activities. "They say now however," Sucre wrote referring to Ponsonby, "that a Lord something or other is on the way over with instructions to mediate" the war. By August, the mission of Ponsonby unfolded in Rio, and it was obvious to Sucre, as he wrote Bolívar, that "Britain is mixing itself in a very direct manner" in the bank question. Was it advisable for American states to rely on a European power to settle their internal quarrels? "I do not know what your opinion is on this but I want to know it very, very much." Sucre knew exactly what Bolívar's opinion was: give the British a green light.[3]

At this juncture, Sucre decided to try to shift the basis of his policy toward the *caudillo* movement in the Argentine interior. Even if the republican politics of the war would thereby be diluted in favor of *caudillo* politics (Rivadavia's point), the conflict in the Eastern Bank would be more of an American object and less of a European one. Sucre proceeded to establish widespread understandings with the Argentine *caudillos*—Bustos, Ibarra, Quiroga, Gorriti—that served as a cover for the decision he made to militarily occupy Tarija—an action that he justified on the grounds of Rivadavia's collusion with the British in the Eastern Bank and his open hostility toward Bolivia. Not only had Rivadavia refused to recognize the Sucre government, but he had applauded (and possibly incited) the actions of a mutinous Colombian cavalry unit, led by Domingo Matute, that had accused Sucre and Bolívar of dynastic aspirations in Bolivia and fled Bolivia into Argentina.[4]

During 1826, Sucre was diverted from his efforts to join with the Argentine *caudillos* by increasing pressure from the Bolivarians in Lima to unite Bolivia to Peru. He could not very well excuse Bolivia from these demands by pleading the cause of trying to find a basis in Argentina for stimulating a challenge to the monarchy in the Eastern Bank conflict. Quite the opposite. The whole Andean empire concept was intended as a Spanish-American accommodation of the Brazilian empire. Therefore, Sucre began to form the concept of an Andean equilibrium of power as the basis on which to excuse Bolivia from unification with Peru. This was the embryo of his American equilibrium idea.

Sucre had given a considerable amount of attention to the effects of Bolívar's departure from Peru. He was convinced that anarchy would soon break out in Peru and that it would inevitably spread into Bolivia and destabilize his government. In the meantime, Sucre had to deal with the Bolivarians who were fighting to stay at the helm in Peru following Bolívar's departure. A large Colombian garrison remained in Lima. But the party's main chance of surviving politically was to effect the federation of Peru and Bolivia through the Bolivian constitution, which both countries had adopted by the end of 1826; this would prove the Bolivarians' "nationalist" credentials. These relations with the Peruvian Bolivarians were bound to be embarrassing for Sucre. They needed what he was determined not to give.

Bolívar's choice of Santa Cruz as the head of Peru's ruling council placed Sucre in a difficult position. Bolívar had instructed Sucre to maintain "perfect harmony" with the Peruvian council. Anticipating Sucre's opposition to the federation of Bolivia and Peru, Bolívar specifically instructed Sucre not to obstruct the proposals for federation that would be forthcoming from Santa Cruz.[5]

Santa Cruz, as head of the council of state, identified his task as that of aiding Bolívar to "move ahead the work of [uniting Peru and Bolivia under the Bolivian constitution] which is that of our salvation." "We have to unite to him more each day," he continued to a Peruvian friend, "as we unite to form an entity that will be a powerful mass [Peru and Bolivia] capable of defeating by its solidarity any attacks, external or internal." If Bolívar would solve the Páez crisis and add Colombia to the structure, so much the better. The stature of the federation would be only increased if Colombia were added to it.[6]

On the eve of Bolívar's departure for Colombia, Santa Cruz wrote him "that if he had to leave Peru, let it be for a temporary period, and that he never remove Peru from his sight, or his authority." To Sucre, Santa Cruz had already started pressing for the federation of Peru and Bolivia. He appealed to Sucre's loyalties. "There are many reasons in favor of it [the federation] especially if Colombia joins at least for the lifetime of Bolívar who ought to preside over the whole." He addressed a possible fear Sucre might have, namely that the federation would dilute the special relationship that Bolívar had with Bolivia. Santa Cruz argued, on the contrary, that the federation would not detract from, but would patently enhance and add to, the Bolivarian foundations of both nations; that by merging those foundations, the role of those foundations in each of the two countries would be more cogent; if they remained separate, it would be unlikely that the Bolivarian order could hold its own in either. "Don't you think that [Bolivia and Peru] can in this way constitute themselves better?"[7]

Santa Cruz's agent in Bolivia, Zeballo Ortiz, was instructed by the state council to bring about through a treaty the "reunion of the two sections of Peru into one, indivisible republic." The two lands, it was argued, shared a common history, race, language, and customs. Politically, they shared a loyalty to Bolívar and his constitution. But even more germane was the fact that Bolivia as a separate state faced the prospect of isolation and of becoming the object of encroachment by neighboring states that were more powerful. These words were prophetic.

> Isolated from easy and direct communications with the Powers of Europe and even with many of the American countries, it would be seen as repudiated by civilization. Its commerce would be precarious, costly and dependent on the will of neighbors. Its exports would be made with great difficulty in times of peace and would cease entirely in times of war. Its imports would be taxed enough to make them unfeasible. The country would be perpetually threatened with agitations endemic to its racial composition and by arguments with the governments of Buenos Aires. And what is worse than anything, it [Bolivia] would always be exposed to being assaulted and insulted with impunity by neighbors as ambitious and powerful as Brazil. These evils are so real that they should capture the serious consideration of Bolivians, to the end that they should adopt the only measure [unification with Peru] which is capable of overcoming. ... [T]he partial inconveniences which may be embarrassing to the federation project [should be] put aside.[8]

Yet, Sucre knew that Santa Cruz faced strong nationalist opposition in Lima; he was a Bolivian and a Bolivarian. Sucre knew that Santa Cruz and the Bolivarians needed the federation of Peru and Bolivia through the Bolivarian system in order to survive politically in Peru. The anti-Colombian Peruvian nationalists did not need federation with Bolivia; their desire was the elimination of Bolívar's authority in Peru and Bolivia. Sucre concluded that avoiding the embarrassing question of the federation might be accomplished by hedging his commitments to Santa Cruz and waiting to see what direction Peruvian nationalism took. Sucre's fundamental paradox was this: The nationalists might settle for the departure of Sucre and his army in order to have them accept the fact of Bolivian independence. Their position corresponded to Rivadavia's—the "issue" in Bolivia was "foreign domination," not its statehood. What the Bolivarians wanted was for Sucre to stay as lifetime president and help use the Bolivarian system to politically unify the two countries.

Sucre had to go through the motions of opening a discussion with Santa Cruz about federating Bolivia and Peru. Bolívar demanded it, and Santa Cruz lost no time pressing ahead. But Sucre was very agile. He emphasized to Santa Cruz that he was only tenuously linked to the lifetime presidency of Bolivia; his opposition to accepting it was well known, and in any case he would be leaving Bolivia for Colombia in 1828. In the meantime, Sucre "promised" to advance the federation project.[9]

Santa Cruz had argued forcefully, and candidly, to Sucre that the Bolivarian system was only the means to the end of uniting Peru and

Bolivia into one country. That end was valid on its merits, for as separate countries Bolivia and Peru would be weak and subject to foreign manipulation. But, united, they would be powerful and able to resist outside pressures. Sucre did not reject this plausible proposition, but he effectively countered it by emphasizing his concurrence in the idea that small states will get swallowed up by large ones. The inference was clearly that Bolivia was in as much danger of being swallowed up by Peru through "federation" than was Peru or Bolivia of being swallowed up separately by other states.[10]

In Arequipa, Sucre sought, as a hedge against the projected union of Peru and Bolivia, to cultivate the strong tradition of resistance to the central authority of Lima. With the break-up of Spain's rule in Peru, Arequipa had advocated a federal constitution for Peru with each of its provinces having a considerable degree of independence from the central government. Now, political opinion in Arequipa saw a new chance to achieve autonomy from Lima by taking advantage of the federation of Peru and Bolivia. Bolívar had pointed out this connection when recommending the federation of Peru and Bolivia. He said that Arequipa, plus Bolivia, would be able to balance Lima's weight within the overall federal structure of three states: Bolivia, northern Peru and Arequipa. This gambit was seized upon in Arequipa and it appeared in an article on the Peru-Bolivian federation appearing in the newspaper *Federal* of Arequipa. The article advocated the separation of Peru into two states; one in the north controlled by Lima and one in the south controlled by Arequipa, which would then enter a federation with Bolivia. The balance of power would therefore be more even: Bolivia would not have to fear domination by a larger Peruvian state, and Arequipa would get the independence from Lima that it was seeking.[11]

This article was appealing to Sucre's new thinking. It vindicated his own thesis that, all things being equal, Bolivia would be dominated by Peru if they were unified. And it provided him with a political opening in Arequipa. It is possible, as was in fact alleged, that Sucre, through Infante, inspired the article. In any case, the Bolivian official newspaper *Condor* published the article with elaborate editorial endorsement. *Condor* supported the proposition that Peru should be divided into two states with Bolivia then joining them. Sucre proceeded to write the prefect of Arequipa in support of the proposition advanced in the *Federal* article as the condition of the Peru-Bolivian federation. "These three states could then have equal weight," he wrote him.[12]

Behind Sucre's concern for the development of military and political influence in Arequipa stood his concern over the Pacific port of Arica. This port was of major importance to the Bolivian economy because it provided the country's only link to maritime trading.

On the morning of January 27, 1827, as José María Pando, Bolívar's chief Peruvian collaborator and Santa Cruz's right hand man, was riding to work in his carriage, he noticed a strange quiet in the streets of Lima. Drawing closer to the central plaza, he spied Colombian sentries on duty; they were stopping all entry to the plaza. Before being turned away, he caught a glimpse of the Colombian Third Division mustered in the middle of the plaza. On the night before, he learned, there had been a mutiny. New Granadian officers, led by Lieutenant Colonel José Busta-mante, had arrested their Venezuelan commanders and taken command of the division. They alleged their action to be in retaliation for Páez's revolt against the authority of the Santander Government in Bogotá. Pando immediately left the capital for Chorillos, a seaside resort, where Santa Cruz was vacationing, to inform him of this cataclysmic event, the roots of which lay in Bogotá. Páez had brought his revolt into the open against the national government in Bogotá. Santander had perceived that Bolívar, now back in Colombia, was planning to ally with Páez against him and against the constitutional system of Colombia. By conniving with New Granadian officers on the scene, Santander and his advisers had orchestrated the mutiny in Lima. Santander intended the revolt in Lima to give Bolívar a taste of his own medicine.[13] The Liberator, seeing his authority flouted in Lima, could now understand how Santander felt in the face of the attacks on the constitutional order of Colombia which were engendered by the Páez revolt. Now Santander had, he said, a "companion in the scandalizing of authority."[14]

The mutiny in Lima accelerated the shift in Sucre's policy toward the idea of an American equilibrium as the proper basis—albeit one with less of a republican foundation—for an American system. The problem of the monarchy for Argentina was the same as the problem of Peru for Bolivia. In other words, the problem of Brazil was its territorial bigness, not its monarchy, just as Peru would become a problem for neighboring states if it became territorially too big through the annexation of Bolivia.

This shift was indicated in a critical article that appeared in *Condor*, on February 1, 1827. The editorial admitted that, because of similarity of race and customs, Bolivia and Peru should be joined, a joining that would be especially appropriate if Peru could be divided into two states so that Bolivia was not dominated. "This (union) is what the exclusive interest of Peru and Bolivia requires but this is not what seems to be required by the equilibrium of the New World" because it does not ensure the independence of Bolivia or effectively allow for the counterbalancing of Brazilian power. The equilibrium called for Bolivia to form an alliance with Argentina and Chile (smaller states than Peru and therefore less threatening to Bolivia's independence), whose function would be to protect Bolivia against Peru, and in the process, to contain Brazil's power on the continent. In the north, Colombia could ally with Mexico and Central America to check the Spanish in the Caribbean. Peru, big enough as it is, could remain alone, protected on both sides by phalanxes of "brother states."[15] This is an elaboration of Sucre's Yungay letter.

In early 1827, Sucre began to feel the need for a Bolivian tie to Argentina that was directed toward checking Peruvian designs against Bolivia. So long as these designs were Bolivarian, Sucre could not pursue outright an Argentine tie as a substitute for them; this would put him in an open conflict with Bolívar's desires. But with the Bolivarian cover for Peru's designs on Bolivia dropped, he could. Sucre felt that Bolivia was safer in a federation with Argentina than with Peru: Peru was bigger and more accustomed to dominate Bolivia than Argentina. Bolivia, he believed, would carry greater weight in a federation with Argentina. "Small nations are swallowed by larger ones and Bolivia is a small nation," he wrote Bolívar, in an effort to convince him that the Argentine tie was better for Bolivia than the Peruvian tie. In March, 1827, Sucre wrote Bolívar that the revolt in Lima had eliminated any remaining chance for a Bolivian-Peruvian federation. The *Condor* editorial proposing that Bolivia unite with Argentina and Chile, he alleged, caused more enthusiasm among Bolivians than unification with Peru. The anarchy of Argentina and the political weakness of Chile ensured that neither would harbor designs on Bolivia, he said. "I am consequently trying to foment this idea in order to get the advantage of having the Republics of America be able to count on containment of the ambitions of the Emperor of Brazil. ... It seems necessary to league together these small states in a way that they will not be the plaything of partisan groups or the prize of anyone with ambitious designs." As the Peruvian revolution developed, and as its anti-Colombian—and therefore anti-Bolivian—tone became more pronounced, Sucre's phrase "anybody with ambitious designs" came to mean Peruvian designs on Bolivia rather than the expansionist designs of Pedro.[16]

Sucre was aware of Lima's plans, including the massing of Peruvian troops on the Bolivian border in midyear and sending Santa Cruz on to Buenos Aires to coordinate this operation with Rivadavia. Sucre's enthusiasm for the federation of Bolivia, Chile, and Argentina increased accordingly and the rationale shifted also away from the inclusion of the containment of Brazil. "The federation is needed," Sucre wrote Bolívar, "to protect Bolivia from the hostile plans of Peru which is showing pretensions of subjugating it and from [Santa Cruz's] diplomatic machinations with Buenos Aires." Sucre informed Bolívar that Domingo Matute, the leader of the renegade Colombian cavalry unit operating in the Argentine provinces, had joined forces with the *caudillos* against Rivadavia. Therefore, a certain common interest had developed between him and Rivadavia in the provinces. Bolivia had leverage there. If that leverage were used, including the possibility of a military strike against Matute and his *caudillo* allies, the control of the central government would be immeasurably increased. The way would be paved toward the federation that Sucre now wanted. He conveyed this remarkable change in his Argentine policy this way to Bolívar:

> All of the interior provinces of Argentina are at the mercy of the enemies of the Government of Buenos Aires. If Buenos Aires continues a hostile policy toward Bolivia, there is now a barrier which will not be removed for three years, and Bolivia can concentrate on the problem of Peru. I believe however, that Buenos Aires will settle things now with Bolivia because that country [Argentina] has nothing to hope for from Peru, while this one [Bolivia] can be of great use to it.[17]

Sucre was not talking essentially about Bolivian help in the war against Brazil. He was talking about the use of Bolivian troops, and possibly some of the remaining Colombians, to help the central government police the provinces. The inclusion of Chile proved to Santa Cruz that Sucre's federation was aimed more against Peru than against Brazil. "Chile's natural offensive role is on the Pacific." Santa Cruz tried during his stop in Santiago to discredit Sucre's initiative with the Chilean Government.[18] In early 1827, Sucre did not appreciate how far a common ground had actually emerged between Canning and Rivadavia; they had come to agreement on the principle of creating a buffer state under the umbrella of British protection in the bank. What he thought would be agreed to by Rivadavia, which was just as bad, was the imposition of a staggering debt on Buenos Aires in the form of an indemnity payment to Brazil, in order to achieve the restoration of the bank to Argentina. If he got out of the war, Sucre predicted that Rivadavia would enter one with the federalists and anarchy would engulf the country. Sucre felt that Rivadavia would fall and that possibly Alvear would be his successor. Through his policy of rapprochement, Sucre hoped to save Rivadavia from this fate—to give him a basis for resisting a British-arranged solution in the bank, and for resisting anarchy in the provinces.[19]

The essence of Sucre's policy was to reduce Rivadavia's reliance on British diplomacy by drawing him into an American equilibrium structure through the federation with Bolivia and Chile. So long as the Bolivarian system had remained intact, Rivadavia's hostility toward him and Bolivia as parts of that system had required Sucre to align with the *caudillos* against Rivadavia. As far as the Eastern Bank war went, Sucre's purpose was to keep Rivadavia too weak and distracted to carry off a deal with the British in the bank. In his new approach, Sucre's purpose was to keep the British role at a minimum by strengthening Rivadavia through the federation. Sucre would not rule out federation resources being committed to the war. More importantly Rivadavia's position in the provinces could be guaranteed, and the recruitment base for the war widened. It could take on a patriotic aspect that would dramatize the fact that it was, in Sucre's phrase, a "purely American war" deserving of an American, that is, non-European solution. At the same time, federation resources would be available to Bolivia and Chile against Peruvian encroachments on either of them.[20]

Sucre's insight was that since the Bolivarian system was in deep trouble because of the Lima revolt, Rivadavia could see that federation with Bolivia and Chile could support the American equilibrium rather than the extension of the principle of "foreign domination," meaning Bolívar's system. Sucre was prepared to offer Rivadavia military help in the provinces against Matute and allied insurrectionists in exchange for Argentine help—military but also political and diplomatic—against Peruvian efforts to insurrect his regime. Mutual assistance to contain domestic revolts in Bolivia and Argentina figured as large in Sucre's plan as mutual help against external attack. Sucre emphasized the domestic help he could give Rivadavia against the *caudillos* because he was not enthusiastic about committing Bolivia in the bank war, especially with a war looming with Peru. He was also vitally interested in increasing Argentine political influence within Bolivia, now that Argentina no longer had to fear Bolívar's power, in order to offset what he saw as an upcoming Peruvian blitz against him in Bolivia. He was willing, however, to dangle military help against Brazil provided that Argentina signed the federation treaty with Bolivia, and Chile. He would also commit Bolivian military forces in the Argentine provinces provided the federation treaty was signed first.

Sucre felt that the American equilibrium would be self-sustaining and therefore exclusive of European supervision. This would be a net American gain. Further, he felt that Spanish-American states could benefit by making the balancing of Brazil's power part of a wider balancing process. His error was to believe that by including the Brazilian empire in an American equilibrium, it would make it possible to construct an overall equilibrium that would serve to protect the weaker Spanish-American states from the predatory behavior of the stronger. Sucre failed to appreciate that in order to include the Brazilian monarchy the South American system had to be shifted onto power foundations and away from republican foundations that the Spanish Americans could relate to in terms of the common aspirations of their struggle for independence. The American equilibrium necessarily implied a weakening of the principle of American unity based on the republican basis of Spanish-American independence. But now Sucre placed the need to keep Bolivia and Peru separate ahead of the need to exclude the monarchy. By excluding the monarchy, the Spanish-American states would have shown the common republican foundation of their shared struggle against Spain. In the absence of a sense of being different from the monarchy and what it stood for and derived from, what was there to prevent the Spanish-American states from fighting among themselves in a manner that simply increased the arrogance of the Brazilian monarchy and the sense of its political and moral superiority—all in the name of "balancing power?"

The Overthrow of Sucre in Bolivia

Rivadavia and his advisers were well aware that Sucre's position in Bolivia was fatally weakened by the Colombian mutiny in Lima. They felt that this eliminated Sucre as an ally of the Argentine *caudillos* and that this would make the latter more amenable to Buenos Aires's control. Rivadavia's main adviser, Julian Segundo de Azuero, wrote to Alvear that "the change that has occurred in Peru, which cannot but be extended to Bolivia, gives us some respite since the anarchists of the interior, whose insolence rested on Sucre (*se apoyaba en Sucre*), appear ready to do their national duty."[21] Theoretically, this would facilitate recruitment in the interior provinces for the centralist army operating in the Eastern Bank under Alvear's command. But not even this calculation, nor the considerable victory that Alvear scored over the imperial army in the battle of Ituzaingo on March 3, 1827, deterred Rivadavia from his effort to achieve a diplomatic, as opposed to military, solution in the Eastern Bank.

In Rivadavia's analysis, the war in the bank was not winnable on land. In a letter to his agent in London, he admitted that Alvear's victory at Ituzaingo was useful, but only to increase the pressure on Pedro in the peace talks being mediated by the British. The decisive factor in the war was the Brazilian naval blockade, which Buenos Aires could not hope to break. A diplomatic settlement was therefore the only alternative. On May 27, 1827, Rivadavia's negotiator, Manuel García, and Pedro initialed a treaty in Rio that effectively left the Eastern Bank under Pedro's control and saddled Buenos Aires with indemnity payments to Pedro! In his haste to get Buenos Aires off the hook with Brazil, García had given away everything. When the treaty became known, an uproar of patriotic indignation spread from the congress meeting in Buenos Aires to the streets. García's home was attacked by a mob. Rivadavia disavowed García's actions. He followed with a public *mea culpa*, which was insufficient in staving off the demands for his resignation, which he duly tendered in late June. Rivadavia was forced to recognize that the war would have to be continued and that recruitment of troops in the provinces was needed. That was not possible, as Dorrego pointed out, so long as Rivadavia remained in office. Only a federalist president, armed with a new constitution, could lead Argentina into a patriotic war against the empire. That man was Dorrego.[22]

The irony for Sucre in these events was that he had come to believe that a Bolivian-Argentine federation would contribute more to the American equilibrium of states through agreement with the centralists than with federalists such as Dorrego. He knew that Dorrego would place more emphasis on Bolivia's military role against Brazil. The federalists would divert Bolivia from attending to the Peruvian threat. An editorial in *Condor* warned that joining the war against Brazil would not help Bolivia resist Peru and might even make it more vulnerable to Peruvian designs. Thus, even as Sucre opened relations with Dorrego through Funes, and even authorizing Funes to discuss the use of Bolivian auxiliaries in the war, he instructed Infante to open relations with Pedro in order to secure Rio's recognition of the Bolivian state.[23]

In late August, Dorrego decided to send Ignacio Bustos, the cousin and envoy of the *caudillo* of Córdoba, to Chuquisaca to negotiate a treaty of alliance with Sucre. Bustos gave Sucre a letter from Dorrego's government. It advised Sucre that the purpose of the mission was to repair "a strange anomaly of politics" by which "two American nations and neighbors, born of the same sacrifices to achieve independence and faced by the same dangers, maintained between them a cold indifference" even while "the blood of one of them is being spilled in a struggle provoked by the injustice and usurpation of another neighbor [Brazil] whose principles will always be very dangerous to the well being of the Republics in this part of the American Hemisphere."[24]

In spite of this declaration, the Bustos-Sucre exchanges are significant because they reveal how the concept of posing a republican challenge to the monarchy had become secondary to the balancing of power among the Spanish-American states. As Sucre and Bustos went through the motions of talking about the un-American character of the monarchy, their framework and vocabulary was that of equilibrium. Sucre had become convinced the war against the monarchy was not the way to assert the American character of the Bolivian-Argentine relationship. He maintained that the relationship should be part of the larger American equilibrium. Even as the two men talked about the American equilibrium, what they really meant was creating a power structure which would be favorable to Argentina at the expense of Peru.

Bustos opened his conversations with Sucre on Saturday, March 29, in Sucre's office at the palace, overlooking the central plaza of Chuquisaca. He stressed to Sucre that the new Dorrego government in Argentina had broken with Rivadavia's policy of trying to isolate Sucre's government in Bolivia. The primary goal of the government now was to "to close the breaches" opened in the Argentine relationship with Bolivia by pursuing "an American policy" based on an "alliance of friendship" between the two countries. In their first substantive talks on April 10, Sucre raised a question about whether enough national authority existed at the present time in Argentina to sign a treaty with Bolivia. But he was willing to be forthcoming. "We will negotiate, Mr. Ambassador," he said, "without the fastidious ceremony of the Europeans, with an American candor devoid of deceit. ... In politics they say that two plus two are not four, but between us there will be no duplicity."[25]

Quickly Tarija came up as a test of the "American" relationship between Bolivia and Argentina. Bustos pressed for restoration to Argentina, noting that it had been occupied on Sucre's orders when Argentina was being hurt in the bank war by Brazil, an action that, on its face, was a breach in American solidarity. Sucre said that at that time Argentina's policy toward Brazil looked more European than American, given Rivadavia's predilection for a British mediation. Now that Argentine policy was becoming more American under Dorrego, Sucre would consider reciprocating it by offering to cooperate on the Tarija question. He suggested arbitration so long as the arbitrator was "an American government, state or person." He did not even rule himself out. After he left the Bolivian presidency, as expected in August, he professed that he could be impartial on the Tarija matter. What was important, Sucre emphasized, was to avoid "the fatal example which had been given by Buenos Aires, of looking to, in regard to [the war with] Brazil, which was purely American, the British as guarantors or mediators, etc."[26]

As the two men groped to put the Argentine-Bolivian relationship on an "American" basis, Sucre's effort, clearly, was to de-emphasize the war with Brazil as the vehicle for that purpose. He was anxious to place the Bolivian-Argentine relationship in the framework of an American equilibrium of states, such that the balancing of Peruvian power, a need of both Bolivia and Colombia, was as much a part of the arrangement between Bolivia and Argentina as the balancing of Brazilian power. While still stressing Bolivia's American duty to support Argentina against Brazil, Bustos elaborated upon this other, larger American framework by stressing Colombia's problem with Peru as a reason for Bolivia solidifying with Argentina. "Lower Peru borders on Colombia," Bustos reminded Sucre, "and however much it extends its influence into Bolivia and not elsewhere, the more jealous Colombia ought to be and the more danger it faces." On the other hand, Argentina was at the other end of the continent from Colombia, which therefore had nothing to fear from it increasing its influence in Bolivia. American policy, Bustos said, "should concern itself with equilibrating the powers of states." Putting it into effect would be an enormous benefit to South America, particularly now when "it could be said that it was in the hands" of Bolívar and Sucre to do it.[27]

Argentine influence in Bolivia began to look more benign to Sucre as he faced, in 1828, the fact of Peruvian troops massing on Bolivia's borders. Buenos Aires should have influence in Bolivia, he said. Since Bolivia would be able to hold its own against Argentina, Argentina's influence in Bolivia was "more convenient to Colombia than the other's [Peru's]." Bolivia's union with Argentina was necessary, Sucre affirmed to Bustos, to "counterbalance the powers of America" and, almost as an afterthought, to "instill respect in the Emperor." He even alleged that Bolívar and he were of one mind on this subject![28]

After several negotiating sessions with Infante, Bustos was able to draft a treaty which he felt covered the area of agreement. There were actually two treaties combined into one. The first one was Sucre's and it comprised Articles 1–4. The emphasis was on a mutual assistance pact to repel aggression "which against one or the other, or both" might occur, and to sustain "the legitimate national government" of each other in the event auxiliary troops were needed for that purpose and were requested. Brazil is not mentioned in these articles. The emphasis upon "domestic support" is more clearly upon Bolivia's need for support against Peruvian attempts to dominate it through internal manipulation. Bustos's instructions were not overly receptive to Sucre's known offer to help Buenos Aires police the Argentine provinces in exchange for Argentine military help in Bolivia. In Article 5, the emphasis therefore shifted to the problem of external invasion. Here, the emphasis was Bolivia's entry into the war against Brazil as Argentina's ally. Bolivia was called upon to enter the fighting after delivering an ultimatum to Pedro asking for his acquiescence in Argentine demands for evacuation of the bank or suffer the consequences of Bolivia opening up a second land front against him. Infante was apprehensive that military aid would not be mutual. Bustos argued that Argentina, with a war against Brazil on its hands, could not promise immediate military help to Bolivia in the event Bolivia were invaded by Peru. Therefore, Argentina was required to announce the mobilization of its resources on Bolivia's behalf in that contingency. Until it was able to intervene militarily, it was obligated to interpose itself diplomatically with Peru in order to have any planned military attack suspended.[29]

Bustos prefaced the draft treaty by saying that the chief threat to the American republics was the absence of unity through solemn pacts made among themselves. Argentina was looking "by means of a purely American policy, for friends among its neighbors." It deeply wanted Bolivia on the other end of that policy. Sucre's long-sought goal—Argentine entry into the American equilibrium by supporting Bolivian independence from Peru—appeared to be near realization. In fact, Argentine policy goals toward Bolivia were becoming ambitious, judging by some of Bustos's communications to Buenos Aires. He argued that an alliance with Bolivia was useful in order that "Argentine policy be the decisive one [in Bolivia] and the one which governs [the Bolivians] who are amateurs at revolution and in want of civilization." He recommended that an Argentine minister stay in Chuquisaca, "in the manner of the Colombian chiefs" to see to it that "Peru, which is the other border state and which can lean on Bolivia or weaken or undermine the advantages of the policy of Argentina, does not occupy the place which [Argentina] should occupy." Argentina, to protect its role in Bolivia should seek to block any Peruvian use of force in that country.[30]

Events aborted this nascent relationship between Argentina and Bolivia. On April 18, a Colombian cavalry unit in Chuquisaca mutinied in emulation of the earlier Matute revolt. In a single-handed attempt to confront the mutineers, Sucre was severely injured in his right arm by a bullet; this gave the Peruvians the opportunity to invade. The mutiny was fomented by some obscure combination of Peruvian propaganda against Sucre and Argentine sedition which had been ongoing in Bolivia since the Rivadavia days. Curiously, Bustos appears to have been involved, although the result of the mutiny—the Peruvian invasion—was certainly not sought by him. But he may have been gambling that the Argentine takeover in Bolivia could have been accelerated by the mutiny.[31]

The political atmosphere in Lima had turned sharply nationalistic and anti-Bolívarian. In an a letter to Santander, which was published in an article appearing in *El Peruano*, the Bolivarian-turned-nationalist, Manuel Vidaurre, wrote that the Andean empire was the basis for creating a throne for Bolívar. It accused Bolívar of conspiring with Pedro to impose "two empires" in South America. This view spread rapidly from Lima into the press and diplomatic correspondence of South America.[32]

La Mar, who eventually came into the Peruvian presidency in the wake of the Colombian army's mutiny in Lima in early 1827, pursued a strategy of trying to ally with Buenos Aires in order to isolate Sucre and attempt to overthrow him in Bolivia, preparatory to confronting Bolívar in the north.

In view of this trend, Sucre decided to accelerate the evacuation of Colombian forces from Bolivia. He correctly feared that the Peruvians would try to reproduce the Colombian mutiny in Lima in Bolivia in order to bring him down. Therefore Sucre rejected the efforts of Bolívar's commanders in Colombia to get him to stay in Bolivia and open a second front against Peru in the event of war.[33]

In fact, the ultimate reason that Sucre wanted the Colombian troops out of Bolivia was that he did not want Bolivia to combine with Bolívar in an invasion of Peru. He feared that this would lead to the restoration of the Bolivarian order in Peru with all of the attendant pressures for unification of Peru and Bolivia. Sucre was not afraid to fight the Peruvians, but that fight, if it had to happen, should be made from Colombian soil for the purpose of protecting Colombian territory against Peruvian attacks, rather than from Bolivia, where the purpose inescapably would be to restore the Bolívarian system in Peru. Sucre was certain that while he was still in Bolivia, even with only a remnant of the Colombian army with him (especially if it included Pichincha, the best regiment), the commander of the Peruvian army, Agustín Gamarra, would not have the nerve to attack. If he did, Sucre was convinced that he would be able to make short work of him even if his army consisted mainly of green Bolivian troops. He was even convinced that if Gamarra attacked after all of the Colombians had left Bolivia, that the Bolivians would fight back. If Gamarra did succeed in occupying Bolivia, the Bolivians would "throw him out within a year, in defense of their independence." In the meantime, Colombia would have Peru "at its discretion." Should Peru manage to dominate Bolivia permanently, Sucre conceded that the Colombian south would become its next target. In that connection, he urged Bolívar to have Colombia give Bolivia a guarantee against a Peruvian invasion.[34]

Gamarra had drawn up a contingency plan for the invasion of Bolivia as early as June 1827. The main variables in the plan were the rate of Colombian evacuation, the rate of recruitment of Bolivian troops to take their place, and the degree of their concentration near the border. Gamarra was apparently not acting on orders from La Mar in regard to the invasion. On the contrary, he clearly saw the invasion as a method of inflating his reputation and wresting control of the presidency away from La Mar, while the latter was distracted by preparation for his looming war against Colombia in the north. In December 1827, Gamarra had two battalions and two squadrons from Tacna and Arequipa stationed at Puno, on Peru's border with Bolivia. At Lampa and Azuangaro, he had two more battalions, which had arrived from Cuzco. His attack force consisted of roughly 4,000 men including 500 cavalry. Sucre had organized a defensive force of 3,000 infantry and 700 cavalry, which he positioned between Oruro and La Paz. These forces were in the majority

Bolivian, but they included Pichincha. So long as Pichincha was in the Bolivian defensive configuration, it was doubtful that Gamarra would attack. But Pichincha was subsequently evacuated from Bolivia on April 15, 1828. This was the work of Miguel Antonio Figueredo, who was named commander of Colombian forces in Bolivia by the Bogotá Congress. His orders were to weaken Sucre.[35]

The revolt of Colombian troops occurred in Chuquisaca three days after Pichincha's departure. Sucre's injury in the revolt caused him to turn the government over to his ministers. The mutiny in Chuquisaca gave Gamarra the chance that he was looking for. He sent his army across the border in late April, announcing that the revolt required this step as a means of Peruvian "mediation" of the turmoil in Bolivia occasioned by the revolt in Chuquisaca. "It is not ambition, desire for conquest, or usurpation which obliges me to take this step; it is the health and life of both Perus." Sucre's death would be a public calamity that Peru could not permit to happen to an "American hero." The Peruvian army would save him![36]

Sucre was not impressed with Gamarra's solicitude for his safety. He wrote the shifty Peruvian general that the invasion was nothing more or less than the application of the law of the strongest on the international level and as such it set a pernicious precedent for the American states. Following Gamarra's example, "Colombia, stronger than Peru and with even more cause, will intervene in Peruvian affairs (under this law). Europe, observing that our public international law is that of power and bayonets will not hesitate to teach us some rules and to dispose of our fate."[37]

Gamarra, however, saw the ultimate purpose of the invasion to allow Bolivia "to have its own being and to belong to itself ... to constitute itself in its own way without the interference from the foreign state [Colombia] which has up to now disposed of its fate." As such, Bolivia could join the ranks of the American republics. The vehicle for the achievement of this result was to be a treaty, which Gamarra had drafted in a "minute" of May 10, 1828. He wanted all of the Colombians out of the country forthwith; the Bolivian constitution abrogated and a "democratic" one promulgated; relations with the Brazilian monarchy, which Sucre had opened, to be suspended in the "interest of identity of principles and common cause" with the rest of the American states, and until Pedro acceded to Argentine demands in the bank.[38]

In Pedro Blanco, a Bolivian commander, Gamarra found a key military traitor. Blanco's defection confused and demoralized Bolivian forces and prevented them from being effectively rallied against the Peruvians. In José María Pérez de Urdininea, he found a political collaborator albeit a reluctant one. Urdininea, in the June treaty negotiations, at first resisted the terms calling for immediate expatriation of the remaining Colombians without payment of back salaries or outstanding prize money. He insisted that this could only be stipulated if the Peruvian troops left along with the Colombians. The fact that Gamarra had waited until Pichincha had left Bolivia to invade, made Urdininea somewhat dubious of Gamarra's protestations that it was solely the presence of Colombians in Bolivia that motivated the invasion. Urdininea also insisted that Sucre was the legitimate president of Bolivia and that his departure should be handled with decorum. Urdininea and Gamarra, however, eventually came to terms as embodied in the Treaty of Piquiza, dated July 6, 1828. Fifteen days were allotted for all remaining Colombian military personnel to leave. Transit rights to Arica would be guaranteed to Colombian units. Sucre would be allowed to address the congress prior to resigning his office and leaving. The Bolivian constitution should be taken under consideration for revision. A new president would be elected by the congress. Both Peru and Bolivia would not open diplomatic relations with Brazil until the Eastern Bank war was settled. The Peruvian army would begin the process of withdrawal to the Desaguadero River. Diplomatic ties between Bolivia and Peru would be established as soon as the Peruvian army was off Bolivian soil.[39]

Sucre and Gamarra, obviously, did not part ways on the best of terms. Sucre, accused the Piquiza treaty of "asserting the conqueror's rights." Gamarra responded that Sucre was a tool of Bolívar who intended to make Peru and Bolivia into client states of Colombia. This was the ultimate distortion of Ayacucho, he said. Gamarra wanted Peru and Bolivia to "belong to their native sons and not be the patrimony of any person." He concluded by noting to Sucre that "it is your person which causes the anxiety of two states [Peru and Bolivia] and not because of [jealousy of] your stature, since that disappeared in the mutiny of last April, but because of your cunning tricks."[40]

Sucre had been placed under arrest by Peruvian troops at Nucco, a *hacienda* outside of Chuquisaca that he frequented on weekends. He was brought, under trying and humiliating circumstances, to Chuquisaca where his address to the congress, which he wrote at Nucco, was read for him.

In his testament, Sucre described his wounded arm as the one which "in Ayacucho ended the war of American independence" and "brought to life Bolivia" (*dió ser a Bolivia*). His most famous sentences (for Bolivians) are these from the testament which are engraved on the equestrian statue of Sucre in the plaza of Chuquisaca:

> I ask only one gift from the nation and its leaders: that of not destroying the fruit of my creation, of preserving in the midst of all dangers the

independence of Bolivia and to suffer complete disgrace and even the death of its sons before losing the sovereignty of the republic.[41]

Sucre left Chuquisaca barely an hour before advance units of Gamarra's army occupied the city. He headed for the Pacific port of Cobija on a mule.

It did not take long for the repercussions of Sucre's overthrow to become evident on the Atlantic side of the continent. Seeing Sucre's downfall as the removal of one of the main supports for escalating the war, Dorrego warmed to a diplomatic settlement arranged by the British. Ponsonby's negotiations with La Valleja had produced agreement on the creation of an independent state in the bank. Ponsonby used this agreement to pressure Dorrego into acceptance. Dorrego's relatively greater ability to broaden the Argentine base of the war, beyond anything that Rivadavia could hope to achieve, combined with the surprising gains made against Brazilian forces by Fructuosa Rivera, the Argentine *caudillo*, dampened Pedro's enthusiasm for more fighting. He became amenable to British proposals for the creation of an independent buffer state in the bank. The big defeat of his imperial army at Ituzaingo had also taken a severe toll on Pedro's popularity among Brazilians. In Rio, on August 28, 1828, the final treaties were signed under Ponsonby's auspices by the representatives of Pedro and Dorrego. With the signing of those treaties a new state—Uruguay—took its place among the Spanish-speaking republics on the South American continent. It was a classic buffer state. Its creation was a harbinger of South America's balance of power system.

The repercussions of Sucre's downfall on the Pacific side of the continent were, however, less favorable to the expansion of British diplomatic influence. The Pacific balance of power pattern was driven by the outbreak of the war between Colombia and Peru in 1829. U.S. diplomacy loomed larger in the mediation of this war than did British diplomacy. This reflected the collapse of Bolívar's Andean empire.

La Mar had led an army across the border into Ecuador in an attempt to fan the flames of revolt against Bolívar that had been ignited there by the mutinous Colombian division under the command of Bustamante. La Mar proceeded to occupy Guayaquil. He was reinforced by the arrival of Gamarra's "victorious" army from Bolivia. By this time, Bolívar had returned to Bogotá after his flirtation with Páez in Venezuela. He broke definitively with Santander who was arrested for complicity in a plot to assassinate Bolívar. The Liberator proceeded to take dictatorial authority over Colombia on June 24, 1828, after he learned that the constitutional convention that he had convened at Ocaña had failed to adopt the Bolivian constitution. He then mobilized his forces to repel the Peruvians and to invade Peru in order to re-establish the Bolivian constitution there and subsequently in Bolivia, where he would undo the effects of Gamarra's invasion. As Bolívar contemplated the attempted overthrow of his system in Peru, Gamarra's invasion of Bolivia, and the prospect of a war between Colombia and Peru, he focussed on the idea of formalizing an alliance between Colombia and Brazil. His reasons were partly tactical. "With our attention turned south," he wrote General Francisco Carabaño, who was his choice as Colombia's first ambassador to Rio, "we should be on good terms with the Emperor of Brazil." But his purposes were also political and ideological. Bolívar saw the Colombian-Brazilian alliance as an axis that would moderate the behavior of the republics. The British envoy in Bogotá, Charles Henderson, pointed out this drift in Bolívar's thinking with evident gratification. He said that Bolívar had become convinced "that the Republican forms of government are chimeras and he is on that account more desirous to maintain relations of intimate friendship with the Emperor of Brazil." The purpose, Henderson stated, "was to give tone to the political institutions of the New States, whose prosperity appears to depend on the adoption of more vigorous and permanent Systems of Government." In expanded instructions to Bogotá's new envoy in Rio, Pedro was to be informed that since 1825 Colombia had shown its desire for good relations with the Brazilian monarchy. The behavior of the other Spanish-speaking states was in stark contrast, as exemplified most recently by Peru's inclusion of a clause in the Treaty of Piquiza that prevented Bolivia from establishing diplomatic relations with the empire.[42]

Since he first developed his idea of an Andean empire, Bolívar had envisaged a tacit collaboration with the Brazilian empire in the organization of the South American system. Now, as the Andean empire became threatened by the Peruvian defection, more explicit collaboration with the Brazilian empire was needed. And, it appeared, a more explicit dynastic cast in Colombia's own domestic order was also desirable in order to present a common cause with the empire in establishing standards of behavior for the unruly Spanish-American republics.[43]

Fearful that he would be seen as a reactionary, he wrote that if "all of America were to denounce his tyranny" over Colombia, Bolívar saw himself "left with the only hope that Europe would do [him] justice." He expected "nothing from any form of American system."[44] He began returning to his old theme. "America needs a regulator," he wrote to his foreign minister Estanislao Vegara, "such that its mediation, protection or influence emanate from a powerful nation of the Old World ... [it should] exercise enough power so that if its policy be ignored and insufficient, it uses force to make the voice of duty heard." Dangers still existed for recolonization of South America by Spain or other European nations, not to mention the hegemonic threat of the United States in the hemisphere. Great Britain, therefore, should be South America's regulator. Its mediation of the Plata war established the precedent. That precedent could be expanded, if need be, in connection with the war against Peru.[45]

<hr>

After a trip of almost three weeks, down the Andes and across the Atacama Desert, Sucre arrived at the Bolivian port of Cobija on the Pacific coast. A bad fall off his mule had almost cost him his life. His wound continued to fester and would not close for another three months. His physical discomfort, combined with bitterness over the Gamarra invasion and the Bolivian capitulation, depressed him. But he was glad to be heading back to Quito.

It was galling for him that his only chance for passage out of Cobija was an English commercial ship, the *Porscopin*. His request to Santander for naval transportation for him and his staff had met with a stony silence. The *Porscopin* was scheduled to stop at Arica and Callao. The latter stop was dangerous personally for Sucre, should his presence on board become known to the Peruvian authorities. On the other hand, Sucre saw an opportunity to act as an intermediary between Bolívar and La Mar to avert the war between Colombia and Peru. Sucre chose the latter course and once at Callao, on September 9, 1828, he announced his arrival and invited the Peruvians to talk. Sensing a trap, he declined an offer to disembark but invited Peruvian envoys to board the *Porscopin*. Judging from Peruvian press editorials, Sucre's decision not to disembark was a wise one. After he had departed Callao for Guayaquil, the government was severely censured for "not making use of the unquestionable right belonging to every nation to take prisoner an enemy general who is trying to arrive in his country at the outbreak of war." Apparently the same "right" did not apply when Santander's man in Bolivia, the Colombian colonel Miguel Antonio Figueredo, surfaced in Lima after Gamarra's invasion of Bolivia. He was treated as an ally by Peruvian officials.[46]

By seeing La Mar, Sucre hoped to persuade him to abandon the idea of war with Colombia in the north by alerting him to the danger to that Gamarra and Santa Cruz represented to his presidency in the south. He had already sought to warn La Mar. Now he had fresh evidence from comments that Gamarra had made in Potosí that Gamarra considered La Mar's presidency illegitimate because since he was from Guayaquil he was a foreigner.[47]

Sucre's invitations to talk on board the *Porscopin* were spurned by La Mar's foreign minister, José María Galdeano. He informed Sucre that "[t]here were well known plans formed in the north and in the south against Peru." Sucre's intervention with "General Bolívar" was unlikely to be availing. In any event, it was a moot point, since Bolívar had declared war against Peru and "suffocated the voice of his own country [Santander] in favor of liberty and the right of Peru to self-determination."[48]

Sucre had been prepared to discuss a plan with the Peruvians that he developed for mediation of the war by the Panama congress which had migrated to Tacubaya, Mexico. As soon as he arrived at Guayaquil, Sucre sent a letter to Bolívar pressing that initiative in an effort to dissuade him from war against Peru. The reason Sucre had stopped in Callao, he informed Bolívar, was that, in his view, Colombia lacked the military preparedness in the south to fight a land war successfully against Peru. Colombia's fleet was in the Caribbean, while Peru's was in the Pacific, giving the latter the option of blockading Colombian ports on the Pacific, especially Guayaquil. In this same letter, Sucre reviewed the events surrounding his overthrow in Bolivia, placing great emphasis on his hope that the Bolivians "who have a country because of me" would free themselves of Gamarra's influence. He also emphasized the imminence of a power struggle between Gamarra and La Mar. All of this was carefully calculated to discourage any punitive action against Peru that Bolívar might be contemplating. Sucre feared that a war between Colombia and Peru might lead to the re-installation of Bolívar's lifetime presidency system into the domestic structure of Peru and from there into Bolivia and Colombia.[49]

Sucre's plan for an American mediation of the war anticipated powerful currents that were already moving in that direction. It was, increasingly, mediation by the United States that was being singled out. As a result of suggestions made by William Tudor, the American envoy to Lima and an ardent foe of Bolívar, La Mar's foreign minister, José Mariategui, had approached Washington and London. In late 1827, he had written to Secretary of State Henry Clay requesting U.S. mediation "in defense of Peru's peace and freedom." Peru would not submit "to being conquered by the combined forces of Bolivia and Colombia." Tudor had prepared Clay for the request by telling him that if the "consequences that would follow" from the forcible extension of "the character and view of Bolívar" through the war, were fully understood, the mediation help by the United States and Great Britain should not only be given "but it should be accompanied by an alternative that would compel its acceptance." He later explained that with Bolívar "obtaining absolute control of the two Perus and once more established in Lima, with Sucre at his old outpost (in Bolivia) the former intrigues will be resumed against Chile and Buenos Aires." Tudor subsequently added Mexico to the list of mediators.[50]

Joaquín Campino, Chile's ambassador in Washington, had proposed to Secretary of State Martin Van Buren, Clay's successor, an American mediation of the war between Colombia and Peru in order to prevent the war from leading, by virtue of a victory by Bolívar, "to a consolidation of territory and the establishment of a military power" that would be dangerous to the liberty of Chile and Argentina. He argued that the interest of the United States would also be prejudiced by the war producing an Andean empire. Van Buren continued Clay's affirmative policy. The proposal of a joint American mediation "did full justice to the United States' deep interest" in preventing the unbalancing of power in Andean South America.[51]

During the year following his arrival in the Colombian south, Sucre played a crucial role, political and military, in the structuring of the Colombian war against Peru. Two cardinal objectives governed his activities. The first was to stop a victory over Peru from leading to the creation of an Andean empire. The second was to stop European mediation of the war. These objectives put Sucre at cross purposes with Bolívar and, more obviously, with Daniel O'Leary, his proxy in the south.[52] O'Leary was blindly loyal to Bolívar. Sucre, despite his personal affection for Bolívar and his respect for the Liberator's enormous accomplishments, had come to doubt his capacity to lead Colombia.

Two distinct purposes, beyond defense of its borders, are ascribable to Colombia's purposes in the war against Peru. First, as Rafael Urdaneta, one of Bolívar's New Granadian generals, suggested, it could be tied to the "political regeneration" of Colombia under Bolívar's dictatorship. This purpose was in turn tied to the re-establishment of the Bolivian constitution in Peru, which the southern Bolívarian commanders felt should be its true purpose. This scenario would have been facilitated if Sucre had cooperated by staying in Bolivia. The second purpose ascribable to the war against Peru was that of re-establishing the equilibrium of the South American states, which was upset by the Peruvian invasion of Bolivia. In this perspective, it was not the ideological structure of Bolivia (or of Peru for that matter) that warranted Colombia's war against Peru. "In light of Peru's invasion of Bolivia," Tomás Heres, Bolívar's Venezuelan aide, wrote to Urdaneta, presumably to discourage this first purpose, "Colombia should make war on Peru to re-establish the political equilibrium of South America." Essential to that equilibrium was "the independence of Bolivia which will serve as a buffer [*cuerpo neutral*] between Peru and Argentina and will always distract Peru [from Colombia]." He concluded his analysis by stating that if Argentina were involved in the war against Brazil, "Colombia's situation would be different because then Argentina would seek to maintain the equilibrium" and push the Peruvians out of Bolivia.[53]

Bolívar called Sucre back from retirement in Quito to take command of the Colombian forces to be used against the Peruvians. In his long military career, Sucre had fought against fellow Spanish Americans, but they had always been under the command of Spaniards or Spanish sympathizers. This time it was different. He was not sure what he was fighting for. He hoped it was only against Peru's territorial aggression. He suspected it was for the Liberator's vanity. Sucre handed Bolívar a deadly victory over the Peruvians at Tarqui. No quarter was given by the Colombians. The carnage left 1,500 Peruvians dead on the field, along with 15 commanders and 60 officers. After the "battle" Sucre wrote Bolívar that he "was not sure if the men were fighting for Colombia or for Bolívar."[54] Sucre signed a generous treaty with the defeated Peruvian officers, led by a chastened and obsequious Agustín Gamarra. It only required that Peru respect the independence of Bolivia, pay its war debt to Colombia and agree to negotiate a border treaty with Colombia—a far cry from requiring the restoration of the Bolívarian order in Peru and Bolivia that Bolívar vehemently wanted. The return of Guayaquil to Colombia, was not even addressed.[55]

Bolívar immediately set about overriding Sucre's treaty by planning an invasion of Peru. He signaled Sucre, through O'Leary, that he was disappointed with the softness of his post-Tarqui treaty but indicated that Sucre could vindicate himself by leading and planning the invasion of Peru. He predicted that as Colombian forces closed on Peru, like those of Napoleon returning to France from Egypt, the Peruvian people would rise up, proclaim him their liberator, and pave the way to the creation of the Bolivarian order in the length and breadth of the Andes. He was heartened by Gamarra's overthrow of La Mar and seizure of power in Lima. Apparently Gamarra was once again a Bolivarian; he was writing admiring letters to Bolívar, inviting him back to Peru as the country's savior.[56]

Sucre advanced many arguments—logistical, political, strategic—against an invasion of Peru.[57] He need not have worried. Páez's activities distracted Bolívar from his plans for Peru. Declaring Venezuela's secession, Páez had massed Venezuelan troops on the border with New Granada. After returning from the southern theater to Bogotá, Bolívar had ordered Sucre to negotiate an accommodation with the Venezuelan commanders at the border. The mission failed; the Venezuelan secession decision was not negotiable. Páez came out in open defiance of Bolívar. (Ecuador followed suit and seceded under the leadership of a local, Venezuelan-born *caudillo*, Juan José Flores.) Bolívar gamely tried to rally support among the *granadino* delegates in the congress to raise an army to invade Venezuela and crush Páez, whom he now recognized as his nemesis. The legislators would have none of it; the time for confrontion had passed and so had the time for Bolívar. With his health completely broken and his prestige at its lowest ebb, the Liberator accepted a pension from the congress and left for a long, melancholy boat ride down the Madgdalena to Cartagena and a planned trip to Europe.

Sucre was prepared to return to Ecuador after his unavailing negotiations with Páez's commanders. He was bittersweet about the prospect. His marriage was not particularly a happy one. Yet his wife had borne him a daughter of whom he was very fond. He decided to make a go of the marriage. Quito was his home now—for better or worse. He was making plans to become a country farmer and to lead a life of quietude and reflection. He planned to read extensively, something his hectic and crowded life had not permitted. Fortunately, his wife's dowry included a large country *hacienda*.

Sucre had ridden to Bogotá from Quito in the company of civilians who were Ecuadorean delegates, along with Sucre, to the Ocaña Convention. He returned with them, following a brief stay in Bogotá where he accepted a commission from the government to prevail upon Flores to repeal his actions and restore his land to Colombia. Traveling with civilians had possibly blunted Sucre's security instincts. Had he been with military companions, signs of danger would probably have been noticed and precautions taken. One particular sign was that the individual in whose hut the party stayed the night, reappeared the following day ahead of them. He turned out to be an accomplice in a conspiracy against Bolívar. Part of the plan was to assassinate the man they feared would be Bolívar's successor.

At seven o'clock in the morning of June 4, 1830, Sucre left the small town of Ventaquemado and began the ascent of the mountain of Berruecos. The rain had stopped and the mountain air was brisk and clear. A few miles up the trail, four shots rang out. Three hit Sucre, one in the head. He died instantaneously and lay face down in the mud for 20 hours until his horrified companions, who fled, dared return. They buried him in a makeshift grave on the roadside.

Bolívar did not make it past Santa Marta on the Caribbean coast. He wanted to sail for Europe, but his health was failing fast. On hearing the news of Sucre's assassination, he clasped his forehead and uttered a curse. It was the last straw. He died six months later at a small farm on the outskirts of Santa Marta. It was one o'clock in the afternoon of December 17, 1830.

Notes

1. Sucre understanding with Alvear and Dorrego: Mariano Pelliza, *Dorrego en la Historia de los Partidos Unitarios y Federales.* Buenos Aires, 1878, 278–81,

which contains letters to this effect from Dorrego in Chuquisaca to various Argentine provincial politicos; Dorrego presidency as part of the plan: in ibid., 276.

2. Sucre to Funes, January 21, 1826, in Biblioteca Nacional de Argentina, A. J. Sucre to Dean Funes, doc. no. 542/67.

3. "Crux of the question": Sucre to Funes, February 7, 1826, Biblioteca Nacional, doc. no. 542/71; "Britain is mixing itself": Sucre to Bolívar, June 6, 1826, and August 4, 1826, Daniel F. O'Leary, *Cartas de Sucre al Libertador.* Madrid, 1919, 34–35, 73 respectively; Sucre's view of the Stuart mission as less threatening than Ponsoby's: Sucre to Funes, October 22, 1826, Biblioteca Nacional de Argentina, folio doc. 542/116.

4. Sucre's objectives in allying with the *caudillos* against Rivadavia: Sucre to Bolívar, August 4, 1827, in Daniel F. O'Leary, *Memorias de General O'Leary*, I: 447; Forbes to Clay, April 12, 1827, in William Manning, *Diplomatic Correspondence of the United States Concerning the Independence of the Latin American Nations.* New York: Oxford University Press, 1925, I, 660–661; Sucre to Funes, August 2, 1826, Biblioteca Nacional de Argentina, folio doc. 542/97; Sucre to Bolívar, December 20, 1826, O'Leary, *Memorias*, I, 417; Matute statement, November 1826, *Documentos Referentes a la Creación de Bolivia*, II, 287. It appeared in the *Colombia Gazette*, no. 288, when it was under Santander's control. When it was under Bolívar's control, after September 1827, its issue no. 330 reported Matute's death, criticized the official applause given to Matute in Colombia and elsewhere, and praised the lifetimers (*vitalícios*) in Bolivia. See *Documentos Referentes a la Creación de Bolivia*, II: 456–57 for no. 330. Rivadavia's "protection" of Matute is cited in a circular n.d. from Geraldino to the provincal governors of Argentina, *Documentos Referentes a la Creación de Bolivia*, II: 291–293. Funes mentions to Sucre Rivadavia's backing of Matute through Arenales. Funes to Sucre, February 18, 1827, in J. Francisco Silva, *El Libertador Bolívar y el Dean Funes.* Madrid, 1916, 370–71. Funes protested the government's support for Matute in Argentina in his letter to Manuel Moreno, minister of foreign relations, December 14, 1827, in Carlos Gonzalo Saavedra, *El Dean Funes y la Fundación de Bolivia.* La Paz, 1976, 83–88. This volume is especially valuable for the Argentine archival material copied into the annexes, 57–94. Sucre's responsibility for Matute's escape into Argentina: O'Connor, 232–39; Sucre to Bolívar, November 27, 1826, in O'Leary, *Memorias*, I: 406. Agustín Geraldino circular to the governors of Salta, Tucumán, La Rioja, Catamarca, Santiago, Córdoba, November 30, 1826, *Documentos Referentes a la Creación de Bolivia*, II, 291–93; Infante to Colombian Foreign Ministry, August 19, 1827, *Documentos Referentes a la Creación de Bolivia*, II: 448. Sucre mentions the accusations against him for inciting the Argentine *caudillos* in the Salta legislature in his letter to Bolívar, September 4, 1827, in *Documentos Referentes a la Creación de Bolivia*, II, 451; "All of Argentina": Sucre to Bolívar, December 27, 1826, in *Documentos Referentes a la Creación de Bolivia*, II: 309. Sucre's protest that it was the centralists who had escalated the conflict by putting Matute in their pay, and his denial of any responsibility for the civil wars in the Argentine provinces, is conveyed by Funes in his letter to the Argentine foreign ministry, December 14, 1827, in Saavedra, 83–85.

5. Sucre mentions Bolívar's admonition not to interfere with Ortiz achieving his objectives in his letter to Bolívar, May 20, 1826, *Documentos Referentes a la Creación Bolivia*, II: 142–143.

6. Santa Cruz to la Fuente July 3, 1826, in *Archivo Histórico de Mariscal Andrés Santa Cruz.* La Paz, Bolivia, 1976, I: 196.

7. "He should never remove Peru from his sight": Santa Cruz to Bolívar (via Heres), August 9, 1826, in ibid., 201–02; "This way constitute themselves better": Ibid., Santz Cruz to Sucre, April 28, 1826, in ibid., 193–94.

8. "Supreme and delicate office of representative of Peru": Pando to Infante, July 13, 1826, in Carlos Ortiz de Zeballos, *La Misión de Ortiz de Zeballos en Bolivia, 1826–1827.* Lima, 1956, 343. The emphasis is added. Long quote from the instructions, in ibid., 8–9.

9. Sucre to Santa Cruz, October 4, 1826, O'Leary, *Cartas,* III: 116–21.

10. Use of Bolívarian system to fuse Bolivia and Peru together: Santa Cruz to Sucre, April 28, 1826, *Archivo Histórico,* 193–94. Danger of Bolivia being swallowed by Peru in the fusion: Sucre to Santa Cruz, August 12, 1826, in *Documentos Referentes a la Creación de Bolivia,* II: 378–79.

11. More autonomy from Lima for Arequipa in the Peru-Bolivian federation: Bolívar to La Fuente, May 17, 1826, in *Documentos Referentes a la Creación de Bolivia,* II: 376. More even "balance of power": Sucre's term in describing the article in *Federal* to Bolívar in his letter of December 4, 1826, O'Leary, *Cartas,* II: 129.

12. Sucre to La Fuente, December 4, 1826, in ibid., 381–84.

13. Events and commentary on the New Granadian revolt in Lima: Tomás Heres, "Account of the Revolt of the Colombian Third Division in Lima," n.d., in O'Leary, *Memorias,* V, 178; Sucre to Bolívar, March 11, 1827, in O'Leary, *Cartas,* II: 150; Anti-Venezuelan racial aspect: Tudor to Clay, May 17, 1826, in Manning, III: 1794–95. Santander commented on the "illiberality" displayed by Sucre in his letters to the Colombian commander in Lima, Bartólome Salom. These were captured by Bustamente, leader of the New Granadian mutiny, and forwarded to Santander. Santander accused Sucre and Salom of efforts to isolate the Colombian Division from Bogotá press reports. Santander to Bustamente, March 14, 1827, in Roberto Cortazar, ed., *Cartas y Mensajes.* Bogotá, 1953–1956, VII: 86–87. Also Jacinto Lara to Santander, January 7, 1827, Roberto Cortazar, ed., *Correspondencia Dirigida al General Santander.* Bogotá, 1964–1970, VI: 80. Favorable appraisal of the mutiny by the anti-Bolívar, pro-Santander U.S. consul in Lima: Tudor to Clay, February 3, 1827, in Manning, III: 1816. Bustamente's anti-Páez protestations: Jesus Henac and Gerardo Arrubla, *History of Colombia.* Trans. and ed. by J. Fred Rippy. Chapel Hill: University of North Carolina Press, 1938, 393. Cristóbal Armero to Bolívar, May 22, 1827, in O'Leary, *Memorias,* IV: 439–41. Santander to Bustamente, March 14, 1827, in Cortazar, *Cartas y Mensajes,* VII: 78–81. Rafael Urdaneta to Mariano Montilla, June 1, 1827, in O'Leary, *Memorias,* VI: 145–48; Jose D. Espinar to Bolívar, March 26, 1827, in ibid., V: 505–6; Tudor to Clay, May 23, 1827, in Manning, III: 1813; Tudor to Clay, March 3, 1827, in ibid., 1825; Arrubula, 405.

14. Santander to Bolívar, n.d., in Cortazar, *Cartas y Mensajes,* VII: 60–65.

15. *Condor,* Bolivian official newspaper, February 1, 1829, 19.

16. Sucre to Bolívar, March 11, 1827, in O'Leary, *Memorias,* I: 424.

17. Sucre to Bolívar, August 4, 1827, in ibid., I: 447.

18. Santa Cruz to Peruvian foreign ministry, May 12, 1828, in *Archivo Histórico,* I: 305–06.

19. Sucre to O'Connor December 22, 1826, O'Connor, 226–27; Sucre to O'Connor, February 7, 1827, in ibid., 228–30; Sucre to Bolívar, March 26, 1827, in O'Leary, *Memorias,* I: 427.

20. Sucre used the phrase "purely American war" to characterize the Plata conflict, in a conversation (Saavedra, 67) with an Argentine envoy, Juan Ignacios Bustos on April 10, 1828. Sucre to Bolívar, July 3, 1827, in O'Leary, *Cartas de Sucre,* II: 168–70; Sucre to Bolívar, July 3, 1827, 439. Ron Seckinger, *The Brazilian Monarchy and the South American Republics.* Baton Rouge, La.: Louisiana State University Press, 1984, (137, n. 14) reports a copy of the text of the proposed federation dated April 4, 1826, is in the Argentine archives.

21. Azuero to Alvear, April 6, 1827, in Rodríguez, II: 321–22

22. Funes to Sucre, July 18, 1827, in Silva, 383–87. Dorrego to Sucre, July 18, 1827, in O'Leary, *Memorias,* XI: 291; Funes to Sucre, July 10, 1827, in Silva, 379–83. Funes to Sucre, July 18, 1827, in ibid., 383–87; Dorrego to Sucre, July 18, 1827 in O'Leary, *Memorias,* XI: 290–93.

23. Sucre to Bolívar, September 4, 1827, in *Documentos Referentes a la Creación de Bolivia,* II: 453. Ibid., 469 copies a "letter from La Paz," carried in the *Colombian Gazette,* no. 329, which argues that Bolivia could not fight Brazil and Peru at the same time. Sucre's decision to open relations with Brazil: Sucre to Bolívar, January 27, 1827, in O'Leary, I: 488; Seckinger, *Brazilian Monarchy,* 139.

24. Dorrego's choice of Bustos for the Bolivian mission: Funes to Sucre, July 10, 1827, in Silva, 382–83; Funes to Sucre, July 18, 1827, in ibid., 383–87; Funes to Sucre, August 26, 1827, in ibid., 387–88; "Strange anomaly of politics": Jose Rondeau, minister of foreign relations, to Sucre, November (n.d.) 1827, in Saavedra, 58–59. Bustos's instructions, December 3, 1827, in Saavedra, 60–61.

25. Bustos conversation with Sucre, April 10, 1828, in Saavedra, 65.

26. Ibid., 67.

27. Ibid., 66.

28. Ibid., 67; Sucre to Bolívar, July 12, 1827, O'Leary, *Cartas,* 173–74.

29. Draft treaty text, Saavedra, 69–70.

30. Bustos to Argentine foreign ministry, n.d., Saavedra, 68.

31. Saavedra, 76–88, documents Bustos's complicity.

32. *Condor,* April 19, 1827, 3–4; Seckinger, 133.

33. Sucre to Flores, February 3, 1827, in O'Leary, *Cartas de Sucre,* II: 419–20.

34. Sucre to Bolívar, January 27, 1828, and March 11, 1828, in *Documentos Referentes a la Creación de Bolivia,* II: 519–20 and 529 respectively. Alfonso Rumazo Gonzalez, *Sucre: Gran Mariscal de Ayacucho.* Madrid, 1963, 305, states Sucre's preference for fighting in Colombia, rather than in Bolivia, against Peru. He, however, stops short of linking this preference to the *vitalicia* issue which, in my own view, is the key to the matter.

35. Sucre to Bolívar, July 3, 1827, in O'Leary, *Cartas de Sucre,* II: 168–70; Sucre to Bolívar, January 27, 1828, in *Documentos Referentes a la Creación de Bolivia,* II: 524–526. Gamarra invasion deployments: Sucre to Bolívar, December 20, 1827, in *Documentos Referentes a la Creación de Bolivia,* II: 483–84.

36. Gamarra to Leon Galindo, April 30, 1828, in Agustín Gamarra, *Epistolario.* Lima, 1952, I: 94–95.

37. Sucre to Gamarra, May 10, 1828, in *Documentos Referentes a la Creación de Bolivia*, II: 560.

38. Gamarra, "Minute on Treaty Terms," May 10, 1828, in *Documentos Referentes a la Creación de Bolivia*, II: 556; Gamarra to La Paz Prefect, July 10, 1828, in *Epistolario*, I: 108–09.

39. Gamarra's use of Blanco and Urdininea: Gamarra to Peruvian Ministry of War, June 15, 1828, in *Epistolario*, I: 104–06; Gamarra to Juan Francisco Reyes, in ibid., 107; Treaty text, July 7, 1828, in *Documentos Referentes a la Creación de Bolivia*, II: 588–91.

40. Gamarra to Sucre, July 17, 1828, in *Epistolario*, I: 110–11.

41. Text of Sucre's testament, *Documentos Referentes a la Creación de Bolivia*, II: 599–618. Quotation, 617.

42. Bolívar to Francisco Carabono, July 9, 1828, in Lecuna and Barret de Nazaris, *Simon Bolívar: Obras Completas*. Havana, Cuba, 1950, II: 911; Seckinger, *Brazilian Monarchy*, 141–43.

43. Harrison to Van Buren, May 27, 1829, in Manning, II: 1334–35.

44. Bolívar to Leandro Palacios, July 27, 1829, in Lecuna and Barret de Nazaris, *Obras Completas*, III: 261; Bolívar to Patrick Campbell, August 5, 1829, in ibid., 278.

45. Bolívar to Vergara, July 6, 1829, in ibid., III: 239–44.

46. "To take prisoner an enemy general": Quoted from *La Prensa Peruana*, Peruvian official newspapaer, in Jorge Basadre, *Historia de la República de Peru*. Lima, 1949, I: 245. Figueredo in Lima: Urdaneta to Mariano Montilla, August 7, 1828, in O'Leary, *Memorias*, VI: 169–70.

47. Santa Cruz to de la Fuente, October 3, 1827, in *Archivo Histórico*, I: 281.

48. José María Galdeano to Sucre, September 11, 1828, in *Documentos Referentes a la Creación de Bolivia*, II: 621–23; Sucre to Galdeano, September 11, 1828, in ibid., 623–24.

49. Sucre to Bolívar, September 18, 1828, in *Documentos Referentes a la Creación de Bolivia*, II: 624–30.

50. "In defense of Peru's peace and freedom": Mariategui to Clay, November 16, 1828, in Manning, III: 1838; "Consequences would follow": Tudor to Clay, November 20, 1827, in Manning, III: 1840–42; August 1, 1829, ibid., 1844–46.

51. Juaquin Campino to Martin Van Buren, May 5, 1829, in Manning, II: 1134; Van Buren to Campino, May 26, 1829, in ibid., I: 304–05.

52. Sucre's disputatious remarks to O'Leary: letter, November 7, 1828, O'Leary, *Memorias*, IV: 490–91.

53. Heres to Urdaneta, September 6, 1828, in O'Leary, *Memorias*, IV: 275–79.

54. Sucre to Bolívar, March 3, 1829, in O'Leary, *Cartas*, II: 283.

55. Arrubula, 408; Basadre, I: 254; Rumazo, 320.

56. Sucre to Bolívar, June 28, 1829, O'Leary, *Cartas*, II: 298–299 refers to Bolívar's criticism of the Giron Treaty brought to Sucre's attention by O'Leary.

57. Sucre to Bolívar, June 28, 1829, in O'Leary, *Cartas*, II: 300.

Bibliography

Books and Articles

Abecia, Valentín. *Historiografía Boliviana.* La Paz, 1973.
———. *Independencia: El Criollismo de La Plata.* La Paz, 1970.
———. *La Revolución de 1809.* La Paz, 1954.
Alcalá, Domingo de. *Para la Historia de la América del Sur.* Lima, 1850.
Alemán, Hugo. *Sucre: Parábola Ecuatorial.* Quito, 1970.
Andrew, "Captain." *Journey from Buenos Aires to Potosí.* London, 1827. 2 vols.
Anna, Timothy E. *Spain and the Loss of America.* Lincoln, Nebraska: University of Nebraska Press, 1983.
Anonymous, by "An Officer, Late in Colombian Service." *The Present State of Colombia.* London, 1824.
Arguedas, Alcides. *Historia de Bolivia, 1809–1921.* La Paz, 1922.
Armitage, John. *History of Brazil.* London, 1836.
Arnade, Charles. *The Emergence of the Republic of Bolivia.* Gainesville: University of Florida Press, 1957.
Arocha Moreno, Jesús. *Las Ideas de Bolívar y Sucre en el Proceso de la Fundación de Bolivia.* Caracas, 1952.
Arze Quiroga, Eduardo. *La Constitución Boliviana de 1826 y la Disintegración Política de la América del Sur.* La Paz, 1973.
———. *Historia de Bolivia. Fases de Proceso Hispanoamericano: Orígines de la Sociedad Boliviana en el Siglo XVI.* La Paz, 1969.
Baldivia Galdo, José María, et al. *La Revolución de 16 de Julio de 1809.* La Paz, 1949.
Baldivieso, Abecia. *Las Relaciones Internacionales de la Historia de Bolivia.* Vol. 1. La Paz, 1972.
Barman, Roderick. *Brazil: The Forging of a Nation.* Stanford, Calif.: Stanford University Press, 1988.
Barnardas, José. *Charcas: Orígenes de Una Sociedad Colonial.* La Paz, 1973.
Barra, Felipe de la. *La Campaña de Junín y Ayacucho.* Lima, 1974.
Basadre, Jorge. *Historia de la República de Peru.* Vol.1, 1822–1868. Lima, 1949.
Belaunde, Victor Andrés. *Bolívar and the Political Thought of the South American Revolution.* Baltimore: Johns Hopkins University Press, 1938.
Beltrán Avila, Marcos. *El Tabú Bolívarista, 1825–1828. Comentario al Margen de los Documentos que Tratan de la Fundación de Bolivia.* Oruro, Bolivia, 1960.
Bendetti, Carlos. *Historia de Colombia.* Lima, 1887.
Bethell, Leslie, ed. *The Cambridge History of Latin America.* Vol. 3. New York: Cambridge University Press, 1985.

————. *George Canning and the Independence of Latin America.* London, 1970.

Bierck, Harold A. *Vida Pública de don Pedro Gual.* Caracas, 1976.

Borrero, Alfonso María. *Ayacucho.* Cuenca, Ecuador, 1974.

Brandt, Joseph A. *Toward the New Spain.* Chicago: University of Chicago Press, 1933.

Bulnes, Gonzalo. *Bolívar en el Peru: Últimas Campañas de la Independencia del Peru.* 2 vols. Madrid, 1919.

Burr, Robert N. *By Reason of Force: Chile and the Balancing of Power in South America, 1830–1905.* Berkeley: University of California Press, 1967.

————. *The Stillborn Panama Congress: Power Politics and Chilean-Colombian Relations during the War of the Pacific.* Berkeley: University of California Press, 1962.

Bushnell, David. *The Santander Regime in Gran Colombia.* Newark, Dela.: University of Delaware Press, 1954.

Camino Calderón, Carlos. *Anecdotario de los Libertadores.* Lima, 1940.

Chapman, C.E. *Colonial Hispanic America.* New York: Macmillan, 1938.

————. *Republican Hispanic America.* New York: Macmillan, 1937.

Chew, Benjamin. *A Sketch of the Politics, Relations, and Statistics of the Western World.* Philadelphia, 1827.

Collier, Simon. *Ideas and Politics of Chilean Independence, 1808–1823.* New York: Cambridge University Press, 1967.

Cortés, Juan Domingo. *Galería de Hombres Célebres de Bolivia.* Santiago, Chile, 1869.

Cortés Vargas, Carlos. *Participación de Colombia en la Libertad de Peru.* 3 vols. Bogotá, 1924.

Costa de la Torre, Arturo. *Romance y descendencia del Gran Mariscal de Ayacucho (Sucre) en la Ciudad de La Paz.* La Paz, 1961.

Cova, J. A. *Sucre, Ciudadano de América.* Caracas, 1943.

Crespo, Alonso. *Santa Cruz, el Condor Indio.* Mexico City, 1944.

Crespo Torral, Regimio. *Pichincha: la Sombra de Sucre.* Cuenca, Ecuador, 1972.

Cresson, W. P. *The Holy Alliance: The European Background of the Monroe Doctrine.* New York: Oxford University Press, 1922.

Díaz Venteo, Fernando. *Las Campañas Militares del Virrey Abascal.* Seville, Spain, 1948.

Dickenson, W. Calvin. ed. *James Harrington's Republic.* Washington, D.C.: University Press of America, 1983.

Domínguez, Jorge I. *Insurrection or Loyalty: The Breakdown of the Spanish American Empire.* Cambridge: Harvard University Press, 1980.

Dos Santos, Luiz Goncalves. *Memórias Para Servir à História do Reino do Brasil.* 2 vols. Rio de Janeiro, 1943.

Dos Santos Lima, Nestor. *La Imágen de Brazil en las Cartas de Bolívar.* Caracas, 1978.

Encina, Francisco A. *Emancipación de la Presidencia de Quito, del Virreinato de Lima y del Alto Peru.* Santiago, Chile, 1954.

Enock, Reginald C. *Peru.* London, 1908.

Eguiguren, Luís Antonio. *Hojas Para la Historia de la Emancipación del Peru.* Vol. 1. Lima, 1959.

Fernandez, Juan José. *La República de Chile y el Imperio del Brasil.* Santiago, Chile: Editorial Andres Bello, 1959.

Fifer, J. Valerie. *Bolivia: Land, Location and Politics Since 1825.* New York: Cambridge University Press, 1972.

Finot, Enrique. *Historia Contemporanea de Bolivia.* La Paz, 1976.

Fisher, J. R. *Government and Society in Colonial Peru: The Intendant System, 1784–1814.* London, 1970.

Flores y Camaño, Alfredo. *Objecciones Históricas.* Lima, 1960.

Forero, Manuel José. *Camilo Torres.* Bogotá, 1960.

Fortoul, José Gil. *Obras Completas.* Vol. 1. *Historia Constitucional de Venezuela.* Caracas, 1953.

Francovich, Guillermo. *El Pensamiento Universtario de Charcas.* Sucre, Bolivia, 1948.

———. *La Filosofía en Bolivia.* La Paz, 1960.

Galvéz, Juan Ignacio. *El Peru Contra Colombia. Ecuador y Chile.* Santiago, Chile, 1919.

Gamarra, Agustín. *Epistolario.* Lima, 1952.

García Camba, Andrés. *Memorias del General García Camba Para la Historia de las Armas Españolas en el Peru, 1809–1821.* 2 vols. Madrid, n.d.

García Ponce, Guillermo. *Las Armas en la Guerra de la Independencia.* Caracas, 1965

Gilmore, Robert L. *Caudillism and Militarism in Venezuela, 1810–1910.* Athens, Ohio: Ohio University Press, 1964.

Gil Novales, Alberto. *Rafael del Riego.* Madrid, 1976.

Giurto, Toto. *Peru Milenario.* Vol. 3. Lima, 1947.

Gomez Hoyos, Rafael. *Hombres, Libros, e Ideas.* Bogotá, 1968.

———. *Revolución Granadina de 1810.* 2 vols. Bogotá, 1962.

Gonzalez, Julio César. *El Proyecto de Puno y el Decreto de La Paz del 9 de Febrero de 1825.* Pamphlet, n.d., Universidad Mayor de San Andrés.

Graham, Richard. *Patronage and Politics in Nineteenth Century Brazil.* Stanford, Calif.: Stanford University Press, 1990.

Grases, Pedro, ed. *Proyecto de Constitución Para la Republica Boliviana.* Caracas, 1978.

Griffin, Charles Carroll. *The United States and the Disruption of the Spanish Empire, 1810–1822.* Reprint. New York: Octagon Books, 1968.

Grisanti, Angel. *El Gran Mariscal de Ayacucho y su Esposa la Marques de Solanda.* Caracas, 1955.

———. *Retratos de Bolívar y de Sucre.* Caracas, 1969.

Guzman Arze, Augusto. *Historia de Bolivia.* La Paz, 1976.

Haigh, Roger Malone. *Martín Guemes: A Study of the Power Structure of the Province of Plata.* University of Florida PhD, 1963. University Microfilms Inc. Ann Arbor, Michigan.

Hale, Charles. *Mexican Liberation in the Age of Mora, 1821–1853.* New Haven: Yale University Press, 1968.

Hann, John. "Burr's Model Applied: The Balance of Power in the Río de la Plata." *Proceedings of the Pacific Coast Council on Latin American Sudies 1974.* 3: 31–44.

Haring, C. H. *The Spanish Empire in America*. New York: Oxford University Press, 1947.

Henac, Jesús and Gerardo Arrubla, *History of Colombia*. Trans. and ed. by J. Fred Rippy. Chapel Hill, N.C.: North Carolina Press, 1938.

Heredia, Enrique. *Planes Españoles Para Reconquistar Hispanoamérica, 1810–1818*. Buenos Aires, 1974.

Herr, Richard. *The Eighteenth Century Revolution in Spain*. Princeton: Princeton University Press, 1958.

———. *Spain*. Englewood Cliffs: Prentice Hall, 1971.

Hill, Lawrence. *Diplomatic Relations between the United States and Brazil*. Durham, N.C.: Duke University Press, 1932.

Hobsbawm, E. J. *The Age of Revolution*. New York: World Publishing Co., 1962.

Hoenigsberg, Julio. *Santander ante la Historia*. Vol. 1. Baranquilla, Colombia, 1969.

Hoover, John M. P. *Admirable Warrior: Marshal Sucre, Fighter for South American Independence*. Detroit, Mich.: Blaine Ethridge, 1977.

Humphreys, R. A. *Liberation of South America, 1806–1827. The Career of James Paroissien*. London, 1952.

Irazabel, Carlos. *Venezuela Esclavo y Feudal*. Caracas, 1964.

Jimenez Fernandez, Manuel. *Las Doctrinas Populistas en la Independencia de Hispanoamérica*. Seville, Spain, 1947.

Jordan Dandoval, *Bolivia y el Equilibrio del Cono Sudamericano*. La Paz, 1978.

Kaufmann, William W. *British Policy and the Independence of Latin America*. New York: Anchor Books, 1967.

Kendall, Lane Carter. "Andrés Santa Cruz and the Peru-Bolivian Confederation." *Hispanic American Historical Review*, 1976, 16: 29–48.

Kissinger, Henry A. *A World Restored*. New York: Grosset and Dunlap, 1964.

Labra, Rafael María de. *América y la Constitución Española de 1812*. Madrid, 1914.

Larrazabal, Felipe. *Vida deLibertador: Simón Bolívar*. 4 vols. Madrid, n.d.

Larrera Alba, Luís. *Sucre: Alto Conductor Político Militar; la Campaña Libertadora de 1821–1822*. Quito, 1925.

Lastarria, J. V. *La América*. Madrid, 1867.

Lecuna, Vicente. *Catálogo de Errores y Calumnias en la Historia de Bolívar*. New York: Colonial Press, 1957.

———. *Crónica Razonada de las Guerras de Bolívar*, 4 vols. New York: Colonial Press, 1950.

Levillier, Roberto. *La Audiencia de Charcas*. Buenos Aires, 1962.

Libermann Z., Jacobo *Tiempo de Bolívar, 1783–1830*. 2 vols. La Paz, 1989.

Lofstrom, William. "Attempted Economic Reform and Innovation in Bolivia under Antonio José de Sucre, 1825–1828," *Hispanic American Historical Review*, 1970. 56: 279–99.

———. *The Promise and Problem of Reform: Attempted Social and Economic Change in the First Years of Bolivian Independence*. Cornell Latin American Studies Pogram. Dissertation Series no. 35. June 1972. Cornell University, Ithaca, N.Y.

Lopez de Mesa, Luis. *De Como Se Ha Formado la Nación Colombiana*. Medellin, Colombia, 1970.

Ludwig, Emil. *Bolívar. The Life of an Idealist.* New York: Alliance Book Corporation, 1942.

Lynch, John. *The Spanish American Revolutions, 1808–1826.* New York: Norton, 1973.

———. *Spanish Colonial Administration , 1782–1810. The Intendant System in the Viceroyalty of Río de la Plata.* New York: Greenwood Press, 1958.

Macaulay, Neil, *Dom Pedro: The Struggle for Liberty in Brazil and Portugal, 1798-1835.* Durham, N.C.: Duke University Press, 1986.

Macera, César. *San Martín, Gobernante del Peru.* Buenos Aires, 1950.

Mackenna, B. Vicuña. *El Washington del Sur.* Madrid, n.d.

Madriaga, Salvador de. *Bolívar.* New York: Pellegrini and Cundahay, 1952.

Mallo, Jorge. *Historia de la Fundación de Bolivia y Lo Que Fue Para Ella la Administración de Sucre.* Pamphlet. La Paz, 1871.

Manchester, Alan K. British *Preeminence in Brazil: Its Rise and Decline.* Chapel Hill: University of North Carolina Press, 1933.

Masur, Gerhard. *Simón Bolívar.* Albuquerque, N.M.: University of New Mexico Press, 1948. Rev. ed., 1969.

May, Ernest R. *The Making of the Monroe Doctrine.* Cambridge, Mass.: Harvard University Press, 1975.

Maxwell Kenneth. *Conflicts and Conspiracies: Brazil and Portugal, 1750–1808.* New York: Cambridge University Press, 1973.

Miller, William. *Memorias de General Miller.* London, 1829, 2 vols.

Millington, Thomas. *Debt Politics after Independence: The Funding Conflict in Bolivia.* Gainesville, Fla.: University of Florida Press, 1992.

Minutolo de Ortiz, Cristina. *Historia de Tarija.* 2 vols. Tarija, 1986.

Mitre, Bartolomé. *Historia de San Martín y de la Emancipación Sudamericana.* 4 vols. Buenos Aires, 1890.

Monslave, José Dolores. *El Ideal Político del Libertador Simón Bolívar.* Bogotá, 1916.

Moreno de Angel, Pilar. *Santander.* Bogotá, 1989.

Morón, Guillermo. *Historia de Venezuela.* 3rd. ed. Caracas, 1961.

Mitre, Bartolomé. *Historia de Belgrano y de la Independencia Argentina.* 4 vols. Buenos Aires, 1927.

Muniz Tavares, *A Revolucão de Pernambuco em 1917.* Recife, Brazil, 1917.

Munoz Cabrera, Juan R. *La Guerra de los Quince Años.* Santiago, 1867.

Navarro, Nicolas E. *Diario de Bucaramanga por L. Peru de Lacroix; un Estudio Crítico.* Caracas, 1935.

Nicholson, Irene. *The Liberators.* New York: Praeger, 1969.

O'Connor, F. Burdett. *Independencia Américana.* Madrid, n.d.

O'Leary, Daniel F. *Bolívar and the War of Indpendence.* Translated and edited by Robert F McNerney, Jr. Austin, Tex.: University of Texas Press, 1970.

Olviera Lima, Manoel de. *Dom João VI no Brasil.* 3 vols. Rio de Janeiro, 1945.

———. *O Movimento da Independencia.* Sao Paulo, 1922.

Ovando-Sanz, Jorge Alejandro. *La Invasion Brasileña a Bolivia en 1825: Una de las Causas del Congreso de Panama.* La Paz, 1977.

Palmer, John, ed., *Foreign Constitutions.* Albany, 1894.

Pandiá, Calogeras. *A Política Exterior do Império.* 2 vols. Rio de Janeiro, 1962.

Pang, Eul-soo. *In Pursuit of Honor and Power: Noblemen of the Southern Cross in Nineteenth Century Brazil.* Tuscaloosa, Ala.: Univeristy of Alabama Press, 1988.

Parra-Perez, Carraciolo. *Bolívar: A Contribution to the Study of His Political Ideas.* Westport, Conn.: Greenwood Press, 1975.

———. *Mariño y la Independencia de Venezuela.* 2 vols. Madrid, 1954.

———. *La Monarquía en la Gran Colombia.* Madrid, 1957.

Pelliza, Mariano. *Dorrego en la Historia de los Partidos Unitarios y Federales.* Buenos Aires, 1878.

———. *Monteagudo, Su Vida y Sus Escritos.* 2 vols. Buenos Aires, 1880.

Paz Soldan, Mariano Felipe. *Historia del Peru Independente, 1822–1827.* 2 vols. Madrid, 1919.

———. *Historia del Peru Independiente; Tercer Período, 1827–1833.* Lima, 1929.

Pentland, Joseph Barclay. *Report on Bolivia, 1827.* London, 1974.

Pereyra Plasencia, H. *La Campaña Libertadora de Junín y Ayacucho.* Lima, 1975.

Perez Sosa, Elias. *Gestas Dialecticas.* Caracas, 1957.

Pereira-Pinto, Juan Carlos. *Temas de Historia Económica y Social Argentina Durante el Siglo XIV.* Buenos Aires, 1975.

Peterson, Harold F. *Argentina and the United States.* New York: State University of New York, 1964.

Piccirilli, Ricardo. *Rivadavia y Su Tiempo.* 3 vols. Buenos Aires, 1960.

———. *San Martín y la Política de los Pueblos.* Buenos Aires, 1960.

Pike, Frederick. *The Modern History of Peru.* New York: Praeger, 1967.

Pinilla, Sabino. *La Creación de Bolivia.* La Paz, 1975.

Puente Candamo, José Agustín de la. *San Martín y el Peru: Planteamiento Doctrinario.* Lima, 1948.

Quevedo, Numa. *Sucre y la Cultura.* Caracas, 1974.

Ravignani, E., ed., *Comisión de Bernadino Rivadavia ante España y Otras Potencias de Europa, 1814–20.* 2 vols. Buenos Aires, 1933.

Rene Moreno, Gabriel. *Ayacucho en Buenos Aires.* Madrid, n.d.

———. *La Audiencia de Charcas.* La Paz, 1970.

———. *Últimos Días Coloniales en el Alto Peru.* La Paz, 1970.

Restelli, Ernesto, ed. *La Gestión Diplómatica del General de Alvear en el Alto Peru.* Buenos Aires, 1927.

Rey de Castro, José María. *Recuerdos del Tiempo Heróico.* Guayaquil, Ecuador, 1883.

Riva Aguero, José de la. *Historia del Peru.* 2 vols. Lima, 1953.

Robertson, William Spence. "Metternich's Attitude toward Revolutions in Latin America." *Hispanic American Historic Review.* 1941. 21: 538–59.

———. *France and Latin American Independence.* New York: Octagon Books, 1967.

———. *Rise of the Spanish-American Republics.* New York: Appleton, 1918.

Rodrigues, José Honório. *Independencia: Revolucao, e Contrarevolucao.* 5 vols. Rio de Janeiro, 1975.

Rodríguez, Gregorio. *Contribución Historica y Documental.* 3 vols. Buenos Aires, 1921.

Rodríguez, Luis. *Ayacucho: La Batalla de la Libertad Americana.* Quito, 1975.

Rojas, Ricardo. *San Martín: Knight of the Andes.* Translation by Herschel Brickell and Carlos Videla. New York: Doubleday. 1945.

Ruiz Rivas, Guillermo. *Simón Bolívar; Más allá del Mito.* Vol. 1. Bogotá, 1964.

Rumazo Gonzalez, Alfonso. *Sucre: Gran Mariscal de Ayacucho.* Madrid, 1963.

Russel-Wood, A.J.R., ed. *From Colony to Nation: Essays on the Inpdependence of Brazil.* Baltimore: Johns Hopkins University Press, 1975.

Saavedra, Carlos. *El Dean Funes y la Creación de Bolivia.* La Paz, 1972.

Seckinger, Ron. *The Brazilian Monarchy and the South American Republics, 1822–1831.* Baton Rouge, La.: Louisiana State University Press, 1984.

———. "The Chiquitos Affair: An Aborted Crisis in Brazilian-Bolivian Relations." *Luso-Brazilian Review.* Summer, 1974. 2(1): 14–19.

———. "Projectada alianza Gran-Colombiana rioplatense contra o Brazil: um documento inédito." *Mensario do Arquivo Nacional.* 1974. 5(1): 33–40.

Silva, J. Francisco. *El Libertador Bolívar y el Dean Funes.* Madrid, 1916.

Sossa, Carlos Urquiza. *La Vida y Obra del Mariscal Andrés Santa Cruz.* 3 vols. La Paz, 1976.

Stoetzer, Carlos, O. *The Scholastic Roots of the Spanish American Revolution.* New York: Fordham University Press, 1979,

Street, John. *Artigas and the Emancipation of Uruguay.* New York: Columbia University Press, 1959.

Temperley, Harold. *The Foreign Policy of Canning, 1822–1827: England, the Neo-Holy Alliance and the New World.* London, 1925.

Trend, J. B. *Bolívar and the Independence of South America.* New York: Macmillan, 1948.

Urdaneta, Rafael. *Memorias.* Madrid, n.d.

Valencia Vega. *El Indio en la Independencia.* La Paz, 1962.

Valladão, Alfredo. *Brasil e Chile na Epoca do Império; Amizade sem Exemplo.* Rio de Janeiro, 1959.

Vallenilla Lanz, Laureano. *Cesarismo Democrático.* Caracas, 1961.

———. *Disgregación y Integración.* 2nd ed. Madrid, 1962.

Vallenilla Lanz, Laureano. *La guerra de Nuestra Independencia Fue Una Guerra Civil.* Caracas, 1959.

Vargas, Carlos Cortés. *El Ejército Colombiano en el Peru.* Bogotá, 1924.

———. *Participación de Colombia en la Libertad de Peru.* Bogotá, 1924.

Vargas Ugarte, R. *Historia del Peru.* Vol. 6. Buenos Aires, 1958.

Varnhagen, Francisco Adolfo de. *História de Independencia do Brasil.* Rio de Janeiro, 1917.

Vasconcelos, José. *Bolívarismo y Monroísmo.* Santiago, Chile, 1937.

Villanueva, Carlos. *La Santa Alianza.* Paris, 1887.

Villanueva, Laureano. *Vida de don Antonio José de Sucre.* Caracas, 1945.

Viotti da Costa, Emilio. *The Brazilian Empire: Myths and Histories.* Chicago: Chicago University Press, 1985.

———. "Introducao ao estudo de emancipacao política do Brasil." Carlos G. Mota, ed. *Brasil em Perspectiva.* São Paulo, 1968.

Waddell, D.A.G. *Gran Bretaña y la Independencia de Venezuela y Colombia.* Caracas, 1983.

Walker, A. *Colombia, Being a Geographical, Statistical, Agricultural, Commercial And Political Account of that Country.* London, 1822.
Webster, Charles. *Britain and the Independence of Latin America.* London, 1938.
Yanes, Francisco Javier. *Historia de la Provincia de Cumaná.* Caracas, 1949.

Letters and Memoirs

Abascal Sousa, Fernando. *Memoria de Gobierno.* (Peruvian viceroyalty.) 2 vols. Ed. by Vicente Rodríguez de Casado and José Antonio Calderon Quijano. Seville, Spain. 1944.

Bolívar, Simón

Cartas de Bolívar, 1823–1825. Ed. by R. Blanco-Fombona, R. Madrid, 1921.
Cartas del Libertador, 1822–1823. Vol. 3. Ed. by Vicente Lecuna. Caracas, 1923.
Cartas del Libertador, 1824–1825. Ed. by Vicente Lecuna, Caracas, 1929.
Correspondencia de Libertador, 1819–1829. Ed. by Vicente Lecuna. Caracas, 1974.
Documentos para la Historia de la Vida Publica del Libertador de Colombia, Peru y Bolivia. Ed. by José Felix Blanco. 14 vols. Caracas, 1875–1878.
Escritos del Libertador. Ed. by Cristóbal Mendoza. Caracas, 1968.
Selected Writings of Bolívar. 2 vols. Ed. by Vicente Lecuna, New York: Colonial Press, 1951.
Simón Bolívar: Obras Completas. 3 vols. Ed. by Vicente Lecuna and Esther Barrett de Nazaris. Havana, 1950.
O'Leary, Daniel. *Memorias del General O'Leary.* 32 vols. Caracas, 1880.

Santa Cruz, Andrés

Archivo Histórico del Mariscal Andrés de Santa Cruz. Ed. by Andrés de Santa Cruz Schuhkrafft. 2 vols. La Paz, 1976.
Sossa, Carlos U. *La Vida y Obra de André Santa Cruz.* 3 vols. La Paz, 1976.

Santander, Francisco Paula de

Archivo Santander. 24 vols. Ed. by Ernesto Restrepo. Bogotá, 1918–1932.
Cartas de Santander. 3 vols. Ed. by Vicente Lecuna. Caracas, 1942.
Cartas y Mensajes de Santander. 10 vols. Ed. by Roberto Cortazar. Bogotá, 1953–1956.
Correspondencia Dirigida al General Santander. Roberto Cortazar. Bogotá, 1964–1970.

Sucre, Antonio José de

Archivo de Sucre. 9 vols. Ed. by Pedro Grases and Esther Barret de Nazaris. Caracas, 1973–1985.
Cartas de Sucre al Libertador. 2 vols. Ed. by Daniel F. O'Leary. Madrid, 1919.
Correspondencia Dirigida al General Santander. Ed. by Roberto Cortazar. Vol. 12. From Sucre. Bogotá, 1968.

Documentos para la Historia de Bolivia: Cartas del General Sucre a León Galindo. La Paz,1918.

Lily Library. Latin America MSS. Antonio José de Sucre. Mutis Daza MS.

Sucre Letters to Funes. Unpublished. See government sources, Argentina.

Urdaneta, Rafael. *Archivo del General Rafael Urdaneta.* 2 vols. Caracas, 1970.

Government Sources

Argentina
Published archival material relating to Bolivia

Ovando-Sanz, Jorge Alejandro. *La Invasión Brasileña a Bolivia en 1825: Una de las Causas del Congreso de Panama.* La Paz, 1977.

Restelli, Ernesto, ed. *La Gestión diplómatica del General de Alvear en el Alto Peru.* Buenos Aires, 1927.

Rodríguez, Gregorio R. *Contribución Histórica y Documental.* 3 vols. Buenos Aires, 1921.

Saavedra, Carlos. *El Dean Funes y la Creación de Bolivia.* La Paz, 1972.

Unpublished material

Sucre letters to Funes. Biblioteca Nacional de Argentina (Buenos Aires). A. J. de Sucre to Dean Funes, 542/37–117, June 18, 1825–November 14, 1826.

Bolivia

Documentos Referentes a la Creación de Bolivia. 2 vols. Ed. by Vicente Lecuna, Caracas, 1975.

Libro Menor de Sesiones Secretas de la Asamblea Constituyente de 1826. La Paz, n.d.

Redactor de la Asamblea de Representantes: Legislatura del Año 1825. La Paz, 1914.

Redactor de la Asamblea Constituyente de 1826. La Paz, 1917.

National Archives at Sucre

GRM Colección Gabriel René-Moreno, Bibioteca Nacional de Bolivia.
Colección Ruck

Brazil

Anais do Parlamento Brasileiro, Assembléia Constiuinte, 1823. Rio de Janeiro, 1874.

Documentos para la História de Independencia. Rio de Janeiro, 1923.

Ministerio das Relacoes Exteriores. Archivo Diplomatico da Independencia. 6 vols. Rio de Janeiro, 1922–1925.

Colombia

Congreso de las Provincias Unidas: Leyes, Actas y Notas. Bogotá, 1924. Vol 33.

Mier, José María de. *Legación a la America Meridional, 1821–1824.* Bogotá, 1987.

State of Colombia: Reports of the Secretaries of State Presented to the First Constitutional Congress in 1823. London, 1824.

Peru

Colección Documental de la Independencia del Peru. Vol. 6. Asuntos Miltares. 9 vols. Lima, 1974.

Ortiz de Zaballos, Carlos. *La Misión de Ortiz de Zeballos en Bolivia, 1826–1827.* Lima, 1956.

———. *Misiones Peruanas, 1820–1826.* Vol. 1. Lima, 1975.

United States

Diplomatic Correspondence of the United States Concerning the Indpendence of the Latin American Nations. 3 vols. Ed. by William R. Manning. New York: Oxford University Press, 1925.

United States Consulate in Lima William Tudor. Dispatches, October 10, 1823–June 19, 1827. National Archives Microfilm Publication. Film no. 2288, Roll 1, microcopy no. 154.

Index

About the Author

THOMAS MILLINGTON is Professor of Political Science at Hobart and William Smith Colleges in Geneva, New York. He is the author of *Latin American Debt Politics after Independence* (1992).

ISBN 0-313-29806-8

90000>

EAN

9 780313 298066

HARDCOVER BAR CODE